Thomas Wright

La Mort d'Arthure.

The History of King Arthur and of the Knights of the Round Table. Compiled by Sir Thomas Malory, Knt. Edited from the text of the edition of 1634, with introduction and notes by Thomas Wright. Second edition

Thomas Wright

La Mort d'Arthure.
The History of King Arthur and of the Knights of the Round Table. Compiled by Sir Thomas Malory, Knt. Edited from the text of the edition of 1634, with introduction and notes by Thomas Wright. Second edition

ISBN/EAN: 9783337820657

Printed in Europe, USA, Canada, Australia, Japan

Cover: Foto ©ninafisch / pixelio.de

More available books at **www.hansebooks.com**

La Mort D'Arthure.

THE
HISTORY OF KING ARTHUR
AND OF THE KNIGHTS OF THE

ROUND TABLE.

COMPILED BY SIR THOMAS MALORY, Knt.

EDITED FROM THE TEXT OF THE EDITION OF 1634,

WITH INTRODUCTION AND NOTES

BY THOMAS WRIGHT, Esq., M.A., F.S.A.,

HON. M.R.S.L. ETC. CORRESPONDING MEMBER

OF THE INSTITUTE OF FRANCE.

VOL. I.

Second Edition.

LONDON:
JOHN RUSSELL SMITH,
SOHO SQUARE.
1866.

INTRODUCTION.

THE origin of the cycle of romances, which have for their subject the adventures of king Arthur and his knights, and which were during many ages so popular throughout nearly all the countries of Europe, appears to be involved in impenetrable mystery, and I will not attempt to discuss it on the present occasion. We first become acquainted with the story which forms the groundwork of them in the pretended History of the Britons, published in the year 1147, by Geoffrey of Monmouth, who acknowledges that his materials came from Britany, which country, therefore, we may perhaps safely regard as the cradle of this branch of mediæval literature. Geoffrey's history was new to everybody in England, (and also, as it appears, in Wales); and it excited not only great interest, but apparently great admiration, for it was seized upon by the metrical chroniclers in Anglo-Norman and English, such as Gaimar and Wace, who were contemporary with Geoffrey of Monmouth himself, and a little later the Anglo-Saxon Layamon, who turned it into verse with more or less of variation and amplification. It is quite evident, nevertheless, from a comparison of these versions with the original, that the various writers had no knowledge of the romantic stories they tell independent of that original, and that their alterations and amplifications were the mere liberties which they considered themselves authorized as poets to take. Nevertheless, in the course of the second half of the twelfth century the story of king Arthur and his knights took suddenly a great development, and presents us with a multitude of new incidents with which Geoffrey of Monmouth could not have been acquainted. It is impossible now to decide from whence these new incidents were derived, or how much of them were the mere invention of the writers, who seem indeed to have worked into their narrative popular stories then current, and derived from various sources, but which had really no relation to it. I will, therefore, not venture upon any discussion of these questions, but proceed simply to state the known facts of the literary history of the long and curious romance of which an edition is given to the public in the present volumes.

The first of these romances, which composed this new development of the story—for the series of which we are speaking consists of several separate narratives—is that of the St. Graal, the holy vessel or "hanap," which had been preserved by Joseph of Arimathea after the death of the Saviour, and which was pretended to have been brought, after many marvellous adventures, into the isle of Britain. This history has no immediate connection with that of king Arthur, but seems to have been founded on some mysterious religious legend, brought perhaps from the East during the age of the crusades. The next in order of date of these compilations is the history of the prophet and enchanter Merlin, which, composed perhaps partly of Breton legends, was certainly built upon the foundation which had been laid by Geoffrey of Monmouth. We have, however, here the events of king Arthur's reign, which had been told briefly by Geoffrey, much amplified, and we are introduced to some of the principal knights of the round table. The third of these romances was that of Lancelot du Lac, which is devoted to the adventures of that hero and to his amours with queen Guenever. This was followed by the Queste du St. Graal, or search of the St. Graal, which had been already partly related in the romance of Lancelot, and which is now conducted more especially by Perceval, Gawaine, Lancelot, and the son of the latter, Galaad or Galahad, who finally succeeds in achieving the adventure. The fifth and last of these romances was that which was more particularly known as the Mort Artus, or Mort d'Arthure, in which Lancelot's intrigues with the queen and the enmity of Gawaine's brothers lead to the war which ended in king Arthur's death, and which concludes the history of all his adventurous knights.

These five romances are written in prose, in the Anglo-Norman dialect of the French tongue; and there can be no doubt that they were compiled by two writers of the reign of Henry II. of England, one who names himself Robert de Borron, and the other a celebrated writer who lived at that monarch's court, and is known popularly by the name of Walter Mapes, though his name is usually written Map in the manuscripts. The first of these writers claims the Roman du St. Graal and the History of Merlin, while Mapes was the author of Lancelot, the Queste du St. Graal, and the Mort Artus.

Subsequently to the appearance of these romances, two

new writers of the same stamp came into the field, one of them giving us his name as Lucas de Gast, the other Helie de Borron, said to have been a kinsman of Robert de Borron. The latter appears to have written as late as the reign of Henry III. To these two writers severally we owe the first and second parts of the romance of *Tristan*, or Tristram, a new hero, unknown to the previous histories of king Arthur and his knights, but who from this time forward assumes a very prominent place among the knights of the round table. For some reason or other—perhaps mere caprice—the two writers of the romance of Tristan take every opportunity of blackening the character of sir Gawaine, who was represented as one of the purest models of knighthood in the previous romances; and it is to them we owe the history of king Pellinore, and of the great feud between his sons and sir Gawaine and his brethren. Helie de Borron also compiled a new and very extensive romance, which, under the title of *Gyron le Courtois*, commemorated a new series of heroes, including Gyron himself, Meliadus of Léonnois, and several others.

This mass of romance soon became popular, as we may judge from the number of manuscripts which still remain, and it formed a sort of code of knight-errantry which exercised a considerable influence on the feudal spirit and sentiments of the thirteenth and fourteenth centuries. A crowd of writers in different languages selected particular incidents from these romances, or abridged the whole, and published them in verse and in more popular forms; and this cycle of romance became thus more and more developed, and in these new forms and editions occupied continually a more important place in the literature of the day. In these

INTRODUCTION.

metrical forms, the romances of king Arthur and his knights might be chaunted in the baronial hall or chamber in the same manner as the Chansons de Geste and the other classes of metrical romances. It would hardly be in place here to give any account of the numerous metrical romances and other poems belonging to this cycle which appeared during the thirteenth and fourteenth centuries. As the feudal manners began to degenerate, and the practice of chaunting the romances was abandoned, the metrical versions, the language of which became sooner obsolete, began also to lose their popularity, and gave way to almost a rage for the romances in prose, which, especially among the great chiefs on the continent, were looked upon with a feeling of reverential respect, as the grand and almost sole repositories of the spirit and principles of feudalism; and this was the state of feeling when the invention of the art of printing came to facilitate the multiplication of copies of books. The French printers of the latter half of the fifteenth century, and of the earlier part of the century following, produced a considerable number of editions, generally in folio, of the long French prose romances relating to the St. Graal, to king Arthur and his knights, and especially to the adventures of sir Tristram, whose story appears to have become permanently the most popular of them all.

Although this cycle of romances had, as we have seen, first made its appearance in England, it seems never to have been so popular here as in France; and it held by no means a prominent place in our literature at the time when so many editions were issuing from the presses of the French printers. A few English metrical romances belonging to this class are found in manuscripts of the fifteenth century, but they are generally unique copies, and I doubt whether they were in any degree of vogue. Even Caxton, who had evidently a taste for French literature, did not think of printing a book on this subject, until he was pressed to do it, as he informs us, by "many noble and dyvers gentylmen of this royame;" and then he seems to have been at a loss to find any book which would suit his purpose, until he was helped out of this difficulty by sir. Thomas Malory, who had compiled a book "oute of certeyn bookes of Frensshe, and reduced it into Englysshe." All we seem to know of sir Thomas Malory is, that he tells us himself, at the conclusion of his book, that he was a knight, and that he completed his compilation in the ninth year of the reign of Edward IV, that is, in the course of the year 1469, or early in 1470, or more than fifteen years before Caxton printed it. The statement of some of the old bibliographers, that he was a Welshman, is probably a mere supposition founded on the character of his book.

We have no exact information as to the method pursued by Malory in his compilation, or as to the materials he used, although it is clear that a large portion of his book is taken from the great prose romances of Merlin, Lancelot, Tristram, the Queste du St. Graal, and the Mort Artus. He has adopted throughout the unfavourable view of the character of sir Gawaine which appears to have been established in France by the popularity of Tristram, although it was quite contrary to the general tone of the English romances. He has considerably modified some parts of the story in the course of abridgment, and omitted many of the most important and characteristic incidents—in Tristram and Lancelot especially—while he sometimes gives incidents which are not found related in the same way elsewhere, and which seem to show that he made use of some materials which are no longer known to exist. Malory takes care to remind us continually that his authorities were in the French language, by his frequent references to the "French book," which references, it may be remarked, are in the greater number of cases omitted in the text from which the present edition is taken.

Caxton tells us that he finished the printing of La Mort Darthur, as he entitles the book, in the abbey of Westminster, on the last day of July, 1485. This book has now become so rare that only one complete copy is known, which was formerly in the Harleian library, and is now in that of the earl of Jersey at Osterley park, Middlesex. An imperfect copy, now in earl Spencer's library, was purchased, as we learn from Lowndes, for the large sum of £320. These, I believe, are the only copies of Caxton's edition known to exist.

Two editions of this work were printed by Caxton's successor in the art of printing, Wynkyn de Worde, one in 1498, the other in 1529. Only one copy of each is at present known to be in existence. Wynkyn de Worde entitled his editions, "The Booke of Kynge Arthur."

William Copland, another well-known early English printer, reprinted this work in 1557, under the title of "The Story of Kynge Arthur, and also of his Knyghtes of the Rounde Table."

This title was also adopted by Thomas East, who printed two editions, one in folio, the other 4to., and both equally without date. It is probable, from the similarity of the title, that East printed from Copland's edition.

We can trace no other reprint of this work until the year 1634, when the last of the black-letter editions was published in three parts, in 4to., with three separate titles. It is proved, by a considerable omission in this edition, that it was printed from a copy of the folio edition by East, in which a leaf in the third part was wanting.[1]

Malory's history of King Arthur appears not to have been printed again until 1816. In that year two different popular editions appeared, undertaken apparently quite independently and unknowingly of each other. Both were printed in the same size, 24mo., the one in three volumes, the other in two. The edition in three volumes is understood to have been edited by Joseph Haslewood, and is spoken of as an especially "correct reprint" of the edition of 1634. This, however, is so little the case, that in reading it over we are led to conclude that the correcting of the text in this edition was left to the printers themselves. Here and there alterations were made to fit the narrative for the taste or understanding of the ordinary modern reader; yet, though alterations of this kind are often made without much judgment, gross and evident misprints of the edition of 1634 are left uncorrected, and others are added which as evidently arose from the misreading of the old black-letter by the modern compositor. Thus, in the very first chapter, the lady Igraine is said to be " passing *wife*," instead of " passing *wise;*" in the thirty-ninth chapter of the third part, the blunder of the edition of 1634, in printing *war wost* instead of *warwolf*, is strictly preserved in the edition ascribed to Haslewood.[2] Again, in the hun-

---

[1] See vol. iii. p. 90, of the present edition.
[2] *Ibid.* p. 270.

INTRODUCTION. xiii

dred and sixty-fifth chapter of the same part, the printer of this modern edition has actually turned the word *Southsexe* (Sussex) into *Southfere*, through a mere mistaking, in the black-letter of the original, of the long *s* for *f*, and of *x* for *r !*[1] The editor of this edition, in an "Advertisement" prefixed to the first volume, complains rather bitterly of the appearance of what he calls the "rival edition," which he seems to treat as though it had been got up in a spirit of opposition to his own.

The edition in two volumes, which appears thus to have come out before Haslewood's, belonged to a series of popular editions known as "Walker's British Classics." The text is quite as little recommendable as that of Haslewood, and the editor, or printer, has taken as great liberties with it in various ways, especially in altering phrases when he did not understand them. Thus, the editor of this edition, not understanding the *war wost* of the text of 1634, boldly changed the whole sentence as follows, "for she made hem well a seven years' *war worse*," which certainly makes a sentence with a meaning, but a meaning that has no relation to the context. This edition gives correctly the words *wise* and *Sussex*, which Haslewood's printer blundered in; but its editor had not discovered the great hiatus in the third part, mentioned above as having risen from the want of a leaf in the copy of East's edition used by the printer of 1634, which was discovered and supplied in the edition ascribed to Haslewood.

Finally, in the year following that of these two editions, in 1817, appeared the well-known 4to. edition of the original text of Caxton, which has gained a reputation, as the pub-

[1] See vol. iii. p. 330.

lishers, no doubt, intended it should, from having the name of Robert Southey attached to it. The text is a mere reprint of Caxton, without any attempt at editing, and was probably left entirely to the care of the printers. It is, therefore, a book useless to the general reader, and is only useful at all because, for reference, it supplies the place of the original, which is inaccessible. The introduction and notes by Southey display the extensive and indiscriminate reading for which the poet was celebrated, but he has done little towards explaining or illustrating his text.

These are all the known editions of the story of king Arthur, as it was given originally to the English reader in the text of sir Thomas Malory and in the types of William Caxton. It is remarkable that the two popular editions published in 1816 have both become rare, and the want of a good edition of this romance has been felt generally. A knowledge of it is, indeed, necessary to enable us to understand the later Middle Ages in one of their important points of view; while it possesses an intrinsic interest, as giving us, in a comprehensive form, a good general sketch of a cycle of romances which through many ages exercised an influence upon literature and art. To meet this want, the present edition has been undertaken. It has been judged advisable to adopt for the text the latest of the old editions, that of 1634; for it is evident that the choice lay between the last and the first, between this we have selected and that of Caxton; as the moment we decided on abandoning Caxton, there was no reason why we should not take that of the reprints which was most readable. This choice was made with the less scruple, as no particular philological value is attached to the language of Caxton's edition, which would

INTRODUCTION.

certainly be repulsive to the modern reader, while all its value as a literary monument is retained in the reprint. On the other hand, the orthography and phraseology of the edition of 1634, with the sprinkling of obsolete words, not sufficiently numerous to be embarrassing, preserves a certain clothing of mediæval character which we think is one of the charms of the book. The edition of 1634 contains the whole text of Malory's work, and presents in general a verbal copy of it. Not unfrequently, however, the words are a little transposed, while some words are here and there added, and others are exchanged, as obsolete, for words that were better understood, with the notion evidently of making the language more correct or more readable. Many of these alterations are probably the mere work of the compositors; but some appear to have been made by design by some better informed person employed to read over the sheets of that or of some of the preceding editions.

In the present edition I have carefully collated the text of 1634 with that of Caxton, and given in the notes any variations in the latter which seem to be of importance or to present any particular interest. I have only ventured to alter the later text in cases where there were evident misprints or omissions. The old printers, especially those of the seventeenth century, when left to themselves, were, as it is well known, extremely careless, and the books of that period, if not corrected by the authors, are generally full of printers' errors. These I have carefully corrected from the text of Caxton, and in general, where the blunders are self-evident, I have not thought it necessary to point them out. If I have erred at all in this respect, it has been by over caution, and as I advanced in the book

INTRODUCTION.

I found it necessary to correct the text rather more than in the earlier part. This was the case especially in the third part, or volume, in which the old compositors and readers appear to have been more careless than usual, and which abounds with omissions of words and sometimes of parts of sentences, which entirely destroy the meaning, while words have often been changed negligently from mere similarity of sound, without being at all equivalent. There are, however, in the course of the book, some evident corrections of Caxton's text, which itself contains a few misprints, and some variations which appear to have been introduced designedly in the editions immediately following Caxton's, and to have been preserved in the text adopted for the present edition. With these I have not interfered.

I have thought it advisable in a work like this, where the obsolete words and phrases are after all not very numerous, to explain them in the notes. Every reader has not at hand a dictionary of obsolete English; nor, if he had, is it convenient, in reading a book of this description, to be interrupted at every page or two in order to trace out a word in a dictionary. When the same obsolete word recurs after some interval, I have, for the same reason, not hesitated to repeat the explanation. I have avoided loading the text with illustrative and what may perhaps be termed historical notes, confining myself to what seemed almost necessary to render the perusal of the text easy and agreeable to a modern reader. It would not be difficult to increase notes and illustrations of this description to an almost indefinite extent.

With these explanations, it is hoped that the present edition of Malory's *Mort d'Arthure* will be a work accept-

INTRODUCTION.

able to the public. It contains, as has been stated before, a good comprehensive condensation of the romantic cycle of king Arthur and his knights, as it first appeared in the great prose compilations of the latter part of the twelfth and beginning of the thirteenth century, and as it remained popular in those same compilations in the fifteenth. Although a similar class of incidents are perhaps too uniformly repeated, yet these romances are full of life and activity, and are often picturesque; while some knowledge of them is absolutely necessary for those who would understand those Middle Ages which have of late years been so much talked of and have excited so much interest. They differ from the Chansons de Geste and the generality of the other mediæval romances in this, that while the former are plain and practical pictures of life in the feudal ages, these embody a sort of mythic code, if I may use such a phrase, of the more elevated principles and spirit of chivalry which the high-minded knight was supposed to labour to imitate. The tone of the morality of this code is certainly not very high; but—it was the morality of feudalism.

14, Sydney Street, Brompton,
May, 1858.

In offering to the public a new edition of these three volumes, I have only to add, that the whole has been carefully revised, that a few errors have been corrected, and that the number of glossarial notes has been somewhat increased, in the hope of making the romance of king Arthur still more acceptable to the general reader.

THOMAS WRIGHT.

October, 1865.

THE MOST ANCIENT AND FAMOVS HISTORY OF THE RENOWNED *PRINCE* ARTHVR

King of *Britaine*,
The firſt Part.

Wherein is declared his Life and Death, *with all his glorious Battailes againſt the* Saxons, Saracens, *and* Pagans, which (for the honour of his Country) he moſt worthily achieued.

As alſo, all the Noble Aɛts, and Heroicke Deeds of his Valiant KNIGHTS of the ROVND TABLE.

Newly refined, and publiſhed for the delight, and profit of the READER.

LONDON,
Printed by *William Stansby*,
for *Iacob Bloome*, 1634.

A PREFACE

OR ADVERTISEMENT TO THE READER AS FOR THE
BETTER ILLUSTRATION AND UNDERSTANDING
OF THIS FAMOUS HISTORIE.

AFTER this kingdome had, for the space of above foure hundred and eighty yeares, borne the intolerable yoke of the Romane servitude, which began by the conquest which Julius Cæsar made here in the raigne of Cassibellan, king of the Brittaines, seventeene yeares before the Incarnation of Christ, and ended in the time of Gratian, which was three hundred seventie six yeares after Christ, who had slaine Maximinianus, the Romane emperour; which Gratian after being slaine, Vortiger of the bloud royall of the Britaine king, did, by usurpation and the murther of Constance, the sonne of Constantius, seize upon the crowne. And being by his wicked life and ill gotten soveraignty, grown odious, and hated by most of his subjects, hee was inforced to send into Germany for the Saxons, to aide and support him. The Saxons having got footing here, never gave over their military diligence till they got full possession of the whole kingdome; chasing the British kings beyond the rivers of Dee and Seaverne in North Wales, in the raigne of Carreticus, in the yeare five hundred eighty sixe. The above said Vortigerne the usurper was deposed, to whom his sonne Vortimer succeeded, but Vortimer was poysoned by Rowan the daughter of Hengist the Saxon, and Vortigerne againe was restored to the crowne; and after nineteene yeares of a troublous raigne, hee and his wife Rowan were burnt in their castle or palace by Aurelius Ambrose, who was of the race of Constance, who formerly had beene murdred by Vortigerne. This Aurelius Ambrose raigned thirty two yeares, to whom succeeded his brother Uter Pendragon, who was the father of Arthur, the great king of Britaine, of whose worthy acts and noble atchievements this history makes mention. King Uter Pendragon begat Arthur of the beauteous Igraine, wife to the duke of Cornwall, which lady king Uter afterward rewarded, and, by the helpe of Merlin the great magitian, Arthur was brought up and educated. He raigned king of Britaine in anno five hundred and sixteene. In his raigne he curbed the insolent power of the domineering Saxons, he wanne and subdued Denmarke and Norway. He ordained and instituted the order of the round table at Winchester, which was honoured with the number of one hundred and fifty knights. He was victorious beyond the seas against the Saracens, and by his conquests made many of those misbeleeving Pagans acknowledge the true God. Whilest he was abroad in these noble and heroicall imployments, his nephew, Mordred, whom hee had put in trust with the government of his realme, being puffed up with ambition and possessed with treason, he caused himselfe to be crowned, and usurped the kingdome; which king Arthur hearing of, hee made quicke expedition into this land, and landed at Dover, where the traytor Mordred was with a mighty army to impeach and hinder the kings arrivall. But in spight of all trayterous and rebellious opposition, king Arthur landed his troupes, and after two set battailes he slue Mordred, and with the losse of his owne life, wonne a glorious victory, and being dead, was buried at the towne of Glastenbury in Somersetshire, after hee had raigned sixteene yeares, to whom next succeeded in the Britaine throne Constantine the fifth, being a kinsman to king Arthur, and sonne to Cadors duke of Cornwall.

All this former narration is set downe to confute the errours of such as are of an opinion that there was never any such man as king Arthur, and though historians doe disagree in their chronologies about times and places, some having written partially, some neglectively, and some fabulously and superstitiously, yet in the mayne points which are most materiall, they doe all conclude of the predecessours and successours of king Arthur, according as I have formerly related. It is apparent in all histories that there were nine most famous and renowmed kings and princes, who for their noble acts and worthy atchievements, are stiled the nine worthies, and it is most execrable infidelity to doubt that there was a Joshua, it is wicked Atheisme to make a question if there was a David, it is hatefull to be diffident of a sometime Judas Macchabeus; besides there are none, of any capacitie, but doe believe there was an Alexander. The world is possest with the acknowledgement of the life and death of Julius Cæsar, and the never dying fame of the illustrious Trojan Hector is perspicuous; we must all approve of the being of that magnanimous prince Godfrey duke of Bulloigne, who was the christian generall at the conquest of Jerusalem, in the yeare 1110. Besides, France, Germany, and all the christian world hath in fresh and admired memory the famous emperour Charlemaigne or Charles the Great.

And shall the Jewes and the Heathen be honoured in the memory and magnificent prowesse of their worthies? shall the French and Germane nations glorifie their triumphs with their Godfrey and Charles, and shall we of this island be so possest with incredulitie, diffidence, stupiditie, and ingratitude, to deny, make doubt, or expresse in speech and history, the immortall name and fame of our victorious Arthur. All the honour we can doe him is to honour our selves in remembrance of him. This following history was first written in the French and Italian tongues, so much did the poets and chronologers of forraine nations admire our Arthur. It was many yeares after the first writing of it, translated into English, by the painfull industry of one sir Thomas Maleore, knight, in the ninth yeare of the raigne of king Edward the Fourth, about one hundred and fifty two yeares past; wherein the reader may see the best forme and manner of writing and speech that was in use at those times. In many places fables and fictions are inserted, which may be a blemish to the reputation of what is true in this history, and it is unfitting for us to raze or blot out all the errours of our ancestours, for by our taking consideration of them, wee may be the better induced to beleeve and reverence the truth. It is 1114 years since king Arthurs raigne, which was long before the dayes of Edward the Fourth, whereby it may be mused what speech they used above 1100 yeares agoe, when as it was so plaine and simple in king Edwards time.

TO THE READER.

And therefore, reader, I advertise thee to deale with this book as thou wouldest doe with thy house or thy garment, if the one doe want but a little repaire thou wilt not (madly) pull downe the whole frame, if the other hath a small spot or a staine thou wilt not cast it away or burne it, gold hath its drosse, wine hath its lees, man (in all ages) hath his errours and imperfections. And though the times are now more accute and sharp-witted, using a more eloquent and ornated stile and phrase in speech and writing then they did, who lived so many yeares past, yet it may be that in the age to come, our successours may hold and esteeme of us as ridiculously as many of our over-nice critickes doe of their and our progenitours, as we are refined in words I wish we were reformed in deeds, and as we can talke better, it were well if wee would not doe worse. Wee perceive their darknesse through our light, let not our light blind us that we may not see our owne ignorance. In many places this volume is corrected (not in language but in phrase), for here and there king Arthur or some of his knights were declared in their communications to sweare prophane, and use superstitious speeches, all, or the most part, of which is either amended or quite left out, by the paines and industry of the compositor and corrector at the presse, so that as it is now it may passe for a famous piece of antiquity, revived almost from the gulph of oblivion, and renued for the pleasure and profit of present and future times.

As (by the favour of Heaven) this kingdome of Britaine was graced with one worthy, let us with thankfulnes acknowledge him; let us not account it our shame, that he hath bin our countries honour; let us not be more cruell then death to smother or murder his name; or let us not be worse then the grave in burying his favour. Thus, reader, I leave thee at thy pleasure to reade but not to judge, except thou judge with understanding. The asse is no competent judge betwixt the owle and the nightingale for the sweetnes of their voices; cloth of Arras or hangings of tapistry are not fit to adorne a kitchin, no more are ketles, pots, and spits to hang in a ladies bed-chamber. Neither is it beseeming for a man to censure that which his ignorance cannot perceive, or his pride and malice will prejudicate or cavill at.

[THE PROLOGUE.]¹

AFTER that I had accomplysshed and fynysshed dyvers hystoryes, as well of contemplacyon as of other hystoryal and worldly actes of grete conquerours and prynces, and also certeyn bookes of ensaumples and doctryne, many noble and dyvers gentylmen of thys royame of Englond camen and demaunded me many and oftymes wherfore that I have not do make and enprynte the noble hystorye of the saynt greal, and of the moost renomed crysten kyng, fyrst and chyef of the thre best crysten and worthy, kyng Arthur, whyche ought moost to be remembred emonge us Englysshe men tofore al other crysten kynges. For it is notoyrly knowen thorugh the unyversal world that there been ix. worthy and the best that ever were, that is to wete, thre paynyms, thre Jewes, and thre crysten men. As for the paynyms, they were tofore the incarnacyon of Cryst, whiche were named, the fyrst Hector of Troye, of whome thystorye is comen bothe in balade and in prose; the second Alysaunder the grete; and the thyrd Julyus Cezar, emperour of Rome, of whome thystoryes ben

¹ This, and what the edition of 1634 calls the preface to the Christian reader, are from Caxton's edition, and they are here printed verbatim from that edition, of which they will serve as a specimen. The headings or titles of the edition of 1634 are given in brackets.

wel kno and had. And as for the thre Jewes, whyche also were tofore thyncarnacyon of our Lord, of whome the fyst was duc Josue, whyche brought the chyldren of Israhel into the londe of byheste; the second Davyd kyng of Jherusalem; and the thyrd Judas Machabeus; of these thre the Byble reherceth al theyr noble hystoryes and actes. And sythe the sayd incarnacyon have ben thre noble crysten men stalled and admytted thorugh the unyversal world into the nombre of the ix. beste and worthy, of whome was fyrst the noble Arthur, whos noble actes I purpose to wryte in thys present book here folowyng; the second was Charlemayn, or Charles the grete, of whome thystorye is had in many places bothe in Frensshe and Englysshe; and the thyrd and last was Godefray of Boloyn, of whos actes and lyf I made a book unto thexcellent prynce and kyng of noble memorye kyng Edward the fourth.[1] The said noble jentylmen instantly requyred me temprynte thystorye of the sayd noble kyng and conquerour kyng Arthur, and of his knyghtes, wyth thystorye of the saynt greal, and of the deth and endyng of the sayd Arthur; affermyng that I ouʒt rather tenprynte his actes and noble feates, than of Godefroye of Boloyne, or ony of the other eyght, consyderyng that he was a man borne wythin this royame, and kyng and emperour of the same.

And that there ben in Frensshe dyvers and many noble volumes of his actes, and also of his knyghtes. To whom I answerd, that dyvers men holde oppynyon that there was no suche Arthur, and that alle suche bookes as been maad of hym, ben but fayned and fables, bycause that somme

[1] *Edward the fourth.*—This book was printed by Caxton at Westminster in 1841, and therefore about three years and a half before the appearance of Caxton's King Arthur.

THE PROLOGUE.

cronycles make of hym no mencyon ne remembre hym noo thynge ne of his knyghtes. Wherto they answerd, and one in specyal sayd, that in hym that shold say or thynke that there was never suche a kyng callyd Arthur, myght wel be aretted grete folye and blyndenesse; for he sayd that there were many evydences of the contrarye. Fyrst ye may see his sepulture in the monasterye of Glastyngburye, and also in Polycronycon, in the v book the syxte chappytre, and in the seventh book the xxiii chappytre, where his body was buryed and after founden and translated into the sayd monasterye. Ye shal se also in thystorye of Bochas in his book *de casu principum*, parte of his noble actes and also of his falle. Also Galfrydus,[1] in his Brutysshe book, recounteth his lyf. And in divers places of Englond many remembraunces ben yet of hym and shall remayne perpetuelly, and also of his knyghtes. Fyrst, in the abbay of Westmestre at saynt Edwardes shryne remayneth the prynte of his seal in reed waxe closed in beryll, in whych is wryton *Patricius Arthurus, Britannie, Gallie, Germanie, Dacie, imperator*. Item, in the castel of Dover[2] ye may see Gauwayns skulle, and Cradoks mantel; at Wynchester,[3] the rounde table; in other places, Launcelottes swerde, and many other thynges. Thenne al these thynges consydered, there can no man reasonably gaynsaye but there was a kyng of thys lande named Ar-

---

[1] *Galfrydus.*—Of course he means Geoffrey of Monmouth.

[2] *Castel of Dover.*— See at the end of the History of King Arthur, vol. iii. p. 329 of the present edition.

[3] *At Wynchester.*—This "rounde table" is still preserved at Winchester, and is a relic of some interest in other points of view, but it is hardly necessary to state that it belongs to a far more recent date than that which Caxton would seem to have given to it.

thur. For in al' places crysten and hethen he is reputed and taken for one of the ix. worthy, and the fyrst of the thre crysten men. And also he is more spoken of beyonde the see, moo bookes made of his noble actes, than there be in Englond, as wel in Duche, Ytalyen, Spanysshe, and Grekysshe, as in Frensshe. And yet of record remayne in wytnesse of hym in Wales, in the toune of Camelot,[1] the grete stones and mervayllous werkys of yron lyeing under the grounde, and ryal vautes, which dyvers now lyvyng hath seen. Wherfor it is a mervayl why he is no more renomed in his owne contreye, sauf onelye it accordeth to the word of God, whyche sayth that no man is accept for a prophete in his owne contreye. Thenne al these thynges forsayd aledged, I coude not wel denye but that there was suche a noble kyng named Arthur, and reputed one of the ix worthy, and fyrst and chyef of the cristen men, and many noble volumes be made of hym and of his noble knyȝtes in Frensshe, which I have seen and redde beyonde the see, which been not had in our maternal tongue, but in Walsshe ben many, and also in Frensshe, and somme in Englysshe, but no wher nygh alle. Wherfore suche as have late ben drawen oute bryefly into Englysshe, I have after the symple connyng that God hath sente to me, under the favour and correctyon of al noble lordes and gentylmen, enprysed to enprynte a book of the noble hystoryes of the sayd kynge Arthur, and of certeyn of his knyghtes, after a copye unto me delyvered, whyche copye

---

[1] *Camelot.*—It is curious that the writer of this preface should have placed Camelot in Wales, contrary to the text of the book itself, which tells us several times that Camelot was Winchester. Both statements are quite erroneous. See vol. i. p. 59.

THE PROLOGUE.

syr Thomas Malorye dyd take oute of certeyn bookes of Frensshe and reduced it into Englysshe. And I, accordyng to my copye, have doon sette it in enprynte, to the entente that noblemen may see and lerne the noble acts of chyvalrye, the jentyl and vertuous dedes, that somme knyghtes used in tho days, by whyche they came to honour, and how they that were vycious were punysshed and often put to shame and rebuke, humbly bysechying al noble lordes and ladyes, wyth al other estates, of what estate or degree they been of, that shal see and rede in this sayd book and werke, that they take the good and honest actes in their remembraunce, and to folowe the same. Wherin they shalle fynde many joyous and playsaunt hystoryes and noble and renomed acts of humanyte, gentylnesse, and chyvalryes. For herein may be seen noble chyvalrye, curtosye, humanyte, frendlynesse, hardynesse, love, frendshyp, cowardyse, murdre, hate, vertue, synne. Doo after the good, and leve the evyl, and it shal brynge you to good fame and renommee. And for to passe the tyme, this book shal be plesaunte to rede in, but for to gyve fayth and byleve that al is trewe that is contayned herin, ye be at your lyberte; but al is wryton for our doctryne, and for to beware that we falle not to vyce ne synne, but texercyse and folowe vertu, by whyche we may come and atteyne to good fame and renomme in thys lyf, and after thys shorte and transytorye lyf to come unto everlastyng blysse in heven, the whyche he graunt us that reygneth in heven the blessyd Trynyte. Amen.

[THE PREFACE OF WILLIAM CAXTON TO THE CHRISTIAN READER.]

THENNE to procede forth in thys sayd book, whyche I dyrecte unto alle noble prynces, lordes, and ladyes, gentylmen, or gentylwymmen, that desyre to rede or here redde of the noble and joyous hystorye of the grete conquerour and excellent kyng, kyng Arthur, somtyme kyng of thys noble royalme, thenne callyd Brytaygne, I, Wyllyam Caxton, symple persone, present thys book folowyng, whyche I have enprysed tenprynte.[1] And treateth of the noble actes, feates of armes, of chyvalrye, prowesse, hardynesse, humanyte, love, curtosye, and veray gentylnesse, wyth many wonderful hystoryes and adventures. And for to understonde bryefly the contente of thys vol-

---

[1] The edition of 1634, in which Caxton's division into "books" is abandoned and the whole is divided into three parts or volumes, omits the remainder of Caxton's "preface," and adds in its place:—
In which all those that dispose them to eschew idlenesse, which is the mother of all vices, may read historicall matters. Some are willing to reade devout meditations of the humanitie and passion of our Saviour Jesus Christ; some the lives and painefull martyrdomes of holy saints; some delight in moralisacion and poeticall stories; and some in knightly and victorious deeds of noble princes and conquerours, as of this present

TO THE CHRISTIAN READER. xxxiii

ume, I have devyded it into xxi bookes, and every book chapytred as here after shal by Goddes grace folowe. The fyrst book shal treate how Utherpendragon gate the noble conquerour kyng Arthur, and conteyneth xxviii chappytres. The second book treateth of Balyn, the noble knyght, and conteyneth xix chapytres. The thyrd book treateth of the maryage of kyng Arthur to quene Guenever, wyth other maters, and conteyneth fyftene chappytres. The fourth book, how Merlyn was assotted, and of warre maad to kyng Arthur, and conteyneth xxix chappytres. The fyfthe book treateth of the conqueste of Lucius themperour, and conteyneth xii chappytres. The syxthe book treateth of syr Launcelot and syr Lyonel, and mervayllous adventures, and conteyneth xviii chapytres. The seventh book treateth of a noble knyght called syr Gareth, and named by syr Kaye Beaumayns, and conteyneth xxxvi chapytres. The eyght book treateth of the byrthe of syr Trystram, the noble knyght, and of hys actes, and conteyneth xli chapytres. The ix book treateth of a knyght named by syr Kaye Le cote male taylle, and also of syr Trystram, and conteyneth xliiii chapytres. The x. book treateth of syr Trystram and other mervayllous adventures, and conteyneth lxxxviii chappytres. The xi book treateth of syr Launcelot and syr Galahad, and conteyneth xiiii chappytres. The xii book treateth of syr Launcelot and his madnesse,

volume, which treateth of the noble acts and featee of armes, of chivalry, prowesse, hardinesse, humanitie, love, courtesie, and gentilnesse, with divers and many wonderfull histories and adventures. And for to understand briefly the contents of this present volume, comprehending the valiant acts of this noble conquerour, with his lamentable death caused by sir Mordred his sonne and the subjects of his realme, I have devided it into three parts, and every part into sundry chapters, as hereafter, by Gods grace, shall follow.

VOL. I.   c

and conteyneth xiiii chappytres. The xiii book treateth how Galahad came fyrst to kyng Arthurs courte, and the quest how the sangreall was begonne, and conteyneth xx chapytres. The xiiii book treateth of the queste of the sangreal, and conteyneth x chapytres. The xv book treateth of syr Launcelot, and conteyneth vi chapytres. The xvi book treateth of syr Bors and syr Lyonel his brother, and conteyneth xvii chapytres. The xvii book treateth of the sangreal, and conteyneth xxiii chapytres. The xviii book treateth of syr Launcelot and the quene, and conteyneth xxv chapytres. The xix. book treateth of quene Guenever and Launcelot, and conteyneth xiii chapytres. The xx book treateth of the pyetous deth of Arthur, and conteyneth xxii chapytres. The xxi book treateth of his last departyng, and how syr Launcelot came to revenge his dethe, and conteyneth xiii chapytres. The somme is xxi bookes, whyche conteyne the somme of v honderd and vii chapytres, as more playnly shal folowe herafter.

CONTENTS.

CHAPTER I.

HOW Utherpendragon sent for the duke of Cornewayle and Igrayne his wife, and of their sodaine departing againe 1

CHAP. II. How Utherpendragon made warre on the duke of Cornewaile, and how by the meanes of Merlyn he lay by the duchesse and begat on her Arthur . 4

CHAP. III. Of the birth of king Arthur, and of his nourishing, and of the death of king Utherpendragon, and how Arthur was chosen king, and of wonders and marvailes of a sword that was taken out of stone by the said Arthur . . . 6

CHAP. IV. How king Arthur pulled out the sword divers times 12

CHAP. V. How Arthur was crowned king, and how he made officers 14

CHAP. VI. How king Arthur held in Wales at a Penticost a great feast, and what kings and lords came to this feast . 15

CHAP. VII. Of the first warre that king Arthur had, and how he wanne the field and overcame his enemies . . . 17

CHAP. VIII. How Merlin counsailed king Arthur to send for king Ban and king Bors, and of their counsaile taken for the warre 19

CHAP. IX. Of a great turney made by king Arthur and the two kings Ban and Bors, and how they went over the sea . . 23

CHAP. X. How eleaven kings gathered a great hoast against king Arthur 25

CHAP. XI. Of a dreame of the king with the hundred knights 27

CHAP. XII. How that the eleaven kings with their hoast fought against king Arthur and his hoast, and of many great feates of the warre 27

CONTENTS.

	Page
CHAP. XIII. Yet of the same battaile	31
CHAP. XIV. Yet more of the said battaile, and how it was ended by Merlin	33
CHAP. XV. Yet of the said battayle	37
CHAP. XVI. How king Arthur, king Ban, and king Bors reschewed king Leodegraunce, and of other incidents . .	41
CHAP. XVII. How king Arthur rode to Carlyon, and of his dreame, and how he saw the questing beast . . .	43
CHAP. XVIII. How king Pellinore tooke king Arthurs horse, and followed the questing beast, and how Merlin met with king Arthur	45
CHAP. XIX. How Ulfius appeaches queene Igrayne, king Arthurs mother, of treason. And how a knight came and desired to have the death of his master revenged . . .	47
CHAP. XX. How Griflet was made knight, and how he justed with a knight	48
CHAP. XXI. How twelve knights came from Rome and asked truage of this land of king Arthur, and how king Arthur fought with a knight	50
CHAP. XXII. How Merlin saved king Arthurs life, and threw an enchauntment upon king Pellinor, and made him to fall on sleepe	53
CHAP. XXIII. How king Arthur, by the meanes of Merlin, gate his sword of Excalibur of the lady of the lake . . .	54
CHAP. XXIV. How tidings came to king Arthur that king Ryence had overcome eleaven kings, and how he desired king Arthurs beard to purfel his mantell	56
CHAP. XXV. How all the children were sent for that were borne upon May day, and how Mordred was saved . . .	57
CHAP. XXVI. Of a damosel which came gyrd with a sword for to finde a man of such vertue to draw it out of the scabbard .	58
CHAP. XXVII. How Balin, arayed like a poore man, pulled out the sword, which afterwards was cause of his death . .	60
CHAP. XXVIII. How the ladie of the lake demanded the knights head that had woune the sword, or the maydens head .	63
CHAP. XXIX. How Merlin told the adventure of the damosell .	65
CHAP. XXX. How Balin was pursued by sir Lanceor, a knight of Ireland, and how Balin slew him	65
CHAP. XXXI. How a damosell which was in love with Lanceor,	

CONTENTS. xxxvii

	Page
slew her selfe for his love, and how Balin met with his brother Balan	67
CHAP. XXXII. How a dwarfe reproved Balin for the death of Lanceor, and how king Marke of Cornewayle found them, and made a tombe over them	69
CHAP. XXXIII. How Merlin prophesied that two of the best knights of the world should fight there, which were sir Lancelot and sir Tristram	70
CHAP. XXXIV. How Balin and his brother, by the counsaile of Merlin, tooke king Rience and brought him unto king Arthur	72
CHAP. XXXV. How king Arthur had a battaile against Nero and king Lot of Orkeney, and how king Lot was deceived by Merlin, and how twelve kings were slaine	73
CHAP. XXXVI. Of the entertainement of twelve kings, and of the prophesie of Merlin, and how Balin should give the dolorous stroke	76
CHAP. XXXVII. How a sorrowfull knight came tofore king Arthur, and how Balin fet him, and how that knight was slaine by a knight invisible	77
CHAP. XXXVIII. How Balin and the damosell met with a knight that was in likewise slaine, and how the damosel bled for the custome of a castle	79
CHAP. XXXIX. How Balin met with the knight named Garlon at a feast, and there he slew him, to have his blood to heale therewith the sonne of his hoast	80
CHAP. XL. How Balin fought with king Pellam, and how his sword brake, and how he gate a speare, wherewith he smote the dolorous stroke	82
CHAP. XLI. How Balin was delivered by Merlin, and saved a knight that would have slaine himselfe for love	83
CHAP. XLII. How that knight slew his love and a knight lying by her, and after how he slew himselfe with his owne sword, and how Balin rode toward a castle where he lost his life	85
CHAP. XLIII. How Balin met with his brother Balan, and how each of them slew other unknowen till they were wounded to death	87
CHAP. XLIV. How Merlin buried Balin and Balan the two brethren in one tombe, and of Balins sword	90

CONTENTS.

	Page
CHAP. XLV. How king Arthur tooke and wedded Guenever unto his wife, which was daughter to Leodegraunce king of the land of Cameliard, with whom he had the round table	91
CHAP. XLVI. How the knights of the round table were ordained, and how their sieges were blessed by the archbishop of Canterbury	93
CHAP. XLVII. How a poore man riding upon a leane mare desired king Arthur to make his sonne a knight	94
CHAP. XLVIII. How sir Tor was knowen for the sonne of king Pellinore, and Gawayne was made knight	96
CHAP. XLIX. How at the feast of the wedding of king Arthur unto Guenever a white hart came into the hall, and thirty couple of hounds, and how a brachet pinched the hart, the which was taken away	97
CHAP. L. How sir Gawayne rode for to fetch againe the hart, and how two brethren fought each againe other for the hart	99
CHAP. LI. How the hart was chased into a castle and there slaine, and how sir Gawaine slew a lady	100
CHAP. LII. How foure knights fought against sir Gawaine and Gaheris, and how they were overcome and their lives saved at the request of foure damosels	102
CHAP. LIII. How sir Tor rode after the knight with the brachet, and of his adventures by the way	104
CHAP. LIV. How sir Tor found the brachet with a lady, and how a knight assailed him for the said brachet	105
CHAP. LV. How sir Tor overcame the knight, and how he lost his head at the request of a lady	107
CHAP. LVI. How king Pellinore rode after the lady and the knight that led her away, and how a lady desired helpe of him, and how hee fought with two knights for that lady, of whom he slew the one at the first strooke	109
CHAP. LVII. How king Pellinore gate the lady, and brought her to Camelot unto the court of king Arthur	111
CHAP. LVIII. How king Pellinore heard two knights, as he lay by night in a valey, and of other adventures	113
CHAP. LIX. How king Pellinore, when he was come to Camelot, was sworne upon a booke to tell truth of his quest	114
CHAP. LX. How Merlin was assotted and doted on one of the	

CONTENTS. xxxix

ladies of the lake, and he was shut in a roche under a stone by a wood side, and there died 116

CHAP. LXI. How five kings came into this land to warre against king Arthur, and what counsaile king Arthur had against them 118

CHAP. LXII. How king Arthur overthrew and slew the five kings, and made the remnant to flee 119

CHAP. LXIII. How the battaile was finished or that king Pellinore came, and how king Arthur founded an abbey where the battaile was 121

CHAP. LXIV. How sir Tor was made knight of the round table, and how Bagdemagus was displeased 123

CHAP. LXV. How king Arthur, king Urience, and sir Accolon of Gaule, chased an hart, and of their marvailous adventures 124

CHAP. LXVI. How king Arthur tooke upon him to fight for to be delivered out of prison, and also to deliver twentie knights that wer in prison 126

CHAP. LXVII. How sir Accolon found himselfe by a well, and he tooke upon him to doe battaile against king Arthur . 128

CHAP. LXVIII. Of the battaile betweene king Arthur and sir Accolon 130

CHAP. LXIX. How king Arthurs sword that he fought with brake, and how he recovered of sir Accolon his owne sword Excalibur, and overcame his enemie 132

CHAP. LXX. How sir Accolon confessed the treason of Morgan le Fay, and how she would have caused her brother king Arthur to be slaine 134

CHAP. LXXI. How king Arthur accorded the two brethren, and delivered the twentie knights, and how sir Accolon died . 135

CHAP. LXXII. How Morgan le Fay would have slaine king Urience her husband, and how sir Ewaine her sonne saved him 137

CHAP. LXXIII. How Morgan le Fay made great sorrow for the death of sir Accolon, and how she stale away from king Arthur the scabbard 139

CHAP. LXXIV. How Morgan le Fay saved a knight that should have beene drowned, and how king Arthur returned home againe to Camelot 141

CONTENTS.

CHAP. LXXV. How the damosell of the lake saved king Arthur from a mantell which should have brent him . . . 143

CHAP. LXXVI. How sir Gawaine and sir Ewaine met with twelve faire damosels, and how they complained upon sir Marhaus 144

CHAP. LXXVII. How sir Marhaus justed with sir Gawaine and sir Ewaine, and overthrew them both 145

CHAP. LXXVIII. How sir Marhaus, sir Gawaine, and Ewaine, met three damosels, and each of them tooke one . . 149

CHAP. LXXIX. How a knight and a dwarfe strove for a lady 150

CHAP. LXXX. How king Pelleas suffered himselfe to be taken prisoner because he would have a sight of his lady, and how sir Gawaine promised him for to get to him the love of his lady 152

CHAP. LXXXI. How sir Gawaine came to the lady Ettarde, and lay by her, and how sir Pelleas found them sleeping . . 155

CHAP. LXXXII. How sir Pelleas loved no more the lady Ettard by the meanes of the damosell of the lake, whom he loved ever after during his life 158

CHAP. LXXXIII. How sir Marhaus rode with the damosell, and how he came to the duke of the South Marches . . 159

CHAP. LXXXIV. How sir Marhaus fought with the duke and his sixe sonnes, and made them to yeeld them . . 161

CHAP. LXXXV. How sir Ewaine rode with the damosell of threescore yeeres of age, and how he gate the prise at a turney . 163

CHAP. LXXXVI. How sir Ewaine fought with two knights, and overcame them 165

CHAP. LXXXVII. How at the yeares end all the three knights with their three damosels met at the fountaine . . . 166

CHAP. LXXXVIII. How twelve aged men, embassadours of Rome, come to king Arthur for to demaund truage for the realme of Brittaine 168

CHAP. LXXXIX. How the kings and lords promised unto king Arthur ayde and helpe against the Romaines . . . 170

CHAP. XC. How king Arthur held a parliament at Yorke, and how hee ordeined in what maner the realme should bee governed in his absence 173

CHAP. XCI. How king Arthur being shipped and lying in his cabin, had a marvailous dreame, and of the exposition thereof 174

CONTENTS. xli

Page

CHAP. XCII. How a man of the countrey told him of a mervailous gyant, and how he fought and conquered him . . 175

CHAP. XCIII. How king Arthur sent sir Gawaine and others to Lucius the emperour, and how they were assailed, and escaped with worship 179

CHAP. XCIV. How Lucius sent certaine spies into ambush for to have taken his knights, being prisoners, and how they were letted 181

CHAP. XCV. How a senatour told to the emperour Lucius of their discomfiture, and also of the great battaile betweene king Arthur and Lucius 183

CHAP. XCVI. How king Arthur, after that he had atchieved the battaile against the Romaines, entred into Almaine, and so into Italy 187

CHAP. XCVII. Of the battaile done by sir Gawaine against a Sarasin, which after was taken and became Christian . 188

CHAP. XCVIII. How that the Sarasins came out of a wood for to rescew their beasts, and of a great battaile . . . 192

CHAP. XCIX. How sir Gawaine returned to king Arthur with his prisoners, and how the king wan a citie, and how he was crowned emperour 193

CHAP. C. How sir Launcelot and sir Lionell departed from the court for to seeke adventures, and how sir Lionell left sir Launcelot sleeping, and was taken 197

CHAP. CI. How sir Ector de Maris followed to seeke sir Launcelot, and how he was taken by sir Torquine . . . 199

CHAP. CII. How foure queenes found sir Launcelot sleeping, and how by enchauntment he was taken and led into a strong castle 200

CHAP. CIII. How sir Launcelot was delivered by the meanes of a damosell 202

CHAP. CIV. How a knight found sir Launcelot lying in his lemans bed, and how sir Launcelot fought with that knight 204

CHAP. CV. How sir Launcelot was received of King Bagdemagus daughter, and how he made his complaint unto her father 205

CHAP. CVI. How sir Launcelot behaved him in a turneyment, and how hee met with sir Turquine leading away sir Gaheris with him 207

CHAP. CVII. How sir Launcelot and Turquine fought together 210

CONTENTS.

CHAP. CVIII. How sir Turquine was slaine, and how sir Launcelot bad sir Gaheris deliver all the prisoners . . . 211

CHAP. CIX. How sir Launcelot rode with the damosel and slew a knight that distressed all ladies, and a villain that kept the passage over a bridge 213

CHAP. CX. How sir Launcelot slew two gyants, and made a castle free 216

CHAP. CXI. How sir Launcelot disguised in sir Kays armour, and how hee smote downe a knight 219

CHAP. CXII. How sir Launcelot justed against foure knights of the round table, and overthrew them 221

CHAP. CXIII. How sir Launcelot followed a brachet into a castle, where as he found a dead knight, and how afterward he was required of a damosell for to heale her brother . 223

CHAP. CXIV. How sir Launcelot came into the chappell perilous, and gat there of a dead corps a peece of the cloath and a sword 224

CHAP. CXV. How sir Launcelot at the request of a lady recovered a fawcon, whereby he was deceived . . . 227

CHAP. CXVI. How sir Launcelot overtooke a knight which chased his wife to have slaine her, and what he said to him 229

CHAP. CXVII. How sir Launcelot came unto king Arthurs court, and how there were recounted of his noble feates and acts . 231

CHAP. CXVIII. How Beaumains came unto king Arthurs court and demanded three petitions of king Arthur . . . 232

CHAP. CXIX. How sir Launcelot and sir Gawaine were wroth because sir Kay mocked Beaumains, and of a damosell which desired a knight for to doe battaile for a lady . . . 235

CHAP. CXX. How Beaumains desired the battaile, and how it was graunted him, and how he desired to be made knight of sir Launcelot 237

CHAP. CXXI. How Beaumains departed, and how he got of sir Kay a speare and a shield, and how he justed and fought with sir Launcelot 238

CHAP. CXXII. How Beaumains told his name to sir Lancelot, and how hee was dubbed knight of sir Lancelot, and after overtooke the damosell 239

CHAP. CXXIII. How sir Beaumains fought and slew two knights at a passage 241

CONTENTS. xliii

Page

CHAP. CXXIV. How sir Beaumains fought with the knight of the blacke launds, and he fought so long with him that the blacke knight fell downe and dyed 243

CHAP. CXXV. How the brother of the knight that was slaine met with sir Beaumains, and fought with sir Beaumains, which yeelded him at the last 245

CHAP. CXXVI. How the damosell alwayes rebuked sir Beaumains, and would not suffer him to sit at her table, but called him kitchin page 247

CHAP. CXXVII. How the third brother called the red knight, justed and fought against sir Beaumains, and how sir Beaumains overcame him 249

CHAP. CXXVIII. How sir Beaumains suffered great rebukes of the damosell, and he suffered it patiently . . . 251

CHAP. CXXIX. How sir Beaumains fought with sir Persaunt of Inde, and made him to be yeelden 254

CHAP. CXXX. Of the goodly communication between sir Persaunt and sir Beaumains, and how he told him that his name was sir Gaureth 256

CHAP. CXXXI. How the lady which was besieged had word from her sister how she had brought a knight to fight for her, and what battailes he had done 258

CHAP. CXXXII. How the damosel and sir Beaumains came to the siege, and came to a sickamore tree, and there sir Beaumains blew an horne, and then the knight of the red launds came to fight with him 260

CHAP. CXXXIII. How the two knights met together, and of their talking, and how they began their battaile . . 261

CHAP. CXXXIV. How after long fighting sir Beaumains overcame the knight, and would have slaine him, but at the request of the lords hee saved his life and made him to yeeld him to the lady 264

CHAP. CXXXV. How the knight yeelded him, and how sir Beaumains made him to goe unto king Arthurs court, and to crie sir Launcelot mercy 266

CHAP. CXXXVI. How sir Beaumains came to the lady, and when he came unto the castle the gates were closed against him, and of the words that the lady said unto him . . . 268

CHAP. CXXXVII. How sir Beaumains rode after for to rescew his dwarfe, and came into the castle where he was . . 270

CHAP. CXXXVIII. How sir Gareth, otherwise called sir Beaumains, came unto the presence of his lady, and how they tooke acquaintance, and of their love 273

CHAP. CXXXIX. How in the night came in an armed knight and fought with sir Gareth, and hurt him sore in the thigh, and how sir Gareth smote off the knights head . . 275

CHAP. CXL. How the same knight came againe the next night, and was beheaded againe. And how at the feast of Pentecost all the knights that sir Gareth had overcome came and yeelded them unto king Arthur 277

CHAP. CXLI. How sir Launcelot and sir Gawaine pardoned him, and demaunded him where sir Gareth was . . 280

CHAP. CXLII. How the queene of Orkeney came to this feast of Pentecost, and how sir Gawaine and his brethren came to aske her blessing 281

CHAP. CXLIII. How king Arthur sent for the lady Liones, and how shee let crie a turnement at the castle, where as came many good knights 283

CHAP. CXLIV. How king Arthur went to the turnement with his knights, and how the lady dame Liones received him worshipfully, and how the knights encountred together . 286

CHAP. CXLV. How the knights bare them in the battaile . 289

CHAP. CXLVI. How sir Gareth was espied by the heraulds, and how he escaped out of the field 293

CHAP. CXLVII. How sir Gareth came unto a castle, where he was well lodged, and how he justed with a knight, and how he slew him 295

CHAP. CXLVIII. How sir Gareth fought with a knight that held within his castle thirtie ladies, and how he slew him 297

CHAP. CXLIX. How sir Gawaine and sir Gareth fought each against other, and how they knew each other by the damosell Linet 299

CHAP. CL. How sir Gareth acknowledged that they loved each other to king Arthur, and of the day of their wedding . 301

CHAP. CLI. Of the great royaltie and what officers were made at the feast of sir Gareth and dame Liones wedding, and of the great justing at the same feast and wedding . . 303

HISTORIE OF KING ARTHUR

AND HIS NOBLE KNIGHTS OF

THE ROUND TABLE.

CHAP. I.—How Utherpendragon sent for the duke of Cornewayle and Igrayne his wife, and of their sodaine departing againe.

IT befell in the dayes of the noble Utherpendragon, when he was king of England and so reigned, there was a mighty and a noble duke in Cornewayle,[1] that held long time warre against him; and the duke was named the duke of Tintagil;[2] and so by meanes king Uther sent for this duke, charging him to bring his wife with him, for shee was called a right faire lady, and a passing wise, and Igrayne was her name. So when the duke and his wife were come to the king, by the meanes of great lords, they were both accorded, and the king liked and loved this lady well, and made her great cheere out of measure, and desired to have lyen by her. But she was a passing good

[1] Called by Geoffrey of Monmouth *Gorlois dux Cornubiæ*, and his wife *Igerna*.
[2] *Tintagil.*—The small town of Tintagell, in Cornwall, is situated on the coast of the Bristol Channel, about four miles from Camelford. The ruins of the castle, which had become so celebrated in medieval romance, are still seen on the brow of a rock, partly insulated, overlooking the sea.

woman, and would not assent to the king. And then she told the duke, her husband, and said: "I suppose that we were sent for that I should be dishonoured, wherefore, husband, I counsell you that we depart from hence sodainely, that we may ride all night[1] to our owne castell." And, like as shee had said, so they departed, that neither the king nor none of his counsell were ware of their departing. As soone as king Uther knew of their departing so sodainly, hee was wonderfull wroth. Then he called to him his privie counsell, and told them of the sodaine departing of the duke and his wife. Then they advised the king to send for the duke and his wife by a great charge; " and, if he will not come at your commandement, then may yee doe your best, for then have you a cause to make mighty warre upon him." So that was done, and the messengers had their answeres, and that was this, shortly, that neither hee nor his wife would not come at him. Then was the king wonderous wroth. And then the king sent him plaine word againe, and bad him bee ready and stuffe him and garnish[2] him, for within threescore[3] dayes he would fetch him out of the strongest castle that hee had. When the duke had this warning, anone he went and furnished and garnished two strong castles of his, of the which the one was Tyntagyll, and that other called Terabyl.[4] So his wife, dame Igrayne, hee put in the castle of Tyntagyll, and hee put himselfe in the castle of Terrabyll, the which had many issues and posternes out. Then in all haste came Uther with a great hoast, and layd a siege about the castle of Ter-

[1] *Ride all night.*—From Camelot in Somersetshire, where Uther is evidently supposed to be holding his court, they would, by riding all night, reach Tintagell before they could be pursued: but not so if, according to the account of Geoffrey of Monmouth, the king had been holding his court in London.

[2] *Garnish.*—To store. The Fr. *garnir*.

[3] *Threescore.*—Caxton's text has *within xl. dayes.*

[4] *Terabyl.*—Geoffrey of Monmouth calls the castle in which duke Gorlois established himself *castellum Dimilioc.* It does not seem now possible to identify the place intended by either of these names.

rabyll, and there hee pight many pavilions. And there was great warre made on both parties, and much people slaine. Then, for pure anger and for great love of faire Igrayne, king Uther fell sicke. Then came to king Uther, sir Ulfius,[1] a noble knight, and asked the king why hee was sicke? "I shall tell thee," said the king, "I am sicke for anger and for love of fair Igrayne that I may not be whole." "Well, my lord," sayd sir Ulfius, "I shal seeke Merlyn,[2] and he shal get you remedy that your heart shal be pleased." So Ulfius departed, and by adventure he met Merlyn in a beggers araye. And there Merlin asked Ulfius whom he sought. And he said he had little adoe to tel him. "Wel," sayd Merlyn, "I know whom thou seekest, for thou seekest Merlin, therfore seeke no further, for I am he, and if king Uther wil wel rewarde me, and bee sworne to me to fulfil my desire, the which shal be his honour and profit more then mine, for I shal cause him to have all his desire." "All this will I undertake," said Ulfius, "that there shal be no thing reasonable, but thou shalt have thy desire." "Well," said Merlyn, "he shal have his intent and desire; and therefore," said Merlin, "ride on your way, for I will not be long behind."

[1] *Ulfius.*—This is one of the names of Teutonic origin which are mixed up so heterogeneously in these strange romances. It is hardly necessary to remark that it is the Latinized form of the Anglo-Saxon name Wulf. Geoffrey of Monmouth calls him *Ulfinus de Ricaradock*. In the early French romances it is *Ulfins*, and the *Ulfius* of the English editions may be a mere misreading.

[2] *Merlyn.*—Merlin is here introduced rather abruptly, and the original story of Merlin's birth and early years, which is here omitted, is altered in the subsequent romances. According to Geoffrey of Monmouth (lib. vi. cc. 18, 19), Merlin had been the court magician since the time of Vortigirn, who had caused him to be sought as the only one capable of relieving him out of the difficulty he had encountered in raising a castle on Salisbury plain. This version of the story also is followed in the early French prose romance of Merlin.

CHAP. II.—How Utherpendragon made warre on the duke of Cornwaile, and how by the meanes of Merlyn he lay by the duchesse, and begat on her Arthur.

THEN Ulfius was glad, and rode on more then a pace til that he came unto king Utherpendragon, and told him he had met with Merlyn. " Where is hee?" said the king. " Sir," said Ulfius, " hee will not tarrie long." Therewithall Ulfius was ware where Merlyn stood at the porch of the pavilions dore. And then Merlyn was bounde to come to the king. When king Uther saw him, he said that he was welcome. " Sir," said Merlyn, " I know all your heart every dele; so you will be sworne to mee, as you be a true king anoynted, to fulfil my desire, you shal have your desire." Then the king was sworne upon the foure Evangelists. " Sir," sayd Merlyn, " this is my desire. The first night that you shall lye by Igrayne you shall get a child on her, and when it is borne that it shall bee delivered to mee for to nourish there as I will have it, for it shall be your worship and the childes availe as much as the child is worth." " I will well," said the king, " as thou wilt have it. " Now make you ready," said Merlyn, " this night shall you lye with Igrayne in the castle of Tintagyll, and you shall be like the duke her husband.[1] Ulfius shall be like sir Brastias, a knight of the dukes, and I will bee like a knight called sir Jordanus,[2] a knight of the dukes. But beware you make not many questions with her, nor with her men, but say you are diseased, and so hye you to bed and rise not on the

[1] *Like the duke.*—It may be remarked that this incident is evidently taken from the fable of Jupiter and Alcmena, which was very popular, under different forms, in the Middle Ages. Arthur, the offspring of this intrigue, answers to the classical Hercules.

[2] *Sir Jordanus.*—Geoffrey of Monmouth calls him *Jordanus de Tintagol;* and according to that writer it was Ulfius who assumed his form, while Merlin assumed that of Briceles, the Brastias of our romance.

morrow till I come to you, for the castle of Tintagill is but ten miles hence." So, as they had devised, it was done. But the duke of Tintagill espied how the king rode from the siege of Terrabill, and, therefore, that night he issued out of the castle at a posterne for to have distressed the kings hoast. And so, through his owne issue, the duke himselfe was slain or ever the king came at the castle of Tintagill. So after the death of the duke, king Uther lay with Igrayne more then three houres after his death and begat on her Arthur the same night, and, ere day came, Merlin came to the king and bad him make him ready; and so he kist the lady Igrayne and departed in all haste. But when the lady hard tell of the duke, her husband, and by all record hee was dead or ever king Uther came to her, then shee marvailed who that might be that lay with her in likenesse of her lord, so shee mourned privily and held her peace. Then all the barons by on assent prayed the king of accord betweene the lady Igrayne and him. The king gave them leave, for faine would hee have beene accorded with her. So the king put al his trust in Ulfius to entreat betweene them, so by that entreat at the last the king and she met together. "Now wil we doe well," said Ulfius, " our king is a lusty knight and wivelesse, and my lady Igrayne is a passing faire lady; it were great joy unto us all and it might please the king to make her his queene." Unto that they were all well agreed, and moved it to the king. And anon like a lusty knight he assented thereto with a good will, and so in all haste they were married in a morning with great mirth and joy. And King Lot[1] of

[1] *King Lot.*—Geoffrey of Monmouth, lib. viii, c. 21, calls him Lot de Loudonesia (Lot of Lothian), and says that he was *consul Leir*, by which he perhaps means " earl" of Leicester. The compilers of the later romances were much given to making their heroes kings. Uther's daughter who married Lot is called by Geoffrey *Anna*. Lot was, according to the same authority, father of Walganus (Gawaine), and Modred. In the English metrical life of Merlin, Lot's wife is called Belicent, and they are said to have had four sons, Gawaine, Guerehes, Agravain, and Gaheriet.

Lowthan and of Orkeny then weded Margawse, that was Gawyns mother. And king Nentres[1] of the land of Garlot wedded Elain. All this was done at the request of king Uther. And the third sister, Morgan le Fay,[2] was put to schole in a nunry, and there shee learned so much that shee was a great clarke of nigromancy,[3] and after shee was wedded to king Urience[4] of the land of Gore, that was sir Ewayns[5] le Blanchemaynes father.

CHAP. III.—Of the birth of King Arthur, and of his nourishing, and of the death of king Utherpendragon, and how Arthur was chosen king, and of wonders and marvailes of a sword that was taken out of stone by the said Arthur.

THEN the queene Igrayne waxed dayly greater and greater, so it fell after within halfe a yeere as king Uther lay by his queen, he asked her by the faith she ought[6] unto him whose was the child within her body. Then was shee sore abashed to give answere. " Feare you not," said the king, " but tell me the truth, and I shall love you the better by that faith of my body." " Sir," said she, " I shal tel you the truth.

---

[1] *King Nentres.*—In the English metrical romance of Merlin he is called Nanters king of Gerlot; his wife is there called Blasine, "eldest daughter" of Utherpendragon, and he is stated to have had a son named Gorlaas.

[2] *Morgan le Fay.*—This celebrated personage of romance was, according to the author of the prose romance of Merlin, an illegitimate daughter of Iguerne, though it is not explained how this happened. It was, we are told, on her mother's marriage with king Uther that she was sent to the nunnery, where she employed herself in studying magic. This may perhaps account for the ill-will she so constantly bore to her half-brother Arthur.

[3] *Nigromancy.*—This was the old English form of what is more correctly called necromancy.

[4] *Urience.*—Urience is the Urianus of Geoffrey, who makes him king of the *Murefenses,* or people of Murray in Scotland. Hist. Brit. ix. 9. The Urien of medieval romance.

[5] *Ewayns.*—Iwayn; a well-known hero of medieval romance.

[6] *Ought.*—i. e. owed.

The same night that my lord was dead, that houre of his death there came into my castle of Tintagil a man like my lord in speech and countenance, and two knights with him in likenes of his two knights Brastias and Jordanus, and so I went to bed with him as I ought to do with my lord, and that same night, as I shal answere unto God, this child was begotten upon mee." "That is truth," said the king, "as you say, for it was I my selfe that came in his likenesse, and, therefore, feare you not, for I am father to the child." And there hee told her all the cause how it was by Merlins counsell. Then the queene made great joy when she knew who was the father of her child. Soone came Merlin unto the king, and said, "Sir, you must provide you for the nourishing of your child." "As thou wilt," said the king, "be it." "Well," said Merlin, "I know a lord of yours in this land that is a passing true man and a faithful, and he shal have the nourishing of your child; his name is sir Ector,[1] and hee is a lord of faire livelyhood in many parts of England and Wales. And this lord sir Ector, let him be sent for, for to come and speake with you, and desire him your selfe, as he loveth you, that hee will put his owne child to nourishing to another woman, and that his wife nourish yours.[2] And when the child is borne, let it bee delivered unto mee at yonder privie posterne unchristned." As Merlin had devised, so was it done, and when sir Ector was come, he made affiance to the king for to nourish the child like as the king desired, and there the king

---

[1] *Sir Ector.*—He is called Sir Antour in the English metrical life of Merlin.

[2] *Nourish yours.*—Southey has given several illustrations of the care which was taken that children of noble birth should not suck the milk of plebeians. This feeling was preserved longest in Spain; and we are told that the mother of Pero Nino having discovered one day that her infant son had sucked another woman, had him tossed about in a cloak till his stomach threw back the stranger's milk. (Southey, notes, p. 460). The sort of relationship formed by this practice of fostering was considered stronger even than the natural relationship of blood.

granted sir Ector great rewards. Then when the queene was delivered, the king commanded two knights and two ladyes to take the child bound in rich cloath of gold, "and deliver him to what poore man you meete at the posterne gate of the castle." So the child was delivered unto Merlin, and so hee bare it forth unto sir Ector, and made an holy man to christen him, and named him Arthur; and so sir Ectors wife nourished him with her owne brests.[1] Then within two yeeres king Uther fell sick[2] of a great maladie; and in the meane while his enemies usurped upon him, and did a great battle upon his men, and slew many of his people. "Sir," said Merlin, "you may not lie so as you doe, for you must to the field though you ride in an horse-litter; for you shall never have the better of your enemies, but if your person be there, and then shal you have the victory." So it was done as Merlin had devised, and they carried the king forth in a horse-litter with a great hoast toward his enemies. And at Saint Albons there met with the king a great hoast of the north; and that day sir Ulfius and sir Brastias did great deedes of armes, and king Uther's men overcame the northen battle and slew much people, and put the remnant to flight. And then the king returned to London, and made great joy of his victorie. And within a while after hee was passing sore sicke, so that three dayes and three nights hee was speecheles, wherefore all the barons made great sorrow, and asked Merlin what counsell were best.

"There is none other remedy," said Merlin, "but God will have his wil. But looke that yee al his barons bee before him to-morrow, and God and I shal make him to speak." So on the morrow al the barons with Merlin came before the king. Then Merlin said aloud unto king Uther:

---

[1] Caxton's text reads *with her owne pappe.*

[2] *King Uther fell sick.*—The incidents of Uther's last battle, of his being carried to it in a litter, and of his subsequent death, are taken from Geoffrey of Monmouth.

"Sir, shall your sonne Arthur bee king after your dayes of this realme, with all the appurtenances?" Then Utherpendragon turned him, and said in hearing of them all: "I give him Gods blessing and mine, and bid him pray for my soule, and righteously and worshipfully that he claime the crowne upon forfeiture of my blessing." And therewith hee yealded up the ghost. And then he was entered as belonged unto a king, wherefore Igraine the queene made great sorrow and all the barons. Then stood the realme in great jepardie a long while, for every lord that was mighty of men made him strong, and many wende to have beene king. Then Merlin went to the archbishop of Canterbury,[1] and counselled him to send for all the lords of the realme, and all the gentlemen of armes, that they should come to London afore Christmasse, upon paine of cursing, and for this cause, that as Jesus was borne on that night, that Hee would of His great mercy shew some miracle as He was come to bee king of all mankind; for to shew some miracle who should be rightwise king of this realme. So the archbishop, by the advise of Merlin, sent for all the lords and gentlemen of armes, that they should come by Christmasse eve to London. And many of them made them cleane of their lives, that their prayer might be the more acceptable to God. So in the greatest church of London (whether it were Paules[2] or not, the French booke maketh no mention) all the states and lords were, long or it was day, in the church for to pray. And when matins and the first masse was done, there was seene in the churchyard, against the hie altar, a great stone foure square, like to a marble stone, and in the midest thereof was an anvile of steele,[3] a foote of height, and therein stooke a faire sword

---

[1] *Archbishop of Canterbury.*—He is called bishop Brice in the English metrical romance.

[2] *Paules*, or, as in Caxton, *Powlis*. The latter was the old spelling. It is hardly necessary to remark that the doubt of the English compiler of this romance was well founded.

[3] Caxton's text says, '*lyke*' an *anvylde of stele*.

naked by the point, and letters of gold were written about the sword that said thus:—WHO SO PULLETH OUT THIS SWORD OF THIS STONE AND ANVILE, IS RIGHTWISE KING BORNE OF ENGLAND. Then the people marvailed and told it to the archbishop. " I commaund you," said the archbishop, " that you keepe you within your church, and pray unto God stil that no man touch the sword til the hie mas be al done." So when al the masses wer don, al the states[1] went for to behold the stone and the sword. And when they saw the scripture, some assaied, such as would have been king. But none might stir the sword nor move it. " He is not yet here," said the archbishop, " that shal achieve[2] the sword, but doubt not God will make him to be knowne. But this is my counsaile," said the archbishop, " that wee let purvey ten knights, men of good fame, and they to keepe this sword." And so it was ordeined; and then there was made a crie that every man should assaic that would for to win the sword. And upon new yeeres day the barons let make a justes and a turneyment, that all knights that would just and turney there might play. And all this was ordained for to keepe the lords together and the commons, for the archbishop trusted that God would make him knowne that should win the sword. So upon new yeeres day, when the service was done, the barons rode to the feild, some to just and some to turney. And so it happened that sir Ector, that had great livelihood about London, rode to the justs, and with him rode sir Key,[3] his sonne, and yong Arthur that was his nourished brother, and sir Key was made knight at all halowmasse afore. So as they rode toward the justes, sir

---

[1] *States.*—*All the lordes*, Caxton. The meetings of estates belonged to the political history of a later period.

[2] *Achieve.*—*Encheve*, Caxton.

[3] *Sir Key.*—Caxton has *Syr Kaynus*. Kay (*Caius*), king Arthur's foster-brother and steward, is one of the most celebrated personages in this cycle of romances. He is understood to have been of a good disposition naturally, but this was mixed with a large amount of envy

Key had lost his sword, for hee had left it at his fathers lodging, and so hee prayed yong Arthur to ride for his sword. " I will with a good will," said Arthur, and rode fast after the sword; and when he came home, the lady and all were gonne out to see the justing. Then was Arthur wroth, and saide to himselfe, " I will ride to the church-yard and take the sword with mee that sticketh in the stone, for my brother sir Key shall not bee without a sword this day." And so when he came to the church-yard Arthur alighted, and tied his horse to the stile, and so went to the tent, and found no knights there, for they were all at the justing; and so hee handled the sword by the handles, and lightly and fiersly hee pulled it out of the stone, and tooke his horse and rode his way till hee came to his brother sir Key, and delivered him the sword. And assoone as sir Key saw the sword, hee wist well that it was the sword of the stone, and so hee rode to his father, sir Ector, and said: " Sir, loe here is the sword of the stone; wherefore I must bee king of this land." When sir Ector beheld the sword, hee returned againe and came to the church, and there they alighted, all three, and went into the church, and anone hee made sir Key to sweare upon a booke how hee came to that sword. " Sir," said sir Key, " by my brother Arthur, for hee brought it to me." " How gate you this sword?" said sir Ector to Arthur. " Sir, I will tell you. When I came home for my brothers sword, I found no body at home for to deliver mee his sword, and so I thought my brother sir Key should not be swordles, and so I came thither egerly and pulled it out of the stone without any paine." " Found yee any knights about this sword?" said sir Ector. " Nay," said Arthur. " Now," said sir Ector to Arthur, " I understand that you must bee

and spitefulness, and some other evil qualities. These defects are ascribed to the fact of his having been taken from his mother's breast to make way for the infant Arthur, and from his thus having sucked a stranger's milk. See before, the note on p. 7.

king of this land." "Wherefore I?" said Arthur; "and for what cause?" "Sir," said sir Ector, "for God will have it so; for there should never no man have drawne out this sword but hee that shall be rightwise king of this land. Now let me see whether yee can put the sword there as it was and pull it out againe." "That is no mastery,"[1] said Arthur; and so hee put it in the stone. Therewith sir Ector assayed to pull out the sword, and failed.

CHAP. IV.—How king Arthur pulled out the sword divers times.

NOW assay you," said sir Ector to sir Key. And anon hee pulled at the sword with all his might, but it would not be. "Now shal ye assay?" said sir Ector to Arthur. "With a good wil," said Arthur, and pulled it out easily. And therewithal sir Ector kneeled downe to the earth, and sir Key also. "Alas!" said Arthur, "mine owne deare father and my brother, why kneele you to me?" "Nay, nay, my lord Arthur, it is not so, I was never your father ne of your bloud, but I wote well that you are of an higher blood then I wende you were." And then sir Ector told him all, how he was betaken him to nourish, and by whose commandement, and by Merlins deliverance. Then Arthur made great mone when hee understood that sir Ector was not his father. "Sir," said sir Ector unto Arthur, "will you bee my good and gracious lord when you are king?" "Else were I too blame," said Arthur, "for you are the man in the world that I am most beholding unto, and my good lady and mother your wife that as well as her owne hath fostred and kept me; and if ever it bee Gods will that I be king, as you say, yee shall desire of mee what I may doe, and I shall not faile you; God forbid I should faile

---

[1] *Mastery.*—This word was formerly used for skill or perfection in any art or science. Arthur means here to say that it wanted no great skill to perform this task.

you." "Sir," said sir Ector, "I will aske no more of you but that you will make my sonne, your fostred brother sir Key, seneshall[1] of all your lands." "That shall be done, sir," said Arthur, "and more by the faith of my body; and that never man shall have that office but hee while that hee and I live." Therewithall they went unto the archbishop, and told him how the sword was achieved, and by whom. And upon the twelfth day all the barons came thither for to assaie to take the sword, who that would assaye. But there afore them al, there might none take it out but onely Arthur; wherefore there were many great lords wroth, and said, "It was great shame unto them all and the realme to bee governed with a boy of no high blood borne." And so they fell out at that time, that it was put of till Candlemasse, and then all the barons should meete there againe. But alwayes the ten knights were ordained for to watch the sword both day and night; and so they set a pavilion over the stone and the sword, and five alwayes watched. And at Candlemasse many more great lords came thither for to have wonne the sword, but none of them might prevaile. And right as Arthur did at Christmasse he did at Candlemasse, and pulled out the sword easily, whereof the barons were sore agrieved, and put it in delay till the high feast of Ester. And as Arthur sped afore, so did hee at Ester; and yet there were some of the great lords had indignation that Arthur should be their king, and put it off in delay till the feast of Penticost. Then the archbishop of Canterbury, by Merlins providence, let purvey of the best knights that might be gotten, and such knights as king Utherpendragon loved best and most trusted in his dayes, and such knights were put about Arthur, as sir Bawdewine of Britaine, sir Key, sir Ulfius, and sir Brastins; all these with many other were alwayes about Arthur day and night till the feast of Penticost.

[1] *Seneshall.*—The seneschal, or steward, was one of the highest and most influential offices about the king's person.

CHAP. V.—How Arthur was crowned king, and how he made officers.

AND at the feast of Penticost, all maner of men assayed for to pull at the sword that would assaye; and none might prevaile, but Arthur pulled it out afore all the lords and comons that were there, wherefore all the comons cryed at once: "We will have Arthur unto our king, we will put him no more in delay; for wee all see that it is Gods will that hee shall bee our king, and who that holdeth against it we will slay him." And therewithall they kneeled downe all at once, both rich and poore, and cryed Arthur mercy because they had delayed him so long. And Arthur forgave it them, and tooke the sword betweene both his hands, and offered it up to the altar where the archbishop was, and was made knight of the best man that was there. And so anone was the coronation made, and there was hee sworne to the lords and commons for to be a true king, to stand with true justice from thenceforth all the dayes of his life: and then hee made all the lords that held off the crowne to come in and to doe him service as they ought to doe. And many complaints were made unto king Arthur of great wrongs that were done since the death of Utherpendragon, of many lands that were bereved of lords, knights, ladyes, and gentlemen. Wherefore king Arthur made the lands for to be rendred againe unto them that ought[1] them. When this was done that the king had stablished all the countries about London, then hee did make sir Key seneshall of England, and sir Bawdewine of Britayne was made constable, and sir Ulfius was made chamberline, and sir Brastias was made warden for to waite upon the north fro Trent forward, for it was that time as for the most part enemie unto the king. But within few yeares after king Arthur wonne all the north,

---

[1] *Ought* here means owned, or had a right to them.

KING ARTHUR. 15

Scotland and all that were under their obeysance. Also a part of Wales held against king Arthur, but hee overcame them all, as hee did the remnant, and all through the noble prowesse of himselfe and his Knights of the Round Table.

CHAP. VI.—How king Arthur held in Wales at a Penticost a great feast, and what kings and lords came to this feast.

HEN King Arthur removed into Wales, and let crie a great feast that it should be holden at Pentecost after the coronation of him at the citie of Carlion.[1] Unto this feast came king Lot of Lowthean and of Orkeney, with five hundred knights[2] with him. Also there came unto this feast king Urience of Gore, which brought with him foure hundred knights. Also to this feast there came king Nentres of Garlothe, and with him seven hundred knights. Also there came unto this feast the king of Scotland, with six hundred knights with him, and hee was but a yong man. And there came unto this feast a king that was called the king with the hundred knights;[3] but hee and his men was passing well beeseene at all points. Also there came the king of Cardos with five hundred knights. Then was king Arthur glad of their coming; for hee wend that all the kings and knights had come for great love, and for to have done him worship at his feast, wherefore the king made great joy, and sent unto the kings and knights great

[1] *Carlion.*—Caerleon-upon-Usk, the Isca Silurum of the Romans, the extensive ruins of which were celebrated at the period of the composition of these romances. See the description of them by Giraldus Cambrensis. It was imagined to be the chief city of Arthur and the legendary British kings of his age.
[2] *Five hundred knights.*—The reader must bear in mind that, as each knight had to appear in the field with a certain number of followers, equally on horseback and armed, this number of knights answers to a considerable force of men.
[3] *The king with the hundred knights.*—This king is called, in the English metrical life of Merlin, *Agrugines.*

presents. But the kings would none receive, but rebuked the messengers shamefully, and said they had no joy to receive gifts of a berdles boy that was come of low blood; and sent him word that they would have none of his gifts, and that they were come to give him gifts with hard swords betweene the neck and the shoulders, and therefore they came thither, so they told the messengers plainly; for it was great shame to all them to see such a boy[1] to have the rule of so noble a realme as this land was. With this answere the messengers departed, and told this answere unto king Arthur. And for this cause, by the advise of his barons, hee tooke him to a strong toure[2] with five hundred good men of armes with him: and all the kings aforesaid in a manner laid a seige afore him, but king Arthur was well vitaled. And within fifteene dayes after Merlin came among them into the citie of Carlion. Then all the kings were passing glad of Merlins comming, and asked him, "For what cause is that berdles boy Arthur made your king?" "Sirs," said Merlin, "I shall tell you the cause. For hee is king Utherpendragons sonne, borne in wedlock, begotten upon faire Igraine the dukes wife of Cornewaile." "Then hee is a bastard," said they all. "Nay," said Merlin, "after the death of the duke more then three houres was Arthur begot, thirteene dayes after king Utherpendragon wedded faire Igrayne, and therefore I prove him hee is no bastard, and who soever saieth nay, he shall bee king and overcome all his enemies, and or that hee die hee shall be long king of all England, and he shall have under his obeysance Wales, Ireland and Scotland, and many moe realmes then I wil now reherse." Some of the kings had mervaile of Merlins words, and

---

[1] *Boy.*—This word was formerly used as a word of contempt or reproach. Below, Caxton's text reads, for *that berdles boy,* simply *that boye Arthur.*

[2] *A strong toure.*—Giraldus speaks of the ruins of an imposing tower at Caerleon, which may perhaps have given the idea of this tower to the romance writer.

KING ARTHUR.

deemed well that it should be as he said; and some of them laughed him to scorne, as king Lot, and moe other called him a witch. But then were they accorded with Merlin that king Arthur should come out and speake with the kings, and for to come safe and goe safe; such assurance was made or Merlin went. So Merlin went unto king Arthur and told him how he had done, and bad him that he should not feare, but come out boldly and speake with them, " and spare them not, but answere them as their king and cheftayne, for you shall overcome them all, whether they will or will not."

CHAP. VII.—*Of the first warre that king Arthur had, and how he wanne the field and overcame his enemies.*

THEN king Arthur came out of his toure, and had underneath his gowne a jesseraunt[1] of double maile, which was good and sure; and there went with him the archbishop of Canterbury, and sir Bawdwin of Britayne, and sir Key the senesshal, and sir Brastias; these were the men of most worship that were with him, and when they were met together there was but little meekenesse, for there was stout and hard words on both sides. But alwayes king Arthur answered them, and said that he would make them to bow and he lived; wherefore they departed with wrath, and king Arthur bad keepe them wel, and they bad the king keepe him wel. So the king returned to the toure againe, and armed him and all his knights. "What wil ye doe?" said Merlin to the kings; "yee are better to stint,[2] for here ye shal not prevaile, though ye were ten times so many." "Be we wel advised to bee afraid of a dreame-reader?"[3]

[1] *Jesseraunt.*—The jesseraunt was a light coat of armour, usually made of small plates of metal overlapping each other, and having no sleeves.
[2] *To stint.*—To cease or stop.
[3] *Dreame-reader.*—An interpreter of dreams. A profession of great importance in the Middle Ages.

said king Lot. With that Merlin vanished away, and came to king Arthur, and bad him set on them fiersly; and in the meane while there were three hundred good men, of the best that were with the kings, that went straight to king Arthur, and that comforted him greatly. "Sir," said Merlin to king Arthur, "fight not with the sword that you had by miracle till you see that you goe to the worst, then draw it out and doe your best." So forthwithall king Arthur set upon them in their lodging. And sir Bawdewinne, sir Key, and sir Brastias slew on the right hand and on the left, and it was marvaile; and alway king Arthur on horseback laid on with a sword, and did marvelous deedes of armes, that many of the kings had great joy of his deedes and hardines. Then king Lot brake out on the back side, and the king with the hundred knights and king Carados,[1] and set on king Arthur fiersly behind him. With that king Arthur turned with his knights and smote behind and before, and king Arthur was in the formost prees[2] till his horse was slaine under him. And therewith king Lot smote downe king Arthur. With that his foure knights received him, and set him on horseback. Then hee drew his sword Excalibar;[3] but it was so bright in his enemies

---

[1] *King Carados.*—He is called in the English metrical romance king of Strangore. But the same romance, a little further on, calls Brangores king of Strangore.

[2] *Prees.*—A crowd.

[3] *Excalibar.*—*Excalibur*, Caxton. This is the first, and rather abrupt, mention in this book of king Arthur's celebrated sword, which appears here to be identified with the miraculous sword he drew from the anvil on the stone, in consequence of which he was made king. The French romance of Merlin gives the following interpretation of the name,—" Escalibort est un nom Ebrieu, qui vault autant à dire en François comme très cher fer et acier, et aussi disoyent-il vrai." According to the English metrical romance of Merlin this celebrated sword bore the following inscription:—

    Ich am y-hote Escalibore;
    Unto a king fair tresore.

And it is added in explanation,

    On Inglis is this writing,
    "Kerve steel and yren and al thing."

eyes, that it gave light like thirtie torches, and therewith hee put them backe, and slew much people. And then all the commons of Carlion arose with clubes and staves, and slew many knights; but all the kings held them together with the knights that were left alive, and so fled and departed. And Merlin came to king Arthur, and counsailed him to follow them no farther.

CHAP. VIII.—How Merlin counsailed king Arthur to send for king Ban and king Bors, and of their counsaile taken for the warre.

SO after the feast and journey, king Arthur drew him to London, and by the counsaile of Merlin the king let call his barons to counsaile. For Merlin had told the king that sixe knights that made warre upon him would in all hast bee avenged on him, and on his lands. Wherefore the king asked counsaile of them all. They could no counsaile give, but said they were enough. "Yee say well," said king Arthur, "and I thanke you for your good courage; but will yee that love mee speake with Merlin? yee know well that hee hath done much for me, and hee knoweth many things; and when he is afore you, I would that yee prayed him hartily of his best advise." And all the barons said they would pray him and desire him. So Merlin was sent for, and was faire desired of all the barons to give them the best counsaile. "I shall tell you, sirs," said Merlin, "I warn you all that your enemies are passing strong for you, and they are good men of armes as any that now live, and by this time they have gotten foure kings more, and a mighty duke also; and but if our king had more chivalrie with him then hee may make himselfe within the bonds of his owne realme, and hee fight with them in battaile, hee shall be overcome and slaine." "What were best to doe in this case?" said all the barons. "I shall tel you," said Merlin, "mine advise; there are two brethren beyond the sea, and they be kings both, and marvelous good men of their hands; the one hight king Ban of Benwicke and that other hight king Bors of Gaule,[1] that is France; and on these two kings warreth a mighty man of men, king Claudas,[2] and striveth with them for a castle; but this Claudas is so mighty of goods, wherof he getteth good knights, that he putteth these two kings for the most part to the worst; wherefore this is my counsaile, that our king send unto the two kings, Ban and Bors, by two trusty knights, with letters well devised, if that they will come and see king Arthur and his court, and so helpe him in his warres, that hee will bee sworne to them to helpe them in their warres against king Claudas. Now what say yee unto this counsaile?" said Merlin. "This is well counsailed," said the king, and all the barons. Right so in all the haste were ordained to goe two knights upon the message unto the two kings. So were there made letters in most pleasant wise, according unto king Arthurs desire. Ulfius and Brastias were made the messengers, and so rode forth well horsed and well armed, as the guyse was that time; and so passed the sea, and rode towards the citie of Benwicke, and there besides were eight knights that espied them. And at the straight passage[3] they mette with sir Ulfius and sir Brastias, and would have taken them prisoners. So they prayed them that they might passe, for they were messengers unto king Ban and Bors sent from king Arthur. "Therefore," said the eight knights, "yee shall die or bee

---

[1] *Ban—Bors.*—These are called in the versions of the romance of Merlin, Ban, king of Benoit, in "Lesser Britany," and Bohort, king of Gannes, (perhaps Vannes.) The former place is, of course, what our romance calls *Benwicke.*

[2] *King Claudas.*—King Claudas of Gaul appears first in the early French prose romance of Merlin by Walter Map, or Mapes. He makes a conspicuous figure in the romance of Sir Launcelot. He is always spoken of as the "tyrant" of Gaul.

[3] Caxton's text has *at a strayt passage.*

our prisoners, for wee be knights of king Claudas." And therewith two of them dressed their speares, and Ulfius and Brastias dressed their speares, and ran together with great strength, and Claudas knights brake their speares and the other two held, and bare the two knights out of their sadels unto the earth, and so left them lying and rode their way. And the other sixe knights rode afore to a passage to meete with them againe, and so Ulfius and Brastias smote other two downe, and so past on their way.

And at the third passage smote downe other two. And at the fourth passage there met two for two, and both were laid to the earth. So there was none of the eight knights but that he was sore hurt or els brused. And when they came to Benwicke it fortuned there were both the kings Ban and Bors. When it was told the kings that there were come messengers, there were sent to them two knights of worship, the one hight Lyonses, lord of the countrie of Payarne,[1] and sir Phariance, a worshipful knight. Anone they asked from whence they came, and they said from king Arthur of England; then they tooke them in their armes and made great joy each of other. But anon as the two kings wist that they were messengers of king Arthurs, no tarrying was made, but forthwith they spake with the knights, and welcomed them in the faithfullest wise, and said they were most welcome unto them before all the kings living; and therewith they kist the letters and delivered them straight, and when king Ban and Bors understood the letters, then were they better welcome then before; and after the haste of the letter they gave them this answere, that they would fufil the desire of king Arthurs writing. And Ulfius and Brastias taryed there as long as they would, and had as good cheere as might be made them in those marches.[2] Then Ulfius and Brastias told the kings of the

[1] *Payarne.*—It would be in vain to attempt to identify this and many other names of places in this romance.
[2] *Marches.*—Border-lands. Preserved in the names of the marches of Wales and the marches of Scotland.

adventure of their passages of the eight knights. "Ha! ha!" said king Ban and Bors, "they were our good frinds. I would I had wist of them, they should not have escaped so." So Ulfius and Brastias had good cheere and great gifts, as much as they might beare away; and had their answere by mouth and by writing, that those two kings would come to King Arthur in all the haste that they might. So the two knights rode on afore, and passed the sea, and came to their lord, and told him how they had sped, whereof king Arthur was passing glad. "At what time suppose yee the two knights will be heer?" "Sir," said they, "afore all hollowmasse." Then the king let purvye for a great feast, and let crie a great justes. And by all holowmasse, the two kings were comen over the sea, with three hundred knights well arayed both for the peace and for the warre. And king Arthur met with them ten miles out of London, and there was great joy as could bee thought or made; and on all halowmasse, at the great feast, sate in the hal the three kings. And sir Key the seneshall served in the hall, and sir Lucas[1] the butler, that was duke Corneus sonne, and sir Griflet,[2] that was the sonne of Cardol; these three knights had the rule of all the service that served the kings. And anone, as they had washed and were risen, all knights that would just made them ready. By than[3] they were ready on horseback there were seven hundred knights. And king Arthur, Ban, and Bors, with the archbishop of Canterbury, and sir Ector, Kay's father, they were in a place covered with cloth of gold, like an hall, with ladies and gentlewomen, for to behold who did best, and thereon to give judgement.

[1] *Sir Lucas.*—Called in the English metrical romance sir Lucan.
[2] *Sir Griflet.*—The English romance of Merlin calls him *Grifles*.
[3] *By than.*—By the time that. An old Anglo-Saxon form.

CHAP. IX.—Of a great turney made by king Arthur and the two kings Ban and Bors, and how they went over the sea.

KING Arthur and the two kings let depart the seven hundred knights in two parties. And there were three hundred knights of the realme of Benwicke, and they of Gaule turned on the other side. Then they dressed their shields, and many good knights couched their speeres. So sir Griflet, was the first that met with a knight that was called Ladynas, and they met so egerly that al men had wonder, and they fought so that their shields fell to peeces, and horse and men fell to the earth, and both the English knight and the French knight lay so long, that al men wend that they had beene dead. And when Lucas the butler saw Griflet lie so, hee quickly horsed him againe; and they two did marvailous deedes of armes with many batchelers. And also sir Key came out of an embushment with five good knights with him, and they sixe smote other sixe downe horse and man. But sir Key did that day marvelous deedes of arms, that there was none that did so well as hee that day. Then there came in fiersly sir Ladinas and sir Grastian, two knights of France, and did passing well, that all men praysed them. Then came there sir Placidas, a good knight, and mette with sir Key and smote him downe horse and man; wherefore sir Griflet was wroth, and mette with sir Placidas so hard that horse and man fel to the earth. But when the five knights wist that sir Key had a fall, they were wonderous wrath, and therwith each of them five bare downe a knight. When King Arthur and the two knights saw them begin to waxe wroth on both parts, they lepte on small hacknyes[1] and let crie that al men

[1] *Hacknyes.*—The hackney (*haquenée*) was a small kind of horse reserved especially for the use of ladies. When the king and his two knights mounted on such horses, it was an unmistakable intimation of his wish to put a stop to all military exercises.

should depart unto their lodging. And so they went home
and unarmed them; and so to even-song[1] and supper.
And after the three kings went into a garden, and gave
the pryce unto sir Key, and to sir Lucas the butler, and to
sir Griflet. And then they went to counsaile, and with
them Gwenbaus, brother unto sir Ban and Bors, a wise
clarke, and thither went Ulfius, and Brastias, and Merlin.
And after they had beene in counsaile, they went to bed.
And on the morrow they heard masse, and after went to
dinner,[2] and so to their counsaile, and made many argu-
ments what were best to doe. At the last they were concluded, that Merlin should goe with a token of king Ban,
and that was a ring, unto his men and king Bors, and
Gracian and Placidas should goe againe and keepe their
castles and their countries, as king Ban of Benwicke and
king Bors of Gaules had ordeined them, and so passed the
sea and came to Benwicke. And when the people saw
king Bans ring, and Gracian and Placidas, they were glad,
and asked how the king fared, and made great joy of their
welfaire and cording.[3] And according unto their soveraigne
lords desire, the men of warre made them readie in al
haste possible, so that they had fifteene thousand on horseback and on foot, and they had great plenty of victuall with
them by Merlins provision. But Gracian and Placidas
were left to furnish and garnish the castles for dread of
king Claudas. Right so Merlin passed the sea, well vic-
tualed both by water and by land. And when he came to
the sea, he sent home the foote men againe, and tooke no
more with him but ten thousand men on horsebacke, the
most part men of armes; and so shipped and passed the sea
into England, and landed at Dover; and through the witte
of Merlin hee led the hoost northward the previest way

[1] *Even-song.*—Even-song, or Vespers, began at four o'clock in the afternoon.
[2] *To dinner.*—The dinner was formerly an early meal. At no great distance of time the dinner hour was ten o'clock in the forenoon.
[3] *Cording.*—Accordance, reconciliation.

that could be thought unto the forrest of Bedgraine,[1] and there in a valey he lodged them secretly. Then rode Merlin unto King Arthur and the two kings, and told them how he had sped, whereof they had great marvaile, that man on earth might speede so soone, and goe and come. So Merlin told them that ten thousand were in the forrest of Bedgraine, wel armed at al points. Then was there no more to say but to horsebacke went all the hoost, as king Arthur had afore purveyed. So with twenty thousand he passed by night and day. But there was made such an ordinance afore by Merlin, that there should no man of warre ride nor goe in no countrie on this side Trent water, but if hee had a token from king Arthur, wherethrough the kings enemies durst not ride as they did before to espie.

CHAP. X.—How eleaven kings gathered a great hoast against king Arthur.

AND so within a little space the three kings came unto the castle of Bedgraine, and found there a passing faire fellowship and well beseene, whereof they had great joy, and vittaile they wanted non. This was the cause of the northern hoast that they were reared for the despite and rebuke that the six kings had at Carlion. And those six kings by their meanes gate to them five other kings, and thus they began to gather their people, and how they swore that for weale nor wo they should not leave each other til they had destroyed king Arthur. And then they made an oath. The first that began the oath was the duke of Candebenet, that hee would bring with him five thousand men of armes which were ready on horseback. Then swore king Brandegoris of Latangor,[2]

[1] *Forest of Bedgraine.*—I cannot at all identify this forest. The English romance of Merlin has Rockingham, both for the forest and for the castle mentioned subsequently; but a little further on (see p. 39) it seems to be identified with Sherwood.

[2] *Latangor.*—Caxton has *Brandegoris of Stranggore.*

that he would bring five thousand men of armes on horse-backe. Then swore king Clariance of Northumberland that hee would bring three thousand men of armes. Then swore the king of the hundred knights, that was a passing good man and a young, that hee would bring foure thousand men on horseback. Then king Lot swore, a passing good knight and sir Gwynas[1] father, that hee would bring five thousand men of arms on horseback. Also ther swore king Urience, that was sir Gwinas[2] father, of the land of Gore, and hee would bring sixe thousand men of armes on horsbacke. Also there swore king Idres of Cornewaile, that hee would bring five thousand men of armes on horseback. Also there swore king Cradelmans to bring five thousand men of armes on horsebacke. Also there swore king Agwisance of Ireland, to bring five thousand men of armes on horse-backe. Also there swore king Nentres to bring five thou-sand men of armes on horsebacke. Also there swore king Carados to bring five thousand men of armes on horsebacke. So their whole hoost was of cleane men of armes on horse-backe fifty thousand. And on foote ten thousand of good mens bodies. Then were they soone redie and mounted upon horse, and sent forth their fore-riders; for these eleaven kings in their wayes laid syege unto the castle of Bedgraine: and so they departed and drew toward Arthur, and left few to byde at the syege, for the castle of Bede-grayne was holden of king Arthur, and the men that were therein were Arthurs.

[1] *Sir Gwynas.*—In Caxton's text it is more correctly given *Sir Gawayns.*
[2] *Sir Gwinas.*—A similar error. Caxton's text has *sir Uwayns fader.*

CHAP. XI.—Of a dreame of the king with the hundred knights.

AND so by Merlins advice there were sent fore-riders to skum[1] the countrie, and there[2] met with the fore-riders of the north, and made them to tell which way the hoost came; and then they told it to king Arthur, and by king Ban and Bors counsaile they let bren and destroyed all the countrie afore them where they should ride. The king with the hundred knights dreamed a wonderfull dreame two nights afore the battaile, that there blew a great wind, and blew downe their castles and their townes, and after that came a water and bare it al away. Al that heard of the dreame said it was a token of great battaile. Then by the counsaile of Merlin, when they wist which way the eleaven kings would ride and lodge that night, at midnight they set upon them as they were in their pavilions; but the scoute watch by their hoost cried, "Lords, at armes![3] for heere be your enemies at your hand.

CHAP. XII.—How that the eleaven kings with their hoast fought against king Arthur and his hoast, and of many great feates of the warre.

THEN king Arthur, and king Ban, and king Bors, with their good and trustie knights, set upon them so fiersly, that they made them overthrow their pavilions on their heads; but the eleaven kings by manly prowesse of armes tooke a faire field. But there was slaine that morrow tide ten thousand of good

---

[1] *Skum.*—Caxton, *skumme.* To skim, to sweep.
[2] *There.*—Caxton, *they.*
[3] *At armes.*—The translation, no doubt, of the French *aux armes!* i. e. arm yourselves, take to your arms.

mens bodies. And so they had afore them a strong passage, yet were they fifty thousand of hardy men. Then it drew toward day. "Now shall you doe by mine advise," said Merlin unto the three kings. "I would that king Ban and king Bors, with their fellowship of ten thousand men, were put in a wood heere besides in an embushement and keepe them prevy, and that they be led or the light of the day come, and that they stirre not till yee and your knights have fought with them long, and when it is daylight, dresse your battaile even afore them and the passage, that they may see all your hoast, for then they will bee the more hardy when they see you have but twenty thousand, and cause them to bee the gladder to suffer you and your hoast to come over the passage." All the three kings and the barons said that Merlin had said passing well, and it was done as hee had devised. So on the morrow when either hoast saw other, the hoast of the north was well conforted. Then to Ulfius and Brastias were delivered three thousand men of armes, and they set on them fiersly in the passage, and slew on the right hand and on the left hand, that it was wonderfull to tell. When the eleaven kings saw that there was so few a fellowship and did such deedes of armes, they were ashamed, and set on them fiersly againe; and there was sir Ulfius horse slaine under him, but he did well and marvelously on foote. But the duke Eustace of Cambenet, and king Clariance of Northumberland, were alway grievous on sir Ulfius. When Brastias saw his fellow so fared withall, he smote the duke with a speare, that horse and man fell downe. That saw king Clariance, and returned to Brastias and either smote other, so that horse and man went to the earth, and so they lay long astonyed, and their horses knees brast to the hard bone. Then came sir Kay the senesshall, with sixe fellowes with him, and did passing well. With that came the eleaven kings, and there was sir Griflet put to the earth horse and man, and Lucas the butler horse and man, by king Grandegors, and king

Idres, and king Agusance.[1] Then waxed the meddle[2] passing hard on both parties. When sir Kay saw sir Griflet on foote, hee rode to king Nentres and smote him downe, and led his horse to sir Griflet and horsed him againe. Also sir Kay with the same spere smote downe king Lot, and hurt him passing sore. That saw the king with the hundred knights, and ran to sir Kay and smote him downe, and tooke his horse and gave him to king Lot, whereof hee said, "gramercie." When sir Griflet saw sir Kay and Lucas the butler on foote, hee tooke a sharpe spere great and square, and rode to Pynell, a good man of arms, and smote downe horse and man, and then hee tooke his horse and gave him sir Kay. When king Lot saw king Nentres on foote he ran to Melot de la Roch, and smote him downe horse and man, and gave king Nentres the horse and horsed him againe. Also the king of the hundred knights saw king Idres on foote; then hee ran unto Guimiart de Bloi, and smote him downe horse and man, and gave king Idres the horse and horsed him againe. And king Lot smote downe Clariance de la Forrest Savage, and gave the horse to duke Eustace. And so when they had horsed the kings againe, they drew them all eleaven kings together, and said they would be revenged of the domage that they had taken that day. In the meane while came in sir Ector with an eger countenance, and found Ulfius and Brastias on foote in great peril of death, which were foule defoyled under the horse feete. Then king Arthur as a lyon ran unto king Cradelmont of Northwales, and smote him through the left side, that the horse and the king fell downe; and then he tooke the horse by the rayne and lad him unto Ulfius, and said, "Have this horse, mine old friend, for great neede hast thou of an horse." "Gramercy,"

---

[1] Agusance occurs in Geoffrey of Monmouth, under the form *Auguselus*, as king of the Scots. Lib. ix. c. 9. The others are mostly arbitrary names introduced by the writers of the romances.

[2] *Meddle.*—The battle; mêlée.

said Ulfius. Then king Arthur did so marvelously in armes that all men had wonder thereof. When the king with the hundred knights saw king Cradelmont on foote, he ranne unto sir Ector, that was well horsed, sir Kays father, and smote downe horse and man, and gave the horse to the king, and horsed him againe. And when king Arthur saw the king ride on sir Ectors horse he was wroth, and with his sword hee smote the king on the helme, that a quarter of the helme and shield fell downe, and the sword kerved downe unto the horse necke, and so the king and the horse fell downe to the ground. Then sir Kay came to sir Morganore sencyall[1] with the king of the hundred knights, and smote him downe horse and man, and lad the horse unto his father sir Ector. Then sir Ector ran unto a knight that hight Kardens,[2] and smote downe horse and man, and lad the horse unto sir Brastias, that had great neede of an horse and was greatly defoyled.[3] When Brastias beheld Lucas the butler, that lay like a dead man under the horse feete, and for rescew him sir Griflet did marvelously, and there were alwayes fourteene knights upon sir Lucas, and then Brastias smote one of them on the helme that it went to the teeth, and hee rode to another and smote him that the arme flew into the fielde. Then hee went to the third and smote him on the shoulder that both shoulder and arme flew into the field. And when sir Griflet saw him rescued,[4] hee smote a knight on the temples, that head and helme went to the earth, and sir Griflet tooke the horse of that knight and ledde him unto sir Lucas, and bad him mount upon the horse and revenge his hurts. For Brastias had slaine a knight tofore, and horsed sir Griflet.

[1] *Sencyall.*—i. e; the seneschal of the king of the hundred knights. The text is literally copied from Caxton, where it appears to be not quite correctly printed.   [2] *Kardens.*—Caxton has *Lardens.*
[3] *Defoyled.*—Bruised.   [4] *Sawe rescowes,* Caxton.

CHAP. XIII.—Yet of the same battaile.

WHEN Lucas saw king Agwysance that late had slaine Moris de la Roche, and Lucas ran to him with a short speare that was great,[1] that he gave him such a fal that the horse fel downe to the earth. Also sir Lucas found there on foote Bloyas de la Flaundres and sir Gwynas, two hardy knights, and in the woodnes[2] that sir Lucas was in, hee slew two batchelers and horsed them againe. Then waxed the battaile passing hard on both parties, but king Arthur was glad that his knights were horsed againe; and then they fought together that the noise and sound rang by the water and the wood, wherefore king Ban and king Bors made them ready and dressed their shieldes and harneys, and they were so couragious that many knights shooke and trembled for egernesse. All this while Lucas, and Guinas, and Briaunt, and Belias of Flaunders, held a strong meddle against sixe kings, that was king Lot, king Nentres, king Brandegoris, king Idres, King Urience, and king Agwisance. So with the helpe of sir Kay and sir Griflet they held these sixe kings hard, that unnethes they had any power to defend them selves. But when king Arthur saw the battaile would not be ended by no manner, he fared like a wood[3] lion, and stirred his horse heere and there on the right hand and on the left, that hee stinted not till hee had slaine twenty knights. Also hee wounded king Lot sore on the shoulder, and made him to leve that ground, for sir Kay and sir Griflet did there, with king Arthur, great deedes of armes. And then sir Ulfius, sir Brastias, and sir Ector, encountred against the duke Eustace, king Cradelmont, king Cardelmans, king Clauriance of Northumberland, king Cardos, and against the king with the hundred knights. So these knights encountred with these

---

[1] *Great.*—i. e. thick and strong.   [2] *Woodnes.*—i. e. furiousness.
[3] *Wood.*—i. e. mad, furious.

kings that they made them to avoide the ground. Then king Lot made great moane for his domages and his fellowes, and said unto the eleaven kings, "But if yee will not doe as I devise, wee shall bee slaine and destroyed. Let me have the king with the hundred knights, king Agwisance, king Idres, and the duke of Cambenet,[1] and we five kings will have fifteene thousand men of armes with us; and wee will goe apart while yee sixe kings hold the meddle with twelve thousand, and as we see that yee have foughten with them long, then will we come on fiersly; and else shall we never match them," said king Lot, "but by this meane." So anone they departed as they had devised, and the sixe kings made their party strong against king Arthur, and made great warre longe. In the meane while brake the embushment of king Ban and Bors, and Lionses and Phariaunce had the vant-guard, and the two kings met with king Idres and his fellowship, and there began a great meddle of breaking of speares and smiting of swords, with sleyng of men and horses, and king Idres was nere at discomfiture. That saw Agwisance the king, and put Lyonses and Phariaunce in point of death, for the duke of Cambenet came on them with a great fellowship. So these two knights were in great danger of their lives that they were faine to returne, but alwaies they rescued themselves and their fellowship marvelously. When king Bors saw those knights put backe, it grieved him sore, then he came on so fast this his fellowship seemed as blacke as the men of Inde.[2] When king Lot had espied king Bors, hee knew him well, then he said: "O Jesus, defend us fro death and horrible maymes, for I see well we ben in great peril of death, for I see yonder a king, one of the most worshipfullest men and one of the best knights of the world, is joyned to his fellowship." "What is he?" said the

[1] *Cambenet.*—Caxton reads *Cunbenec.*
[2] *As blak as Inde,* Caxton. *Inde* was the name of a colour, a very dark blue.

king with the hundred knights. "It is,"[1] said king Lot, "king Bors of Gaule; I marvaile how they com into this countrey without weting of us all." "It was by the advise of Merlin," said a knight. "As for him," said king Carados, "I will encounter with king Bors, if yee will rescewe me when it is neede." "Go on," said they al, "we wil doe al that we may for you." Then king Carados and his hoost rode on a softe pace til they came as nigh king Bors as a bow shotte. Then either battaile let their horses runne as fast as they might, and sir Bleoberis, that was god-sonne unto king Bors, bare his chiefe standard, which was a passing good knight. "Now shall we see," said king Bors, "how these northern Britons can beare their armes." And king Bors encountred with a knight and smote him throughout with a speare that hee fell downe dead unto the earth, and after drew his sword and did mervailous deedes of armes, that both parties had great wonder thereof, and his knights failed not, but did their part; and king Carados was smitten to the earth. With that came the king with the hundred knights, and rescued king Carados mightily by force of armes, for he was a passing good knight, and was but a young man.

CHAP. XIV.—Yet more of the said battaile, and how it was ended by Merlin.

Y then came into the field king Ban as a fierce lion, with bandes of grene, and thereupon gold. "Ha, ha," said king Lot, "now shall we be discomfited, for yonder I se the most valiant

---

[1] *It is.*—It may perhaps be well to explain, for the benefit of the general reader, that, in the later feudal age, king Bors would be known by his coat of arms, blazoned on his shield. This was the great object of armorial bearings; and it was an important branch of the education of a knight to know people by their arms. They could not be known by their faces, as these were covered by the helmet.

knight of the world, and the man of most renowne; for such two brethren as is king Ban and king Bors are not living, wherefore we must needs void or die; and but we avoid manly and wisely ther is but death." When king Ban came into the battle, he came in so fiersly, that the strok redounded againe fro the wood and the water; wherefore king Lot wept for pittie and sorrow, that he saw so many good knights take their end. But through the great force of king Ban they made both the northern batailes that were departed to hurtle[1] together for great dread; and the three kings with their knights slew downe right, that it was pitie to behold, and a great multitude fled.

But king Lot and the king with the hundred knights, and king Morganore, gathered the people together passing knightly, and did great deedes of armes, and held the battaile all that day like hard. When the king with the hundred knights beheld the great domage that king Ban did, hee thrust unto him with his horse, and smote him a mighty stroke upon the helme, which astonied him sore. Then was king Ban wroth with him, and set upon him fiersly. When that other saw that, hee cast up his shield and spurred his horse forward, but the stroke of king Ban fell downe and carved a cantell[2] of the shield, and the sword slod downe by the hawberke behinde his backe, and cut in twaine the trappour[3] of steele and the horse also in two peeces that the sword fell to the ground. Then the king with the hundred knights voyded the horse lightly, and with his sword hee broched the horse of king Ban through and through. With that king Ban with great diligence voyded the dead horse, and came and smote at the other so egerly upon the helm that hee fell to the earth. Also in that ire he felled king Morganore, and there was great slaughter of good knights and much people. By that time

---

[1] *Hurtle.*—To rush together in a crowd.
[2] *Cantell.*—A small piece.
[3] *Trappour.*—Caxton, *trappere.* The trapper or harness.

came into the presse king Arthur, that found king Ban standing among dead men and dead horses, fighting on foote as a wood lion; that there came none nigh him as farre as hee might reach with his sword, but that hee caught a grievous buffet, whereof king Arthur had great pitie. And king Arthur was so bloody that by his shield no man might know him, for all was blood and brains on his sword. And as king Arthur looked by him, he saw a knight that was passing well horsed, and therewith he ranne to him and smote him on the helme with such force, that his sword cutt him in two peeces, that the one halfe fell on the one side and the other on the other side,[1] and king Arthur tooke the horse and led him unto king Ban, and said: "Faire brother, have this horse, for yee have great neede thereof, and me repenteth sore of your great domage." "It shall be sooue revenged," said king Ban, "for I trust in God mine hurt is not much, but some of them may sore repent this." "I will well," said king Arthur, "for I see your deedes full actual; neverthelesse I might not come at you at that time." But when king Ban was mounted on horsebacke, then there began a new battaile, which was sore and hard, and passing great slaughter.

And so through great force king Arthur, and king Ban, and king Bors, made their knights a litte[2] to withdraw them. But alwayes the eleaven kings with their chivalrie never turned backe; and so withdrew them to a little wood, and so over a little river, and there they rested them, for on the night they might have no rest in the field. And then the eleaven kings and their knights assembled them all on an heape together, as men adread and all discomforted. But there was no man might passe them, they held them so

[1] This was evidently intended as an improvement upon Caxton's text, which reads, *and therewith syre Arthur ranne to hym, and smote hym on the helme that his sworde wente unto his teeth, and the knyght sunke doune to the erthe dede.*
[2] *Litte*, more usually written *lite*, a little.

hard together, both behinde and before, that king Arthur had marvaile of their great deedes of armes, and was passing wroth. "Ah, sir Arthur," said king Ban and king Bors, "blame them not, for they doe as good men ought to doe; for by my faith," said king Ban, "they are the best fighting men and knights of most prowes that ever I saw or hard speak of; and those eleven kings are men of great worship, and if they wer belonging to you, there were no king under heaven had such eleven knights, and of such worship." "I may not love them," said king Arthur, "they would destroy me." "That know we wel," said king Ban and king Bors, "for they are your mortall enemies, and that hath ben proved aforehand, and this day they have done their part, and that is great pittie of their wilfullnesse." Then all the eleaven kings drew them together, and then said king Lot: "Lords, yee must take other wayes then you doe, or els the great losse is behinde; yee may see what people we have lost, and what good men wee leese, because alwayes we waite upon those foote men, and ever in saving one of the foote men wee leese tenne horsemen for him, therefore this is mine advise, let us put our foote men fro us, for it is almost night. For king Arthur wil not tary upon the foote men, therefore they may save them selves, the wood is neare hand. And when we horseman be together, looke that everyche[1] of you kings make such an ordinance that none breake upon paine of death. And who that seeth any man dresse him for to flee, lightly that he be slaine, for it is better that we slay a coward, then through a coward all we be slaine. How say ye?" said king Lot; "answere unto mee, all yee kings." "It is well said," quoth king Nentres; and so said the king with the hundred knights, and the same said king Carados and king Urience, so did king Idres and king Brandegoris, and so did king Cardelmans and the duke of Cambenet; the same said king Clariance and king Agwy-

---

[1] *Everyche.*—Every one, each.

sance. And they swore that they would never faile the one unto the other, neither for life nor for death. And who that fled, but did as they did, should be slaine. Then anone they amended their harnyes, and righted their shieldes, and tooke new speares, and set them on their thighes, and stood stil as it had beene a plompe[1] of wood.

CHAP. XV.—Yet of the said battayle.

WHAN kinge Arthur, and kynge Ban, and kinge Bors behelde them and all their knyghts, they praised them greatly for their noble cheere of chyvalry, for the hardyest fyghters that ever they heard or sawe. With that there dressed them a fortie noble knyghtes, and sayd unto the three kings that they would breake theyr batayle, these were theyr names: Lyonses, Pharyaunce, Ulfyus, Brastias, Ector, Key, Lucas the butler, Griflet le Fyse de Dieu, and Meryet of the Rocke,[2] Guynas de Bloy, and Briant de la Forest Savage, Ballaus and Moryans of the Castel of Maydens, Flanedrius of the Castell of Ladies, Annecians, which was kinge Bors god-sonne, a valyaunt knight, Ladinas de la Rouse, Emeraus, Caulas, and Gracience le Castleyn, one Bloyse de la Case, and sir Colgrevaunce of Gorre. All these fortie knightes rode on afore, with great speres on their thyghes, and spurred theyr horses myghtely as fast as theyr horses might runne. And the eleaven kinges, with part of their good knightes, rushed with their horses as fast as they might with theyr speres, and there they did on both parties mervaylous deedes of armes. So came into the thyckest of the presse kinge Arthur, Ban, and Bors, and slewe downe ryght on both handes, that theyr horses went in bloode up to the fytlockes. But ever the eleaven kinges

[1] *Plompe.*—A clump of trees is still called a *plump* in the dialects of the north of England.
[2] *Mariet de la Roche,* Caxton.

and theyr hoost were alwayes in king Arthurs vysage. Wherefore king Ban and Bors had great mervaill consyderinge the great slaughter that there was, but at the last they were driven backe over a lytle ryver. With that came Merlyn upon a great black horse, and sayde to king Arthur, "Ye have never done; have ye not done ynough? of three score thousand ye have left on lyve but fifteene thousand; it is tyme for to saye ho,[1] for God is wrothe wyth you that you wyll never have done, for yonder eleaven kinges at this tyme will not bee overthrowen; but and if yee tary upon them any longer, all your fortune wyll turne, and theirs shall encrease, and therefore withdrawe you to your lodginge, and there rest you as soone as you may, and rewarde well your good knightes wyth gold and silver, for they have ryght well deserved it, for there may no ryches be too deere for them, for of so fewe men as ye have, there were never men did more prowesse than they have done this day, for yee have this day matched with the best fyghters of the worlde." "That is trouth," sayde king Ban and Bors. "Also," said Merlin, "wythdraw you where you lyst, for these three yeres I dare undertake they shall not hurt ne greeve you, and by than ye shall here newe tydinges." And than Merlyn said to king Arthur, "These eleaven kinges have more in hand thán they are ware of, for the Sarasyns are landed in their countries more than fortie thousand that brenne and sley, and have layde seyge at the castell Wandsbrought[2] and made great destruction; therefore dreade ye not these three years. Also, sir, all the goods that ye have gotten at this battaile let it be searched, and when ye have it in your handes, let it be given freely to these two kings that be here, Ban and

[1] *Ho.*—This was the formal exclamation used by the king or umpire of a tournament to command the combatants to cease.
[2] *Wandsbrought.*—Caxton, *Wandesborow.* Perhaps this is the ancient camp of Vandlebury, on the Gogmagog hills, near Cambridge, concerning which a legend is related by Gervase of Tilbury. There is, however, a Wanborough in Wiltshire.

Bors, that they may reward their knightes withall, and that shall cause straungers to be of a better wyll to doe you service at a neede. Also ye be able ynough to reward your owne knights of your owne goods when so ever it lyketh you." "It is well sáyde," quod king Arthur, "and as thou hast devised so shall it be done." Whan it was delivered to kinge Ban and king Bors, they gave the goodes as freely to their knights as it was given them.

Than Merlyn tooke his leave of king Arthur and of the two kinges, for to goe see his master Bleise[1] which dwelt in Northumberland; and so departed and came to his master, which was passing glad of his comming, and there he told him how kinge Arthur and the two kinges had sped at the great battayle, and how it was ended, and tolde him the names of every kinge and knyght of worship that was there. And so Bleyse wrote the battayle word by worde as Merlyn tolde him, how it began, and by whom, and in like wise howe it was ended, and who had the worst. All the batayles that were done in king Arthurs dayes Merlyn caused Bleyse his master to write them. Also he caused hym to wryte all the batayles that every worthy knyght did of king Arthurs court. After this Merlyn departed from his master and came to kinge Arthur that was in the castell of Bedegraine, that was one of the castels that stood in the forrest of Sherwood, and Merlyn was so disguysed that king Arthur knewe him not, for he was all furred in black sheeps skynnes, and a great payre of bootes, and a bow and arowes, in a russet gowne, and brought wild geese in his hand, and it was on the morow after Candelmasse daye, but king Arthur knew him not. "Syr," sayde Merlyn to king Arthur, "will yee give mee a gift?" "Wher-

---

[1] *His master Bleise.*—Blaise, according to the legend of Merlin, was a holy hermit who had protected the mother of Merlin from the fiend, and had undertaken his education after he was born. It is pretended that Merlin afterwards employed Blaise as his historiographer, and communicated to him, as they occurred, the events in which he took a part, or which he witnessed.

fore," sayde the king, "should I give thee a gift, thou chorle?" "Syr," sayde Merlyn, "yee were better to give mee a gyft, the which is not in your hands, than to leese great riches. For here in the same place where as the great battayle was, is great treasure hid in the earth." "Who told thee so, chorle?" sayd king Arthur. "Merlyn told me so," saide he.

Than Ulfius and Brastias knew him well ynough, and smiled at him. "Syr," sayde these two knightes, "it is Merlyn that speaketh so unto you." Than king Arthur was greatly abasshed, and had mervaile of Merlyn, and so had king Ban and king Bors, and so they had great sport at him. So in the mean while there came a damoysell which was an earles daughter, and hir fathers name was Sanam, and her name was Lyonors, a passing fayre damoysell, and so she came thyther for to doe homage, as other lords did after the great bataile. And kinge Arthur set his love greatly upon hir, and so did she upon him, and the king had adoe with hir, and begate upon hir a childe, and his name was Borre, that was after a good knight of the round table. Than there came word that kinge Ryence of North Wales made strong warre upon king Leodegraunce of Camelyarde.[1] For the which thinge kinge Arthur was wrothe, for hee loved him well and hated king Ryence, because hee was alwayes agaynst him. So by the ordinance of the three kinges that were sent home to Benwycke, they all would depart for dreade of king Claudas, and Pharyaunce, and Antemes, and Gracians, and Lyonses, Payarne, with the leaders of those that should keepe the kings lands.

[1] *Camelyarde.*—Cameliard is apparently the district called *Carmelide* in the English metrical romance of Merlin, on the border of which was a town called Breckenho (? Brecknock). Further on in the same poem the capital of Carmelide is said to be Carohaise.

CHAP. XVI.—How king Arthur, king Ban, and king Bors
reschewed king Leodegraunce, and of other incidents.

WHEN king Arthur, and king Ban, and king Bors departed with their felowship, about twentie thousand, and came within six dayes into the countrie of Camelyard, and there rescewed king Leodegraunce, and slewe there much people of king Ryence, unto the number of ten thousand of men, and put him to flight. And than had these three kings great chere of king Leodegraunce, and thanked them of their great goodnes that they woulde revenge him of his enemies. And there had king Arthur the first sight of Guenever,[1] daughter unto king Leodegraunce, and ever after he loved hir. And afterward they were wedded, as it shall be shewed hereafter. So brevely to make an ende, these two kings tooke their leave to go into their owne countrie, for king Claudas did great distruction on both their landes. Than said king Arthur, " I will goe with you." " Nay," sayde the two kings, " yee shall not at this time, for yee have yet much to doe in these lands; therfore wee will depart, and with the great goods that we have gotten in these landes by your gyfts, we shall wage many good knyghts, and withstand the malyce of king Claudas, for, by the grace of God, if wee have need, we will send to you for succour. And if yee have need, send for us, and we will not tarry, by the faith of our bodies." " It shall not neede," said Merlyn, " that these two kings come againe in the way of warre, but I know well that the noble king Arthur may not be long from you, for or twelve

---

[1] *Guenever.*—Geoffrey of Monmouth, the head of all these legends, calls the lady Guanhumara, and tells us that she was of a noble Roman family, and the most beautiful woman in the whole island. Her unfaithfulness to her illustrious husband is well known to every reader, and was proverbial in the later Middle Ages.

moneths[1] be past ye shall have great need of him, and
than he shall revenge you on your enemies, as ye have
revenged him on his. For these eleaven kings shall dye
all in one day, by the great might and prowesse of armes
of two valiant knights, as it shall be shewed hereafter; their
names ben Balyn le Savage and Balan his brother, which
bene mervaylous good knightes as any be now living."

Nowe turne we unto the eleaven kings, which returned
to a city that hyght Sorhaute, which city was wythin king
Uryence land, and there they refreshed them as well as
they myght, and made leches[2] to search their woundes,
and sorowed greatly for the death of their people. With
that there came a messenger and told them that there was
comen into their lands people that were lawlesse as well as
Sarasins fortie thousand, and have brent and slayne all the
people that they may come by without mercy, and have layd
seige unto the castel of Vandesborugh. "Alas," saide
the eleaven kings, "here is sorrow upon sorrow, and if we
had not warred against king Arthur as we had done, hee
would soone revenge us; and as for king Leodegraunce,
he loveth king Arthur better than us; and as for king
Ryence, hee hath ynough to doe with king Leodegraunce,
for he hath layde seige unto him." So they consented
to keepe all the marches of Cornewayle, of Wales, and of
the north. So first they put king Idres in the city of
Nauntes in Brytayne, with foure thousand men of armes
for to watch both the water and the land. Also they put
in the city of Windesan king Nentres of Garlot, with
foure thousand knights, for to watch both the water and the
land.

Also they had of other men of warre more than eight
thousand, for to fortify all the fortresses in the marches of
Cornewayle. Also they put moe knyghtes in all the marches of Wales and of Scotland, with many good men of

---

[1] *Twelve moneths.*—Caxton reads, *within a yere or two.*
[2] *Leches.*—i.e. physicians.

armes. And so they keept them togither the space of three yere, and ever alyed them with mighty kings, dukes, lords, and gentlemen. And to them fell king Ryence of North Wales, which was a mighty man of men, and also Nero, that was a mighty man of good men also. And al this while they furnyshed and garnyshed them of good men of armes and vytale, and of al manner of ordynaunce that belongeth to warre, for to avenge them of the battayle of Bedegrayne, as it is rehersed in the booke of adventure following.

CHAP. XVII.—How king Arthur rode to Carlyon, and of his dreame, and how he sawe the questing beast.

HEN after that king Ban and king Bors were departed, king Arthur rode unto Carlyon, and thyther came to him Lots wyfe of Orkeny in manner of a messenger, but shee was sent thither to espye the court of king Arthur, and she came richly beseene with hir foure sonnes, Gawayne, Gaherys, Agravayne, and Gareth, with many other knights and ladies, and she was a passing fayre lady; wherefore the king cast great love unto her and desired her to lye by her. So they were agreed, and hee begate upon her Mordred, and she was his sister on the mothers side Igrayne. So there shee rested her a month, and at the last she departed. Than on a time the king dremed a mervaylous dreame, whereof he was right sore adread. But all this time king Arthur knewe not that king Lots wife was his sister. This was king Arthurs dreame. Him thought that there was comen into this lande many gryffons[1] and serpents, and him thought[2] that they brent and slew all the people in the land, and then him thought that he fought with them, and

---

[1] *Gryffons.*—Flying dragons.
[2] *Him thought.*—It seemed to him. The verb *thinke* had two senses in old English—to think and to seem.

that they did him passing great domage and wounded him full sore, but at the last hee slewe them all. Whan the king awoke, hee was passing heavy and right pensive of his dreame. And so for to put away al these thoughts, hee made him ready with many knights to ryde on hunting. As soone as hee was in the forest, the king saw a great hart afore him. "This hart will I chace," said King Arthur; and so he spurred his horse and rode long after, and so by fine force oft he was like to have smitten the hart; where as the king had chaced the hart so long, that his horse had lost his breath and fell downe dead. Then a yeoman fet the king another horse. The king saw the hart embushed, and his horse dead; he sat him down by a fountaine, and there he fel in great thoughts, and as he sat there alone, him thought he heard a noise of hounds to the number of thirtie. And with that the king saw comming toward him the strangest beast that ever he saw or heard tell of; so the beast went to the fountaine and dranke, and the noise was in the beasts belly like unto the questyn[1] of thirtie couple of hounds, but all the while that the beast dranke there was no noyse in the beasts belly, and therewith the beast departed with a great noyse, whereof the king had great mervaile, and so he was in great thought, and therewith he fel on sleepe. Right so there came a knight on foote to king Arthur, and said, "Knight, full of thought and sleepy, tel me if thou sawest a strange beast passe this way?" "Such one saw I," said king Arthur unto the knight, "that is past two miles. What would you with that beast?" said king Arthur. "Sir, I have followed that beast long time, and have killed my horse, so would God I had another to follow my quest." Right so came one with the kings horse, and when the knight saw the horse hee prayed the king to give him that horse,—"For I have followed this quest these twelve monethes, and either

---

[1] *Questyn.*—To *queste*, in the language of hunting, means to give tongue as hounds when on the scent of game.

I shall acheave him or bleede of the best blood of my body." King Pellinore that time followed the questing beast, and after his death sir Palomides followed it.

CHAP. XVIII.—How king Pellinore tooke king Arthurs horse, and followed the questing beast, and how Merlin met with king Arthur.

SIR knight," said king Arthur, "leave that quest and suffer mee to have it, and I will follow it other twelve moneths." " Ah, foole," said the knight to king Arthur, " thy desire is in vaine, for it shall never be acheaved but by me, or by my next kynne." Therewith he stert to the kings horse and mounted into the saddle, and said, " Gramercy, this horse is mine." " Well," said king Arthur, " thou maist take my horse by force, but and I might prove thee whether thou wert better on horseback or I, I would be content." " Well," said the knight, " seeke me here when thou wilt, and here nigh this well thou shalt find me," and so passed forth on his way. Then sat king Arthur in a great study, and bad his men fetch his horse as fast as ever they might. Right so came Merlin like a child of foureteene yeeres of age, and saluted the king, and asked him why he was so pensive and heavy. " I may well be pensive and heavy," said the king, "for here even now I have seene the most marvailous sight that ever I saw." " That knowe I well," said Merlin, " as well as thy selfe, and of all thy thoughts ; but thou art but a foole to take thought, for it will not amend thee. Also I know what thou art, and also who was thy father, and also on whom thou wert begotten ; king Utherpendragon was thy father, and begat thee on Igraine." " That is false," said king Arthur ; " how shouldest thou know it, for thou art not so old of yeeres for to know my father ?" " Yes," said Merlin, " I know it better then you, or any man living." " I will not beleeve thee," said king Arthur, and was wroth with the child. So Merlin departed, and came againe in the likenesse of an old man of foure score yeeres of age, whereof the king was glad, for hee seemed to be a right wise man. Then said the old man, "why are you so sad?" "I may wel be heavy," said king Arthur, "for divers things; also here was a child and told me many things that me seemeth he should not know, for he was not of age for to know my father." "Yes," said that old man, "the child told you the truth, and more would hee have told you and you would have suffered him. But you have done a thing late wherefore God is displeased with you, for you have lyen by your sister,[1] and on her you have gotten a child that shall destroy you and all the knights of your realme." "What are you," said king Arthur, "that tell me these tidings?" "I am Merlin, and I was hee in the childs likenesse." "Ah!" said king Arthur, "yee are a marvailous man, but I marvaile much of thy words, that I must die in battaile." "Mervaile not," said Merlin, "for it is Gods will that your body be punished for your foule deedes. But I may well be sory," said Merlin, "for I shal die a much[2] shameful death, as to be put into the earth all quicke, and yee shall die a worshipfull death." As they thus talked, came one with the kings horse,[3] and so the king mounted on his horse and Merlin on another, and so rode to Carlion. And anon the king asked Ector and Ulfius how hee was begotten. And they told him that Utherpendragon was his father, and queene Igraine his mother. Then king Arthur said unto Merlin, "I will that my mother be sent for that I may speake with her, and if shee say so her selfe, then will I beleeve it." In all hast the queene was sent for; and she came anon, and brought with

---

[1] *Your sister.*—Lot's wife is said to have been a daughter of Igraine, born before her intercourse with Utherpendragon. See before, p. 43. As, according to the following chapter, Arthur did not yet know who was his father or mother, his incest was involuntary.

[2] *Much.*—This word was not unusual in the sense of very.

[3] *Horse.*—Corrected from Caxton's text; the edition of 1634 has *horses*, in the plural.

her Morgan le Fay hir daughter, that was as faire a lady as any might be. And the king welcomed Igraine in the best manner.

CHAP. XIX.—How Ulfius appeaches queene Igrayne, king Arthurs mother, of treason. And how a knight came and desired to have the death of his master revenged.

RIGHT so came Ulfius, and said openly, that the king and all that were there might heare:— "Yee are the falsest lady of the world, and the most traytresse unto the kings person." "Beware, Ulfius," said king Arthur, "what thou sayst, for thou speakest a great word." "I am well ware," said sir Ulfius, "what I speak, and heare is my glove for to prove it upon any man that saith the contrary, that this queene Igraine is cause of all your domage, and of your great warre that yee have had, for and shee would have uttered in the life of king Utherpendragon of the birth of you and how you were begotten, yee should never have had halfe the mortall warres which ye have had. For the most part of your great lords, barons, and gentlemen of your realme knew never whose sonne ye were, nor of whom you were begotten; and she that bare you of her body should have made it knowne openly in excusing of her worship and yours, and in likewise to all the realme. Wherefore I prove her false to God and you, and to all your realme, and who will say the contrary, I will prove it upon his body." Then spake Igraine, and said, "I am a woman, and may not fight; but rather then I should be dishonoured, there would some good man take my quarell. More," she said, "Merlin knoweth well, and you, sir Ulfius, how king Uther came to me in the castle of Tintagill, in the likenesse of my lord, that was dead three houres tofore, and thereby gat a child that night upon me. And after the thirtenth day king Uther wedded me, and by his commandement when the child was borne, it was delivered to Merlin, and nourished by him; and so I saw the child never after, nor wote not what is his name, for I never knew him yet." And then sir Ulfius said unto the queene, "Merlin is more to blame then ye." "I wote well," said the queene, "that I bare a child by my lord king Uther, but I wote not where he is become." Then Merlin tooke the king by the hand, saying, "This is your mother." And therwith sir Ector bare witnesse how he nourished him by king Uthers commandement. And therewith king Arthur tooke his mother, queene Igraine, in both his armes and kissed her, and either wept upon other. And then the king let make a feast which lasted eight dayes. Then on a day there came into the court a squire on horsebacke, leading a knight before him wounded to the death, and told him there was a knight in the forest that had reared up a pavilion by a well side, " and hath slaine my master, a good knight, and his name was Miles; wherefore I beseech you that my master may be buried, and that some good knight may revenge my masters death." Then was in the court great noise of the knights death, and every man said his advise. Then came Griflet, that was but a squire,[1] and he was but young, of the age of king Arthur, so he besought the king, for all his service that he had done, to give him the order of knighthood.

CHAP. XX.—How Griflet was made knight, and how he justed with a knight.

"THOU art full young and tender of age," said king Arthur, "for to take so high an order upon thee." "Sir," said Griflet, "I beseech you to make me a knight." "Sir," said Merlin, "it were pittie to leese Griflet, for he will be a passing good man when he commeth to age, abiding with

[1] *But a squire.*—It is perhaps hardly necessary to remark that the position of squire was that of the young noble before he obtained the dignity of knighthood.

you the terme of his life; and if he adventure his body with yonder knight at the fountaine, he shall bee in great perill if ever he come againe,[1] for he is one of the best knights of the world, and the strongest man of armes." "Well," said king Arthur. So, at the desire of Griflet, the king made him knight.

"Now," said king Arthur to sir Griflet, "sithen that I have made thee knight, thou must graunt me a gift." "What ye will, my lord," said sir Griflet. "Thou shalt promise me, by the faith of thy body, that whan thou hast justed with the knight at the fountaine, whether it fall that ye be on foot or on horsebacke, that in the same manner ye shall come againe unto mee without any question or making any more debate." "I will promyse you," said Griflet, "as ye desire." Then sir Griflet tooke his horse in great hast, and dressed his shield, and tooke a great spere in his hand, and so he rode a great gallop[2] till he came to the fountaine, and thereby he saw a rich pavillion, and thereby under a cloth stood a fayre horse well sadled and brideled, and on a tree a shielde of divers colours, and a great spere. Than sir Griflet smote upon the shielde with the end[3] of his spere, that the shield fell downe to the ground. With that came the knight out of the pavilion, and said, "Fayre knight, why smote ye downe my shield?" "For I will just with you," said sir Griflet. "It were better ye did not," said the knight, "for ye are but young and late made knight, and your might is nothing to mine." "As for that," said sir Griflet, "I will just with you." "That is mee loth," said the knight, "but syth I must needs, I will dresse me thereto; but of whence be ye?" said the knight. "Sir, I am of king Arthurs court." So they ran together that sir Griflets spere all to-shevered, and therwithall he smot sir Griflet through the shield and the left side, and

---

[1] i.e. in danger of never returning.
[2] *Gallop.*—Caxton has, *he rode a grete wallop.*
[3] *End.*—Caxton has, *with the bott of his spere.*

brake his spere, that the tronchon stacke in his body, that horse and knight fell downe.

CHAP. XXI.—How twelve knights came from Rome and asked truage of this land of king Arthur, and how king Arthur fought with a knight.

WHEN the knight sawe him lye so on the ground, hee alighted and was passing heavy, for he wend he had slaine him, and than he unlaced his helme and gave him wind, and so with the tronchon he set him upon his horse and betooke him to God, and said he had a mighty heart, and if he might live he would prove a passing good knight. And so sir Griflet rode to the court, where as great mone was made for him; but through good leeches he was healed, and his life saved. Right so came in the court twenty[1] knights, and were aged men, and they came from the emperour of Rome, and asked of king Arthur truage[2] for this realme, or els the emperour would destroy him and his land. "Well," said king Arthur, " yee are messengers, therfore may ye say what ye will, or els ye should die therfore. But this is mine answere: I owe the emperour no truage, nor none will I send him; but upon a fayre field I shall give him my truage, that shall be with a sharpe spere, or els with a sharpe swerd, and that shall be within these few dayes, by my fathers soule." And therwith the messengers departed passingly wroth, and king Arthur was as wroth as they, for in an evill time came they then, for the king was passing wroth for the hurt of sir Griflet. And by and by he commaunded a prevy man of his chamber, that or it be day his best horse and armour with al that belonged to his person "that it be without the citie or to morrow day." Right so in the morning afore day he mette

[1] *Twenty.*—In Caxton it is twelve. Geoffrey of Monmouth, from which this part of the romance is taken, agrees with Caxton in the number of ambassadors.
[2] *Truage.*—Fealty.

KING ARTHUR. 51

with his man and his horse, and so mounted up and dressed his shield, and tooke his spere, and badde his chamberlayne tary there till he came againe. And so king Arthur rode but a soft pace till it was day, and then was he ware of three chorles[1] which chased Merlin, and would have slaine him. Than king Arthur rode unto them a good pace, and cried to them: "Flee, chorles." Than were they afrayde whan they saw a knight,[2] and fled away. "O, Merlin," said king Arthur, "heere haddest thou bene slaine for all thy craft, had I not bene." "Nay," said Merlin, "not so, for I could save my selfe if I would, and thou art more necre thy death then I am, for thou goest toward thy death, and[3] God be not thy friend." So, as they went thus talking, they came to the fountaine, and the rich pavilion by it. Than king Arthur was ware where a knight sate all armed in a chayre. "Sir knight," said king Arthur, "for what cause abidest thou heere? That there may no knyght ryde this way but if he do just with thee?" said the king. "I reade thee leeve that custome," said king Arthur. "This custome," said the knight, "have I used and will use, maugre who saith nay; and who is grieved with my custome, let him amende it that will." "I will amend it," said king Arthur. "And I shall defend it," said the knight. Anone he tooke his horse, and dressed his shield, and tooke a spere, and they met so hard either on others shield, that they all to-shevered their speres. Therewith king Arthur drew his swerde. "Nay, not so," said the knight, "it is fayrer that we twayne ren more together with sharpe speres." "I will well," said king Arthur, "and I had any mo speres." "I have speres ynough," said the knight. So there came a squire, and brought two good speres, and king Arthur tooke one and he another,

[1] *Chorles.*—i. e. peasants.
[2] *Saw a knight.*—In the feudal ages the aristocratic class treated the peasantry with such brutal tyranny, that a peasant gladly avoided encountering a knight.
[3] *And.*—i. e. if.

so they spurred their horses, and came together with al
their might, that either brake their speres in their hands.
Than king Arthur set hand to his swerd. "Nay," said
the knight, "ye shall do better, ye are a passing good
juster as ever I met withal, for the love of the high order
of knighthood, let us just it once again." "I assent me,"
said king Arthur. Anon, there were brought two good
speres, and every knight gate a spere, and therwith they
ran together, that king Arthurs spere all to-shivered. But
the knight hit him so hard in the middes of the shield, that
horse and man fell to the earth, wherwith king Arthur
was sore angred, and drew out his swerd, and said: "I
will assay thee, sir knight, on foot, for I have lost the
honour on horsebacke." "I will bee on horsebacke," said
the knight. Then was king Arthur wroth, and dressed his
shield toward him with his swerde drawen. When the
knight sawe that, hee alighted for him. He thought it was
no worshippe to have a kuight at such avauntage, he to be
on horsbacke, and the other on foot, and so alight, and
dressed him to king Arthur. And there began a strong
battaile, with many great strokes, and so hewed with their
swerds, that the cantels[1] flew in the fields, and much blood
they bled both, so that all the place where they fought was
all bloody, and thus they fought long, and rested them, and
then they went to battayle agayne, and so hurtled together
like two wilde bores,[2] that either of them fell to the earth.
So at the last they smote together, that both their swerds
met even together. But the swerd of the knight smote
king Arthurs swerd in two peeces, wherfore he was heavy.
Than said the knight to the king: "Thou art in my
daunger,[3] whether me lyst to save thee or sley thee, and
but thou yeeld thee as overcome and recreaunt, thou shalt

[1] *Cantels.*—Fragments.
[2] *Bores.*—Caxton's text has, *lyke two rammes.*
[3] *In my daunger.*—The original meaning of *danger* was lordship or
dominion; to be in the danger of any one, meant to be in his power.

dye." " As for death," said king Arthur, "welcome be
it when it commeth, but as to yeeld me to thee as recreaunt,
I had lever die than to be so shamed." And therwithall
the king lept unto Pellynore, and tooke him by the middle,
and threw him downe, and raced off his helme. Whan
the knight felt that, hee was adread, for hee was a passing
big man of might, and anone he brought king Arthur
under him, and raced[1] off his helme, and would have
smitten off his head.

CHAP. XXII.—How Merlin saved king Arthurs life, and threw an
enchauntment upon king Pellinor, and made him to fall on sleepe.

HEREWITHALL came Merlin, and said:
"Knight, hold thy hand, for and thou sley that
knight, thou puttest this realme in the greatest
domage that ever realme was in, for this
knight is a man of more worship then thou wottest of."
" Why, who is he?" said the knight. " It is king Arthur." Then whould he have slaine him for dread of his
wrath, and heaved up his sword, and therwith Merlin cast
an enchauntment on the knight, that he fell to the earth
in a great sleepe. Then Merlin tooke up king Arthur,
and rode forth upon the knights horse. " Alas," said king
Arthur, " what hast thou done, Merlin? hast thou slaine
this good knight by thy craftes? there lived not so worshipfull a knight as hee was; I had lever than the stint[2] of
my land a yeare, that he were on live." " Care yee not,"
said Merlin, " for he is wholer than ye, for he is but on
sleepe, and will awake within three houres. I told you,"
said Merlin, " what a knight he was; heere had yee beene
slaine had I not beene. Also, there liveth not a better
knight then he is, and he shall doe you hereafter right
good service, and his name is Pellinore, and he shal have
two sonnes, that shal be passing good men, and save one,

---

[1] *Raced.—Reaced of*, Caxton. [2] *Stint.*—The loss.

they shall have no fellow of prowesse and of good living;
the one shall be named Percivale[1] of Wales, and the other
Lamerocke of Wales, and they[2] shall tell you the name of
your own begotten sonne upon your sister, that shall be
the distruction of all this realme."

CHAP. XXIII.—How king Arthur, by the meanes of Merlin, gate
his sword of Excalibur of the lady of the lake.

RIGHT so the king and he departed, and went
unto an hermitage where as was a good man
and a great leache.[3] So the hermit searched
all his woundes, and gave good salves, and the
king was there three dayes, and then were his wounds wel
amended that he might ride and goe. And so Merlin and
he departed, and as they rode king Arthur said, " I have
no sword." " No force,"[4] said Merlin, " here by is a sword
that shall be yours and I may." So they rode til they
came to a lake, which was a faire water and a broade, and
in the middes of the lake king Arthur was ware of an arme
clothed in white samite,[5] that held a faire sword[6] in the
hand. " Lo," said Merlin to the king, " yonder is the
sword that I spake of." With that they saw a damosell
going upon the lake. " What damosell is that?" said the
king. " That is the lady of the lake," said Merlin, " and
within that lake is a roch, and therein is as faire a place[7] as
any is on earth, and richly beseene, and this damosell will
come to you anone, and then speak faire to her that she will
give you that sword." Therewith came the damosell to

[1] *Percivale.*—Caxton, *Persyval.*
[2] *They.*—Caxton has, *he,* no doubt the correct reading.
[3] *Leache.*—A physician.   [4] *No force.*—No matter.
[5] *Samite.*—A rich silk, often interwoven with gold or silver thread.
[6] *Sword.*—This, according to the title of the chapter, was the celebrated sword Excalibur, which our romance gives to Arthur at an earlier period. See p. 18.
[7] *Place.*—i. e. a dwelling, or mansion.

king Arthur and saluted him, and he her againe. "Damosel," said the king, "what sword is that which the arme holdeth yonder above the water? I would it were mine, for I have no sword." "Sir king," said the damosell of the lake, "that sword is mine, and if yee wil give me a gift when I aske it you, yee shal have it." "By my faith," said king Arthur, "I will give you any gift that you will aske or desire." "Well," said the damosell, "goe ye into yonder barge, and rowe your selfe unto the sword, and take it and the scabbard with you, and I will aske my gift when I see my time." So king Arthur and Merlin alighted, tyed their horses to two trees, and so they went into the barge. And when they came to the sword that the hand held, king Arthur tooke it up by the handles and tooke it with him; and the arme and the hand went under the water; and so came to the land and rode forth. Then king Arthur saw a rich pavilion. "What signifieth yonder pavilion?" "That is the knights pavilion that yee fought with last, sir Pellinore, but hee is out, for he is not there, hee hath had adoe with a knight of yours, that hight Egglame, and they have foughten together a great while, but at the last Egglame fled, or else he had beene dead, and hath chased him to Carlion, and we shall anone meete with him in the high way." "It is well said," quoth king Arthur, "now have I a sword, and now will I wage battaile with him and be avenged on him." "Sir, ye shall not doe so," said Merlin, "for the knight is weary of fighting and chaceing, so that ye shall have no worship to have adoe with him; also he wil not lightly be matched of one knight living; and therefore my counsaile is that ye let him passe, for he shall doe you good service in short time, and his sonnes after his dayes. Also ye shall see that day in short space, that ye shall be right glad to give him your sister to wife." "When I see him," said king Arthur, "I will doe as ye advise me." Then king Arthur looked upon the sword, and liked it passing well. "Whether liketh you better," said Merlin, "the sword or the scabbard?" "Me liketh better the sword," said king Arthur. "Ye are more unwise," said Merlin, "for the scabbard is worth ten of the sword, for while ye have the scabbard upon you ye shall leese no blood be ye never so sore wounded, therefore keepe well the scabbard alway with you." So they rode on to Carlion, and by the way they met with sir Pellinore. But Merlin had done such a craft that Pellinore saw not Arthur, and so he passed by without any words. "I marvaile," said the king, "that the knight would not speake." "Sir," said Merlin, "he saw you not, for and he had seene you he had not lightly departed." So they came unto Carlion, whereof the knights were passing glad; and when they heard of his adventures, they marvailed that he would jeopard his person so alone. But all men of worship said it was mery to be under such a chiefetaine that would put his person in adventure as other poore knights did.

CHAP. XXIV.—How tidings came to king Arthur that king Ryence had overcome eleaven kings, and how he desired king Arthurs beard to purfel his mantell.

THE meane while came a messenger hastely from king Ryence[1] of Northwales, and he was king of all Ireland, and of many iles; and this was his message, greeting wel king Arthur in this manner wise, saying, that king Ryence had disconfited and overcomen eleaven kings, and everiche of them did him homage, and that was this, they gave him their beards cleane flayne of as much as there was; wherefore the messenger came for king Arthurs beard, for king Rience had purfeled[2] a mantell with kings beards, and there lacked for

[1] *King Ryence.*—He is called in the English metrical romance of Merlin, Ryance king of Ireland. In other romances he is called king Ryon.
[2] *Purfeled.*—Trimmed, or hemmed.

one place of the mantell, wherefore he sent for his beard, or else hee would enter into his lands " and brenn and sley, and never leave till he have thy head and thy beard." " Well," said king Arthur, " thou hast said thy message, which is the most vilainous and lewdest message that ever man heard sent to a king. Also thou mayest see my beard full young yet for to make a purfell of, but tell thou the king this. I owe him none homage, ne none of mine elders, but or it belong he shall doe to me homage on both his knees, or else he shal leese his head, by the faith of my body, for this is the most shamefulest message that ever I heard speak of; I see well the king met never yet with a worshipful man, but tell him I will have his head without he doe homage unto me." Then the messenger departed. " Now is there any heere," said king Arthur, " that knoweth king Ryence?" Then answered a knight that hight Naram: " Sir, I know him well, hee is a passing good man of his body as few beene living, and a passing proude man, and, sir, doubt yee not hee will make warr on you with a mighty puissance." " Well," said king Arthur to the knight, " I shall ordayne for him, and that shall he finde."

CHAP. XXV.—How all the children were sent for that were borne upon May day, and how Mordred was saved.

HEN king Arthur let send for all the children[1] that were borne on May day, begotten of lords and borne of ladies. For Merlin told king Arthur that he that should destroy him should be borne on May day, wherefore he sent for them al upon paine of death. And so there were found many lords sons, and all were sent unto the king, and so was Mordred sent by king Lots wife, and all were put in a shippe to the sea,

---

[1] *All the children.*—The idea of this incident is evidently taken from that of the murder of the innocents in the New Testament.

and some were foure weekes olde, and some lesse.[1] And so by fortune the shippe drove unto a castle, and was al to-riven and destroied the most part, save that Mordred was cast up, and a good man found him, and nourished him til he was fourteene yeeres old, and then he brought him to the court, as it is rehearsed afterward, toward the end, of the death of king Arthur. So many lords and barons of this realme were sore displeased, because that their children wer so lost, and many put it on the wit[2] of Merlin more then on king Arthur. So what for dread, and what for love, they held their peace. But when the messenger came to king Ryence, then was he wood out of measure for anger, and purveied him for a great hoast, as it is rehersed afterward in the booke of Balin le Savage that followeth next after, and how by adventure Balin gate the sword.

CHAP. XXVI.—Of a damosel which came gyrd with a sword for to finde a man of such vertue to draw it out of the scabbard.

AFTER the death[3] of king Utherpendragon reigneth king Arthur his sonne, which had great warre in his dayes, for to get all England into his hands; for there were many kings at that time within the realme of England, in Wales, in Scotland, and in Cornewayle. So it befel upon a time

[1] *And some lesse.*—One does not clearly understand how, all being borne on May-day, if some were four weeks old, others could be less. Yet this is literally copied from Caxton's text. It must have been intended for "and some more."

[2] *Wit.*—The printer of the edition of 1634 has mistaken Caxton's text, which here reads, *and many put the* wyte *on Merlyn*, i. e. many threw the *blame* on Merlin.

[3] *After the death.*—Here commences in Caxton's text, the second book; it appears, as indicated at the close of the preceding chapter, to have been taken for, or to have been abridged from, a separate romance, and it opens accordingly with a statement of the accession of king Arthur, as though that event had not been already related in detail.

when king Arthur was at London, there came a knight that brought the king tydings how that king Ryence of Northwales had reared[1] a great number of people, and were entred into the land, and brent and slew the kings true liege people. "If that be true," said king Arthur, "it were great shame unto mine estate but that he were mightily withstanden." "It is troth," said the knight, "for I saw the hoast my selfe." Then king Arthur let make a crie, that all the lords, knightes, and gentlemen of armes should draw unto a castle that was called in those dayes Camelot,[2] and there the king would let make a counsaile generall, and a great justes. So when the king was comen thither with all his baronage, and lodged as them seemed best, there came a damosell which was sent on message from the great lady Lyle of Avelyon.[3] And when she came before king Arthur, shee told him from whom she came, and how she was sent on message unto him for these causes, and she let her mantle fall that was richly fured, and then was she girded with a noble sword, wherof the king had great marvaile and said: "Damosell, for what cause are ye gird with that sword? it bescemeth you not." "Now shall I tell you," said the damosell; "this sword that I am gird withall doth me great sorrow and encombrance, for I may not be delivered of this sword but by a good knight, and hee must be a passing good man of his hands and of his deedes, and without vilany or trechery; if I may finde such a knight that hath all these vertues, he may draw out this sword of the scabbard. For I have beene at king Ryence, for it

[1] *Reared.*—i. e. raised.
[2] *Camelot.*—This was the place now called Camel, near South-Cadbury, in Somersetshire, where the vast entrenchments of an ancient town or station are still seen. Strangely enough, our romance, a little further on, see chap. xliv., identifies Camelot, very erroneously, with Winchester; and Caxton, as appears by his preface, imagined it to be in Wales.
[3] *Avelyon.*—No doubt Avallon the celebrated island in which Glastonbury was built. Perhaps the original was merely *la dame de l'yle d'Avelyon,* the lady of the isle of Avelyon.

was told that there were passing good knights, and he and al his knights have assayed it, and none can speede."

"This is a great mervaile," said king Arthur; "and it be soothe, I will my selfe assay to draw out the sword, not presuming upon my selfe that I am the best knight, but that I will beginne to draw at your sword, in giving example to al the barons, that they shall assay every one after other when I have assayed." Then king Arthur took the sword by the scabard and by the girdel and pulled at it egerly, but the sword would not out. "Sir," said the damosell, "yee neede not to pull halfe so hard, for he that shall pul it out, shall doe it with little might." "Ye say well," said king Arthur, "now assay ye, all my barons; but beware ye be not defiled with shame, trechery, ne guile." "Then it will not availe," said the damosell, "for he must be a cleane knight without villany, and of gentell streame[1] of father side and mother side." Most of all the barons of the round table that were there at that time assayed all by rowe;[2] but none might speede, wherefore the damosel made great sorrow out of measure, and said: "Alas! I wend in this court had beene the best knights without trechery or treason." "By my faith," said king Arthur, "heere are good knights as I deeme any beene in the world, but their grace is not to helpe you, wherefore I· am greatly displeased.

CHAP. XXVII.—How Balin, arayed like a poore man, pulled out the sword, which afterward was cause of his death.

IT happened so at that time that there was a poore knight with king Arthur, that had beene prisoner with him halfe a yeare and more, for sleying of a knight which was cossen to king Arthur. This knight was named Balin le Savage, and

[1] *Streame.*—Caxton has, correctly, *strene*, i. e. race, progeny.
[2] *By rowe.*—i. e. in turn, one after the other.

KING ARTHUR. 61

by good meanes of the barons hee was delivered out of prison, for hee was a good man named of his body, and hee was borne in Northumberland. And so he went privily into the court, and saw this adventure, whereof his heart raysed,[1] and would assay it as other knights did, but, for because he was poore and poorely arayed, he put him not farr in presse. But in his heart he was fully assured to doe as well (if his grace happened him) as any knight that was there. And as that damosell tooke her leave of king Arthur and al the barons, this knight Balin caled unto her and said, " Damosell, I pray you of your courtesie to suffer me as well to assay as these lords; though I be poorely cloathed, in mine heart me seemeth I am fully assured as some of these other lords, and me seemeth in my heart to speede right well." The damosell beheld the poore knight, and saw hee was a likely man; but because of his poore aray she thought he should be of no worshippe without vilany or trechery. And then she said to the knight Balin, " Sir, it is no neede to put me to any more paine or labour, for it beseemeth not you to speede there as other have failed." " Ah, faire damosell," said Balin, " worthynesse and good taches,[2] and good deedes, are not all onely in rayment, but manhood and worship is hid within mans person, and many a worshipfull knight is not knowen unto all people, and therefore worship and hardinesse is not in rayment and clothing." " By God," said the damosell, " ye say troth, therefore yee shall assay to doe what ye may." Then Balin tooke the sword by the girdell and scabbard, and drew it out easily, and when hee looked upon the sword it pleased him much. Then had the king and all the barons great marvaile, that Balin had done that adventure, and many knights had great spite at Balin. " Truely," said the damosell, " this is a passing good knight, and the best man that ever I found, and most

---

[1] *Raysed.*—Rose.   [2] *Good taches* — Good qualities.

of worship without treason, trechery, or villany, and many marvailes shall he atcheave. Now gentle and courteous knight," said the damosell, " give mee the sword againe." " Nay," said Balin, " for this sword will I keepe, but it be taken from me by force." " Well," said the damosell, " yee are not wise to keepe the sword from me, for ye shall sley with the sword the best friend that ye have, and the man that ye most love in this world, and the sword shall be your destruction." " I shall take the adventure," said Balin, " that God will ordaine to me, but the sword ye shall not have at this time by the faith of my body."

" Ye shall repent it within a short time," said the damosell, " for I would have the sword more for your availe then for mine, for I am passing heavy for your sake, for ye will not beleeve that the sword shall be your destruction, and that is as great pittie as ever I knew." With that the damosell departed, making the greatest sorrow that might be. Anon after Balin sent for his horse and his armour, and so would depart fro the court, and tooke his leave of king Arthur. " Nay," said the king, " I suppose ye will no depart so lightly fro this fellowship. I beleeve yee are displeased that I have shewed you unkindenesse, blame me the lesse, for I was misenformed against you; but I wend[1] you had not beene such a knight as ye are of worship and prowesse, and if ye will abide in this court with my good knights, I shall so avaunce you that ye shall be well pleased." " God thanke your highnesse," said Balin, "for your bountie and highnesse may no man praise halfe to the value; but as now at this time I must needes depart, beseeching you alway of your good grace." " Truely," said king Arthur, " I am right wroth for your departure; I beseech you, faire knight, that ye wil not tarry long, and ye shall be right welcome to me and to all my barons, and I shall amend al that is amisse and that I have

---

[1] *Wend.*—Thought, A. S. *wened*, from *wenan*.

done against you." "God thanke your lordship," said Balin, and therewith made him ready to depart. Then the most part of the knights of the round table said that Balin did not this adventure all onely by might, but by witchcraft.

CHAP. XXVIII.—How the ladie of the lake demanded the knights head that had wonne the sword, or the maydens head.

THE meane while that this knight was making him ready to depart, there came into the court a lady, which hight the lady of the lake, and she came on horsebacke richly beseene, and saluted king Arthur, and there she asked him a gift that he had promised her when she gave him the sword.

"That is sooth," said king Arthur, "a gift I promised you; but I have forgotten the name of the sword which ye gave me." "The name of it," said the lady, "is Excalibur,[1] that is as much to say as cutte-steele." "Ye say well," said king Arthur, "aske what ye will, and ye shall have it, if it lye in my power to give it." "Wel," said the lady of the lake, "I aske the head of the knight that hath wonne the sword, or else the damosels head that brought it; and though I have both their heads I force[2] not, for he slew my brother, a full good knight and a true, and that gentlewoman was causer of my fathers death." "Truely," said king Arthur, "I may not graunt you neither of their heades with my worshipe, therefore aske what ye will else and I shall fulfill your desire." "I will aske none other thing of you," said the lady. When Balin was redy to depart he saw the lady of the lake there, by whose meanes was slaine his owne mother, and he had sought her three yeeres. And when it was told him that she demanded his head of king Arthur, he went strait to her and said, "Evill be ye found, ye would have my head,

---

[1] *Excalibur.*—See before, pp. 18, 54. [2] *Force.*—I care.

and therefore ye shall loose yours;" and with his sword lightly he smote of her head, in the presence of king Arthur. "Alas, for shame!" said the king, "why have you done so? you have shamed me and all my court, for this was a lady that I was much beholden unto, and hither she came under my safe conduite; I shall never forgive you that trespasse." "My lord," said Balin, "me forthinketh[1] much of your displeasure, for this lady was the untruest lady living, and by her enchauntement and witchcraft she hath beene the destroyer of many good knights, and she was causer that my mother was brent through her falsehood and trechery." "What cause soever ye had," sayd king Arthur, "ye should have forborne her in my presence; therefore thinke not the contrary, ye shal repent it, for such another despite had I never in my court afore, therefore withdraw you out of my court in all the haste ye may." Then Balin tooke up the head of the lady and bare it with him to his hostry,[2] and there he met with his squire, that was sorry he had displeased king Arthur. And so they rode foorth out of the towne. "Now," said Balin, "we must heere depart; take you this head and bare it to my friends, and tell them how I have sped, and tel my friends in Northumberland that my most foe is dead; also tell them how I am out of prison, and also what adventure did befall me at the getting of this sword." "Alas," said the squire, "ye are greatly to blame for to displease king Arthur." "As for that," said Balin, "I will hie me in all the haste I may to meete with Rience, and destroy him, or else to die therefore; and if it may happen me to winne him, then will king Arthur be my good and gracious lord." "Where shall I meete with you?" said the squire. "In king Arthurs court," said Balin. So his squire and he departed at that time. Then king Arthur and all the court made great dole,[3] and had great shame of the death of the lady of the lake. Then the king full richly buried her.

[1] *Forthinketh.*—Repenteth.
[2] *Hostry.*—An inn, or lodging.   [3] *Dole.*—Grief.

CHAP. XXIX.—How Merlin told the adventure of the damosell.

AT that time there was in king Arthurs court a knight that was the kings sonne of Ireland, and his name was Lanceor, and he was a proude knight, and hee counted himselfe one of the best knights of the court, and he had great spite at Balin for the atcheaving of the sword, that any should be accounted of more prowesse than he was; and he asked king Arthur if he would give him leave to ride after Balin and to revenge the dispite that he hath done. "Doe your best," said king Arthur, "for I am right wroth with Balin; I would hee were quite of the dispite that he hath done to me and to my court." Then this Lanceor went to his hostrie to make him redy. In the meane while came Merlin to king Arthurs court, and there it was told him of the adventure of the sword, and of the lady of the lake. "Now shall I say to you," said Merlin, "this damosell that here standeth, that brought the sword unto your court, I shal tel you the cause of her comming, she is the falsest damosel that liveth." "Say not so," said they, "she hath a brother a passing good knight of prowesse and a full true man, and this damosell loved another that held her to paramour, and this good knight her brother met with the knight that held her to paramour, and slew him by force of his hands. When this false damosell understood this, she went to the lady Lile of Avelyon, and besought her of helpe to be avenged on her brother.

CHAP. XXX.—How Balin was pursued by Sir Lanceor a knight of Ireland, and how Balin slew him.

AND so this lady Lile of Avelion tooke her this sword which she brought with her, and told that there should no man draw it out of the scabbard, but if he were one of the best knights of this realme, and he should be hardy and ful of prowesse, and with that sword he should sley her brother. This was the cause that the damosell came into this court." "I know it, as well as yee doe," said Merlin, " would to God she had never come into this court, for she came never in fellowship of worshippe to doe good, but alway great harme; and that knight which hath acheaved the sword shal be destroyed by that sword, wherfore it shall be great domage, for there is not living a knight of more prowesse then he is, and he shall doe unto you, my lord king Arthur, great honour and kindenesse, and great pittie it is for he shall not endure but a while, and as for his strength and hardinesse, I know not his match living." So the knight of Ireland armed him at all points, and dressed his sheild on his shoulder and mounted up on horsebacke, and tooke his speare in his hand, and rode after as fast as his horse could run, and within a little space on a mountaine he had a sight of Balin, and with a loude voice he cried to him, and said: "Abide knight, for ye shall abide whether ye will or will not, and the sheild that is tofore you shall not helpe you."

When Balin heard that noyse, he turned his horse fiersly, and said, "Faire knight, what will you with me, will yee just with me?" "Yea," said the Irish knight, "therefore am I come after you." "Peradventure," said Balin, "it had beene better to have holden you at home, for many a man weneth to put his enemy to a rebuke, and often it falleth to himselfe. Of what court be ye sent fro?" said Balin. "I am come fro the court of king Arthur," said the knight of Ireland, "that am come hither for to revenge the despite that ye have done this day to king Arthur and to his court."

"Well," said Balin, "I see well I must have adoe with you, which me forethinketh[1] for to greive king Arthur or any of his knights; and your quarell is full simple to me,"

---

[1] *Forethinketh.*—i. e. repenteth.

said Balin, "for the lady that is dead did great domage, and else I would have beene as loth as any knight that liveth for to sley a lady." "Mak you ready," said the knight Lanceor, "and dresse you to me, for one of us shall abide in the field." Then they tooke their speares in all the haste they might, and came together as fast as their horses might drive, and the kinges sonne of Ireland smote Balin upon his shield, that his speare went all to shivers. And Balin smote him with such a might that it went through his shield, and perished the hawberke, and so pearced through his body and the horse croupe, and Balin anone turned his horse fiersly, and drew out his sword, and wist not that he had slaine him, and then he saw him lye as a dead corps.

CHAP. XXXI.—How a damosell which was in love with Lanceor, slew her selfe for his love, and how Balin met with his brother Balan.

THEN he looked by him and was ware of a damosell that came riding as fast as her horse might gallop, upon a fair palfray; and when she espied that sir Lanceor was slaine, then she made sorrow out of measure, and said, "O Balin, two bodyes haste thou slayne and one heart, and two hearts in one body, and two soules thou hast lost." And therewith she tooke the sword from her love that lay dead, and as she tooke it shee fell to the ground in a swoone, and when she arose she made great dole out of measure, which sorrow greeved Balin passing sore, and went to her for to have taken the sword out of her hands, but she held it so fast, that in no wise he might take the sword out of her hands, but if he should have hurt her; and sodainly she set the pomel of the sword to the grounde and runne her selfe through the body. And when Balin saw her dead, he was passing heavy in his heart, and ashamed that so faire a damosell had destroyed her selfe for the great love she had unto sir Lanceor. "Alas," said Balin, "me repenteth sore the death of this knight for the love of this damosell, for there was much true love betweene them both." And for sorow might no longer behold them, but turned his horse and looked toward a forrest, and there hee espyed the armes of his brother Balan. And when they were met, they put off their helmes and kissed together, and weept for joye and pittie. Then said Balan, "I wend[1] little to have met with you at this sodaine adventure; I am right glad of your deliverance out of your dolorous prisoning, for a man told me in the Castle of Foure Stones that ye were delivered, and that man had seene you in king Arthurs court, and therefore I came hither into this country, for here I supposed to finde you." And anone Balin told unto his brother of all his adventures of the sword and of the death of the lady of the lake, and how king Arthur was displeased with him, "Wherefore he sent this knight after me that lieth here dead, and the death of this damosell greiveth me ful sore." "So doth it me," said Balan, "but ye must take the adventure that God will ordaine unto you." "Truely," said Balin, "I am right heavy of minde that my lord king Arthur is displeased with me, for he is the most worshipfulest knight that reigneth now on the earth, and his love I will get or else I will put my life in adventure; for king Ryence of Northwales lieth at a syege at the castle Terrabill, and thither will wee draw in al haste, to prove our worship and prowesse upon him." "I will well," said Balan, "that we doe so, and we will helpe each other as brethren ought to doe."

[1] *Wend.*—Thought, expected.

KING ARTHUR. 69

CHAP. XXXII.—How a dwarfe reproved Balin for the death of Lanceor, and how king Marke of Cornewayle found them, and made a tombe over them.

"BROTHER," said Balin, "let us goe hence, and well bee we met." The meane while as they talked, there came a dwarfe from the citie of Camelot on horsebacke as fast as hee might, and found the dead bodyes, wherefore he made great dole, and drew his haire for sorrow, and said, "Which of you knights hath done this deede?" "Whereby askest thou it?" said Balin. "For I would wite," said the dwarfe. "It was I," said Balin, "that slew this knight in my defence, for hither came he to chace me, and either I must sley him or he me, and this damosell slew her selfe for his love, which me sore repenteth, and for her sake I shall owe all women the better love and favour." "Alas," said the dwarfe, "thou haste done great domage unto thy selfe, for this knight that is here dead was one of the most valiantest men that lived, and trust thou well, Balin, that the kinne of this knight will chace thee through the world till they have slaine thee." "As for that," said Balin, "I feare it not greatly; but I am right heavie because I have displeased my soveraigne lord king Arthur, for the death of this knight." So, as they talked together, there came a king of Cornewaile riding by them, which was named king Marke,[1] and when he saw these two bodies dead and understood how they were dead by one of the two knights above said, then made king Marke great sorrow for the true love that was betweene them, and said: "I wil not depart from hence til I have on this earth made a tombe." And there he pight his pavilions, and sought through all the

[1] *King Marke.*—This personage is so celebrated among the heroes of the romances of king Arthur, that it is hardly necessary to give any particular account of him here, especially as we shall find him acting a more prominent part further on.

countrie to finde a tombe. And in a church they found one was rich and faire, and then the king let put them both in the earth, and put the tombe on them, and wrote both their names on the tombe. "Here lieth Lanceor, the kings sonne of Ireland, that at his owne request was slayne by the hands of Balin, and how his lady Colombe and paramour slew her selfe with her loves sword for dole and sorrow."

CHAP. XXXIII.—How Merlin prophesied that two of the best knights of the world should fight there, which were sir Lancelot and sir Tristram.

THE meane while as this was in doeing, came Merlin unto King Marke, and seeing all his doing, said, "Here in this place shall be the greatest battaile betweene two knights that ever was or ever shall bee, and the truest lovers, and yet none of them shall sley other." And there Merlin wrote their names upon the tombe with letters of gold that should fight in that place, whose names were Lancelot du Lake and Tristram de Liones.[1] "Thou art a marvailous man," said king Marke unto Merlin, "that speakest of such marvailes, thou art a boistrous fellow and an unlikely to tell of such deedes. What is thy name?" said king Marke. "At this time," said Merlin, "I will not tell, but at that time when sir Tristram shal be taken with his soveraigne lady, then ye shall knowe and heare my name; and at that time yee shall heare tydings that shall not please you." Then said Merlin to Balin, "Thou hast done thy selfe great hurt, because thou did not save this lady that slew her selfe, that might have saved her if thou had would." "By the faith of my body," said Balin, "I could not nor might not

[1] The history of sir Tristam, or more properly sir Tristan, one of the most celebrated heroes of mediæval romance, occupies a large place in a subsequent part of the present work.

KING ARTHUR.

save her, for she slew her selfe sodainely." "Me repenteth," said Merlin, "because of the death of that lady, thou shalt strike a stroke the most dolorous that ever man stroke, except the stroke of our Lord; for thou shalt hurt the truest knight and the man of the most worship that now liveth, and through that stroke three kingdomes shall be in great povertie, miserie, and wrechednesse twelve yeeres, and the knight shall not be whole of that wound in many yeeres." And then Merlin tooke his leave of Balin. Then said Balin, "If I wist that it were sooth that ye say, I should doe such a perilous deede as that I would slay my selfe to make thee a lyer." And therewith anon Merlin sodainly vanished away. Then Balin and his brother tooke their leave of king Marke.

"First," said the king, "tel me your name." "Sir," said Balan, "ye may see he beareth two swords, thereby ye may call him the knight with the two swords." And so departed king Marke, and rode to Camelot to king Arthur, and Balin and his brother took the way to king Rience, and as they rode together they met with Merlin disguised, but they knew him not. "Whether ride ye?" said Merlin. "We have little to doe," said the two knights, "for to tell thee; but what is thy name?" said Balin. "As at this time," said Merlin, "I will not tell thee." "It is full evil seene," said the two knights, "that thou art a true man, when thou wilt not tell thy name." "As for that," said Merlin, "be it as it may, but I can tel you wherefore yee ride this way, for to meete king Rience, but it wil not availe you without you have my counsail." "Ah!" said Balin, "ye are Merlin. We wil be ruled by your counsaile." "Come on," said Merlin, "ye shall have great worship, and looke that ye doe knightly, for yee shall have great neede." "As for that," said Balin, "dread ye not, we will doe what we may."

CHAP. XXXIV.—How Balin and his brother, by the counsaile of Merlin, tooke king Rience and brought him unto king Arthur.

THEN Merlin lodged them in a wood amongst leaves beside the highway, and took off the bridles of their horses, and put them to grasse, and laid them downe to rest them till it was nigh midnight. Then Merlin bad them arise and make them ready, for the king was nigh them, that was stolen away from his hoast with three score horses of his best knights, and twenty of them rode tofore to warn the lady de Vauce that the king was comming, for that night king Rience should have layen with her. "Which is the king?" said Balin. "Abide," said Merlin, "here in a straight way ye shal meete with him." And therwith he shewed Balin and his brother where he rode. Anone Balin and his brother met with the king, and smote him downe, and wounded him fiersly, and laid him to the ground, and ther they slew on the right hand and on the left, and slew moe then fortie of his men, and the remnant fled. Then went they againe to king Rience, and would have slaine him, if he had not yeelded him to their grace. Then said the king againe, "Knights full of prowesse, slay me not, for by my life ye may winne and by my death yee shal winne nothing." Then said these two knights, "Ye say sooth and troth." And so laid him on an horse litter. With that Merlin was vanished and came to king Arthur afore hand, and told him how his most enemy was taken and disconfited. "By whom?" said king Arthur. "By two knights," said Merlin, "that would please your lordship, and to-morrow ye shall know what they be." Anone after came the knight with the two swords and Balan his brother, and brought with them king Rience, and there delivered him to the porters and charged them with him; and so they two returned againe in the springing¹ of the day. King Arthur came to king Rience and said, " Sir king, you are welcom, by what adventure come ye hither?" " Sir," said king Rience, " I came hither by an hard aventure." " Who wan you?" said king Arthur. " Sir," said Rience, " the knight with the two swords and his brother, which are two marvilous knights of prowes." " I know them not," said king Arthur, "but much I am beholden unto them." " Ah," said Merlin, " I shall tell you, it is Balin that atcheaved the sword, and his brother Balan, a good knight, there liveth not a better in prowesse and worthinesse ; and it shal be the greatest dole of him that ever was of knight, for he shall not long endure." " Alas," said king Arthur, " that is great pittie, for I am greatly beholden unto him, and I have full evill deserved it unto him for his kindenesse." " Nay," said Merlin, "he shall doe much more for you, and that shall ye know or it be long. But, sir, are ye purveyed?" said Merlin, " for to morrow the hoast of Nero, king Rience brother, will set upon you afore diner with a mighty hoast, therefore make you ready, for I will depart from you."

CHAP. XXXV.—How king Arthur had a battaile against Nero and king Lot of Orkeney, and how king Lot was deceived by Merlin, and how twelve kings were slaine.

HEN king Arthur made ready his hoast in ten battailes, and Nero was ready in the field afore the castle Terrabil with a mightie hoast, for hee had ten battailes, with much more people than king Arthur had. So Nero himselfe had the vaward² with the most party of his people ; and Merlin came to king Lot, of the yle of the Orkeney, and held him with a tale of prophesie till Nero and his people were destroyed. And

¹ *Springing.*—Caxton has *in the daunyng of the day.*
² *Vuward.*—The van-guard, or avant-guard.

there sir Kay the seneshall did passing well, that all the dayes of his life he had thereof worship. And sir Hervis de Revel did marvailous deedes with king Arthur. And king Arthur slew that day twentie knights, and maimed fortie. At that time came in the knight with the two swords, and his brother Balan; but they two did so marvelously that the king and al the knights had great marvaile thereof, and all that beheld them said that they were sent from heaven as angels, or as divels from hell; and king Arthur said himselfe that they were the best knights that ever he saw, for they gave such stroks that al men had wonder of them. In the meane while came one to king Lot, and told him that while he taried there Nero was destroyed and slaine with al his people. "Alas! I am shamed," said king Lot, "for through my default is slaine many a worshipfull man; for if wee had beene together there had beene no hoast under heaven that had beene able to match us. This fayter[1] with his prophecie hath mocked me." All that did Merlin, for he knew well that if King Lot had beene there with his body at the first battaile, king Arthur and all his people should have beene destroied and slaine. And Merlin knew wel that one of the kings should be dead that day, and loth was Merlin that any of them both should be slaine; but of the twaine he had lever king Lot had beene slaine then king Arthur.

"Now, what is best to doe," said king Lot, "whether is it better for to treat with king Arthur, or to fight, for the most part of our people are slaine and destroyed?" "Sir," said a knight, "set upon king Arthur, for he and his men are weary of fighting, and we be fresh." "As for me," said king Lot, "I would that every knight would doe his part as I will doe mine." And then they advanced their baners and smote together, and al to-shivered their spears; and king Arthurs knights, with the helpe of the knight with the two swords and his brother Balan, put king

---

[1] *Fayter.*—A flatterer, or deceiver.

Lot and his hoast to the worst; but alway king Lot held him in the formost, and did great deedes of armes, for all his hoast was borne up by his hands, for he abode and withstood al knights. Alas! he might not ever endure, the which was great pittie that so worthy a knight as he was should be over-matched, and that of late time afore had beene a knight of king Arthurs, and had wedded king Arthurs sister; and because king Arthur lay by king Lots wife and begat upon her Mordred, therefore king Lot held against king Arthur. So there was a knight that was called the knight with the strange beast, and at that time his right name was Pellinore, which was a good man of prowesse, and he smote a mightie stroke at king Lot as he fought with his enemies, and he failed of his stroke, and smote the horse necke that he fell to the ground with king Lot, and therewith anone sir Pellinore smote him a great stroke through the helme, and hewed him to the browes. And then all the hoast of Orkeney fled for the death of king Lot, and there was slaine many a mothers sonne. But king Pellinore bare the wit[1] of the death of king Lot; wherefore sir Gawaine revenged the death of his father the tenth yeare after he was made knight, and slew king Pellinore with his owne hands. Also there was slaine at the battaile twelve kings on king Lots side with Nero, and all were buried in the church of Saint Stevens, in Camelot; and the remnant of knights and of other were buried in a great roche.[2]

[1] *Wit.*—Blame. An Anglo-Saxon word.
[2] *Ruche.*—A rock.

CHAP. XXXVI.—Of the entertainement of twelve kings, and of the prophesie of Merlin, and how Balin should give the dolorous stroke.

SO at the entertainement[1] came king Lots wife Morgause, with her foure sonnes Gawaine, Agravaine, Gaheris, and Gareth. Also there came thither, king Urience, sir Ewaynes father, and Morgan le Fay his wife, that was king Arthurs sister. All these came to the entertainement. But of all these twelve knights king Arthur let make the tombe of king Lot passing richly; and his tombe stood by it selfe apart, and then king Arthur let make twelve images of latin[2] and of coper, and made them to be overgilt with fine gold, in signe and token of the twelve kings; and every image held a taper of waxe, which brent night and day. And king Arthur was made in signe of a figure standing above them all, with a sword drawen in his hand. And all the twelve figures had countenance like unto men that were overcomen. All this made Merlin by his subtill craft, and there he said to king Arthur, "When I am dead, the twelve tapers shall burne no longer. And soone after this the adventures of the holy sancgreall shall come among you, and shall also be atcheaved." Also hee told unto king Arthur how Balin the worshipfull knight, should give the dolorous stroke, "whereof shall fall great vengeance." "O where is Balin and Balan and Pellinore?" said king Arthur.

"As for sir Pellinore," sayd Merlin, "he will meete with you anone; and as for Balin he will not be long from you; but the other brother Balan will depart, and ye shall see him no more." "Now, by my faith," said king Arthur, "they are two marvailous knights, and namely Balin passeth of prowesse farre of any knight that ever I found, for I am much beholden unto him; would to God that he

[1] *Entertainement.*—In Caxton's text it is, evidently more correctly, *at the enterement.*
[2] *Latin.*—A mixed metal, resembling brass.

would abide still with me." "Sir," said Merlin, "looke that yee keepe well the scabbard of Excalibur; for, as I told you, yee shall lose no blood as long as yee have the scabbard upon you, though yee have as many wounds upon your body as yee may have." So afterward for great trust king Arthur betooke the scabbard to Morgan le Fay his sister; and she loved another knight better then her husband king Urience, or king Arthur, and she would have had king Arthur slaine; and therefore she let make an other scabbard like it by enchauntement, and gave the scabbard of Excalibur to her love, a knight named sir Accolon, which after had nigh slaine king Arthur. After this, Merlin told unto king Arthur of the prophecie that there should be a great battaile beside Salisbury, and that Mordred his owne sonne should be against him. Also he told him that Basdemegus was his cossen, and germaine unto king Uryence.

CHAP. XXXVII.—How a sorrowfull knight came tofore king Arthur, and how Balin fet[1] him, and how that knight was slaine by a knight invisible.

WITHIN a day or two king Arthur was somewhat sicke, and he let pitch his pavilion in a medow, and there he laid him downe on a pallet to sleepe; but he might have no rest. Right so he heard a great noyse of a horse, and therewith the king looked out at the porch of the pavilions dore, and saw a knight comming by him making great sorrow. "Abide, faire sir," said king Arthur, "and tell me wherefore thou makest this sorrow." "Yee may little amend it," said the knight; and so passed forth unto the castle of Meliot. Anone after there came Balin, and when he saw king Arthur, anon he alighted off his horse and came to the king on foote, and saluted him.

[1] *Fet.*—Fetched.

"By my head," said king Arthur, "yee be welcome, sir. Right now came riding this way a knight making great. sorrow, and I can not tel for what cause, wherefore I would desire you of your courtesie and gentilenesse that yee will fetch that knight againe, either by force, or else by his good wil." "I will doe more for your lordship then that," said Balin; and so rode more than a pace,[1] and found the knight with a damosell in a forrest, and said, "Sir knight, ye must come with me unto my lord king Arthur, for to tell him the cause of your sorrow." "That will I not," said the knight; "for it would scath[2] me greatly, and doe you non availe." "Sir," said Balin, "I pray you make you ready, for yee must needes go with me, or else I must fight with you, and bring you by force, and that were I loth to doe." "Will ye be my warrant," said the knight to Balin, "if I goe with you?" "Yea," said Balin, "or else I will die therefore." And so he made him ready to goe with the good knight Balin, and left there the damosell. And as they were afore king Arthurs pavilion there came one invisible, and smote this knight that went with Balin throughout the body with a speare.

"Alas!" said the knight, "I am slaine under your conduct and guarde with a traitrous knight called Garlon; therefore take my horse the which is better then yours, and ride to the damosel, and follow the quest that I was in where as shee wil leade you, and revenge my death when yee may best." "That shall I doe," said Balin, "and thereof I make avowe to you, by my knighthood." And so he departed from this knight, making great sorrow. So king Arthur let burie this knight richly, and made a mention upon the tombe, how there was slaine Herleus le Berbeus, and also how the trechery was done by the knight Garlon. But ever the damosell bare the truncheon of the speare with her, that sir Herleus was slaine withall.

[1] *Pace.*—A step. *Pas*, from the Latin *passus*, meant originally a certain extent of ground.   [2] *Scath.*—To grieve; injure.

CHAP. XXXVIII.—How Balin and the damosell met with a knight that was in likewise slaine, and how the damosell bled for the custome of a castle.

SO Balin and the damosell rode into a forrest, and there met with a knight that had beene on hunting, and that knight asked Balin for what cause he made so great sorrow. "Me list not to tell you," said Balin. "Now," said the knight, "and I were armed as ye be, I would fight with you." "That should little neede," said Balin, "for I am not afraid to tell it you;" and told him all the cause how it was. "Ah," said the knight, "is this all? heere I ensure you by the faith of my body never to depart from you as long as my life lasteth." And so they went to the hostry[1] and armed him, and so rode forth with Balin. And as they came by an hermitage fast by a churchyard, there came the knight Garlon invisible, and smote this good knight Perin de Mountbelyard with a speare through the body. "Alas!" said the knight, "I am slaine by this traitour knight that rideth invisible." "Alas!" said Balin, "it is not the first despite that he hath done to me." And there the hermit and Balin buried the knight under a rich stone and a tombe royall. And on the morow they found letters of gold written how sir Gawaine shall revenge king Lots death his father upon king Pellinore. And anone after this, Balin and the damosell rode till they came to a castle, and there Balin alighted, and he and the damosell wend[2] to have gone into the castle. And anone as Balin came within the castle gate, the portecolis fel downe at his backe, and there came many men about the damosell, and would have slaine her. And when Balin saw that, he was sore grieved, because he might not helpe the damosell. And then he went upon the walles and lept over into the ditch and hurt

---

[1] *Hostry.*—The hostelry, or inn where he lodged.
[2] *Wend.*—Thought.

him not; and anon he pulled out his sword and would have foughten with them. And they all said that they would not fight with him, for they did nothing but the old custom of the castle, and told him how their lady was sicke, and had layen many yeares, and shee might not be whole but if shee had a silver dish full of blood of a cleane maide and a kings daughter; and therefore the custome of this castle is, that there shall non passe this way but that shee shal bleede of her blood a silver dish full. " Well," said Balin, " shee shall bleede as much as she may bleede, but I will not that shee leese her life while my life lasteth." And so Balin made her to bleede by her good will. But her blood helped not the lady. And so he and shee rested there all that night, and had there right good cheare; and on the morrow they passed on their way. And as it telleth afterwards in the sancgreall that sir Percivalles sister helped that lady with her blood, whereof she died.[1]

CHAP. XXXIX.—How Balin met with the knight named Garlon at a feast, and there he slew him, to have his blood to heale therewith the sonne of his hoast.

HEN they rode three or foure dayes, and never met with adventure; and by happe they were lodged with a gentleman that was a rich man and well at ease. And as they sate at their supper, Balin heard one complaine grievously by him in a chaire. "What noyse is this?" said Balin. "Forsooth," said his hoast, "I will tell you; I was but late at a justing, and there I just with a knight that is brother unto king Pellam, and twice I smote him downe; and then he promised to quit[2] me on my best friend, and so he wounded my sonne that cannot be whole till I have of that knights blood, and he rydeth alway invisible, but I know not his name."

[1] See the third part of this romance, chapters 91 and 92.
[2] *To quit.*—To quite, to repay or revenge.

"Ah," said Balin, " I know that knight, his name is Garlon, he hath slaine two knights of mine in the same maner, therefore I had rather meet with that knight then all the gold in this realme, for the despite that he hath done mee." " Well," said his hoast, " I shall tell you : king Pellam, of Listenise,[1] hath made a crie in all this country a great feast that shal bee within twentie dayes ; and no knight may come there but if he bring his wife with him, or his paramour ; and that knight, your enemie and mine, yee shall see that day." " Then I behote you," said Balin, " part of his blood to heale your sonne withal." " We will be forward to-morrow," said his hoast. So on the morrowe they rode all three toward Pellam, and had fifteene dayes journey or they came thither ; and that same day began the great feast. And they alight, and stabled their horses, and went into the castle ; but Balins hoast might not be let in, because he had no lady. Then was Balin wel received, and brought to a chamber and unarmed him ; and there were brought him robes to his pleasure, and would have had Balin leave his sword behinde him.[2] " Nay," said Balin, " that will I not doe, for it is the custome of my countrey a knight alway to keepe his weapon with him, and that custome will I keepe, or else I will depart as I came." Then they gave him leave to were his sword. And so he went to the castle, and was set among knights of worship, and his lady afore him. Soone Balin asked a knight, " Is there not a knight in this court whose name is Garlon ?" " Yonder he goeth," said the knight, " he with that blacke face ; he is the marvailest knight that is now living, for he destroyeth many good knights, for he goeth invisible."

"Ah, wel," said Balin, " is that he?" Then Balin ad-

---

[1] *Listenise.*—*Lystyneyse,* Caxton.

[2] It was the ancient custom for a visitor to give up his arms at the entrance to the hall or to the castle. He was there under the protection of his host, and it was required as a precaution against the sanguinary scenes which might take place when the guests became drunk and quarrelsome.

vised him long: "If I slay him heere, I shall not scape; and if I leave him now, peradventure I shall never meete with him againe at such a steven;[1] and much harm he will doe and he live." Therewith this Garlon espied that this Balin beheld him, and then he came and smote Balin on the face with the backe of his hand, and said, "Knight, why beholdest thou me so? for shame, therefore, eate thy meate, and doe that thou came for." "Thou saist sooth," said Balin; "this is not the first despite that thou hast done me, and therefore I will doe that I came for;" and rose up fiersly, and clave his head to the shoulders. "Give me the troncheon," said Balin to his lady, "wherewith he slew your knight." Anone she gave it him, for alway she bare that troncheon with her; and therewith Balin smote him through the body, and said openly, "With that troncheon thou hast slaine a good knight, and now it sticketh in thy body." And then Balin called to him his hoast, saying, "Now may yee fetch blood inough to heale your sonne withall."

CHAP. XL.—How Balin fought with king Pellam, and how his sword brake, and how he gate a speare, wherewith he smote the dolorous stroke.

ANONE all the knights rose up from the table for to set on Balin. And king Pellam himselfe arose up fiersly, and said, "Knight, why hast thou slaine my brother? thou shalt dye therefore, or thou depart." "Wel," said Balin, "then doe it your selfe." "Yes," said king Pellam. "there shall no man have adoe with thee but my selfe for the love of my brother." Then king Pellam caught in his hand a grim weapon, and smote egerly at Balin, but Balin put the sword betweene his head and the stroke, and therewith his sword burst in sunder; and when Balin was weponlesse he ranne into a chamber for to seeke some weapon, and so from

[1] *At such a steven.*—On such a favourable occasion.

chamber to chamber, and no weapon could he find, and alway king Pellam followed him; and at the last he entred into a chamber that was marvelously well dight and richly, and a bed arayed with cloth of gold, the richest that might be thought, and one lying therein; and thereby stood a table of cleane gold, with foure pillars of silver that bare up the table, and upon the table stood a marvailous speare strangely wrought. And when Balin saw the spere, hee gat it in his hand, and turned him to king Pellam, and smote him passingly sore with that speare, that king Pellam fell downe in a swowne, and therewith the castle rove,[1] and walls brake and fell to the earth, and Balin fel downe so that he might not stir hand nor foot. And so the most part of the castle that was fallen downe through that dolorous stroke lay upon king Pellam and Balin three dayes.

CHAP. XLI.—How Balin was delivered by Merlin, and saved a knight that would have slaine himselfe for love.

THEN Merlin came thither, and took up Balin, and gat him a good horse, for his horse was dead, and bad him ride out of that countrey. "I would have my damosell," said Balin. "Loe," said Merlin, "where shee lieth dead." And king Pellam lay so many yeeres sore wounded, and might never be whole till Galahad the haut[2] prince healed him in the quest of the sancgreal, for in that place was part of the blood of our Lord Jesus Christ that Joseph of Arimathy[3] brought into this land; and there himselfe lay in that rich

[1] *Rove.*—i. e. split, became riven. King Pellam, as well as his brother Garlon who went about invisible, appear to have been living in a state of enchantment.
[2] *Haut.*—High, lofty.
[3] *Joseph of Arimathy.*—According to the legend, Joseph of Arimathea, after the death of our Saviour, obtained possession of the hanap, or cup, from which Christ had served the wine at the Last Supper, which he brought with him to Britain, the inhabitants of which he is represented to have converted to Christianity. This cup was the holy grail, or, as it is called in our romance, the *sancgreal.*

bed. And that was the same speare that Longius[1] smot
our Lord to the heart. And king Pellam was nigh of
Josephs kinne, and that was the most worshipfull man that
lived in those dayes, and great pittie it was of his hurt, for
the stroke turned him to great dole, tray, and teene.[2] Then
departed Balin from Merlin, and said, "In this world we
shal never meete more." So hee rode forth through the
faire countries and cities, and found the people dead on
every side. And all that were on live cryd, "O Balin, thou
hast caused great domage in these countries; for the dolorous
stroke that thou gavest unto king Pellam three countries
are destroyed, and doubt not but the vengeance will fall on
thee at the last." When Balin was past the countries hee
was passing faine,[3] so he rode eight dayes or he met with
adventure, and at the last he came into a faire forrest in a
valley, and was ware of a towre, and there beside he saw a
great horse of warre tied to a tree, and there beside sate a
faire knight on the ground, and made great mourning, and
he was a likely man and a well made. Balin said, "God
save you, why be yee so heavie, tell me, and I will amend
it and I may to my power." "Sir knight," said hee againe,
"thou doest me great griefe, for I was in mery thoughts,
and now thou puttest me to more paine." Balin went a
little from him, and looked on his horse; then Balin heard
him say thus: "Ah, faire lady, why have yee broken my
promise, for ye promised me to meete me heare by noone,
and I may curse you that ever ye gave me this sword, for
with this sword I wil slay my selfe," and pulled it out; and
therewith Balin stert to him, and tooke him by the hand.
"Let goe my hand," said the knight, "or else I shall slay
thee." "That shall not neede," said Balin, "for I shall

---

[1] *Longius.*—This was the name given in the Middle Ages to the knight, or soldier, who pierced the side of the Saviour with his spear to ascertain if he were dead.

[2] *Tray.*—Vexation. *Teene.*—Grief.

[3] *Faine.*—Glad.

promise you my helpe to get you your lady, if you will tell me where she is." " What is your name?" said the knight. " My name is Balin le Savage." " Ah, sir, I know you well inough; ye are the knight with the two swords, and the man of most prowesse of your hands living." " What is your name?" said Balin. " My name is Garnish of the Mount, a poore mans sonne, but by my prowesse and hardinesse a duke hath made me knight and gave me lands; his name is duke Hermell, and his daughter is she that I love, and she me, as I deemed." " How farre is shee hence?" said Balin. " But sixe miles," said the knight. " Now ride we hence." said the two knights. So they rode more then a pace, till that they came unto a faire castle well walled and ditched. " I will into the castle," said Balin, " and looke if she be there." So he went in, and searched from chamber to chamber, and found her bed, but shee was not there; then Balin looked into a faire little garden, and under a laurel tree he saw her lye upon a quilt of greene samite,[1] and a knight in her armes fast halsing[2] either other, and under their heades grasse and hearbes. When Balin saw her lye so with the foulest knight that ever he saw, and she a faire lady, then Balin went through all the chambers againe, and told the knight how he had found her as she had slept fast, and so brought him in the place there she lay fast sleeping.

CHAP. XLII.—How that knight slew his love and a knight lying by her, and after how he slew himselfe with his owne sword, and how Balin rode toward a castle where he lost his life.

AND when Garnish beheld her so lying, for pure sorrow his mouth and nose brast out on bleeding, and with his sword he smote off both their heads, and then he made sorrow out of mea-

---

[1] *Samite.*—A rich silken stuff. See before, p. 54.
[2] *Halsing.*—Holding one another in their arms.

sure, and said, "Oh, Balin, much sorrow hast thou brought to me, for haddest thou not shewed me that sight I should have passed my sorrow." "Forsooth," said Balin, "I did it to this intent, that it should aswage thy courage, and that yee might see and know their falshood, and to cause you to leave that ladyes love. God knoweth, I did none other but as I would you did to me." "Alas!" said Garnish, "now is my sorrow double that I may not endure; now have I slaine that I most loved in all my life." And therewith sodainely he rove himselfe on his owne sword unto the hilts. When Balin saw that, he dressed him from thence, least folke should say that he had slaine them; and so he rode forth, and within three dayes he came by a crosse, and thereon was letters of gold written, that said: "It is not for a knight alone to ride toward this castle." Then saw he an old hore gentleman comming toward him, that said, "Balin le Savage, thou passest thy bounds this way, therfore turne againe, and it will availe thee." And he vanished away anone, and so he heard an horne blow, as it had beene the death of a beast. "That blast," said Balin, "is blowen for me, for I am the prise, and yet am I not dead." And therewith he saw an hundred ladyes and many knights that welcomed him with faire semblant, and made him passing good cheere unto his sight, and led him into the castle; and there was daunsing and ministralsy and al maner of joy. Then the chiefe lady of the castle said, "Knight with the two swords, ye must have ado and just with a knight here by that keepeth an iland, for there may no man passe this way but hee must just or hee passe." "That is an unhappie custome," said Balin, "that a knight may not passe but if he just." "Yee shall have adoe but with one knight," said the lady. "Well," said Balin, "sith I shall, thereto am I ready, but traviling men are often weary, and their horses also; but, though my horse be weary, my heart is not weary, I would be faine there my death should bee." "Sir," said a knight to Balin, " me thinketh your shield is not good, I wil lend you a bigger." " Thereof I pray you ;" and so tooke the shield that was unknowen, and left his owne, and so rode unto the iland, and put him and his horse in a great boate ; and when he came on the other side, he met with a damosell, and shee said, " O knight Balin, why have you left your owne shield, alas ! ye have put your selfe in great danger, for by your shield you should have beene knowen ; it is great pittie of you as ever was of knight, for of prowesse and hardinesse thou hast no fellow living."

" Me repenteth," said Balin, " that ever I came within this country, but I may not turne now againe for shame ; and what adventure shall fall to me, be it life or death, I will take the adventure that shall come to me." And then he looked on his armour, and understood he was well armed, and therewith blessed him, and mounted upon his horse.

CHAP. XLIII.—How Balin met with his brother Balan, and how each of them slew other unknowen till they were wounded to death.

THEN afore him hee saw come riding out of a castle a knight, and his horse trapped al in red, and himselfe in the same colour. And when this knight in the red beheld Balin, him thought it should be his brother Balin because of his two swords, but because he knew not his shield, he deemed that it should not be he. And so they aventred[1] their speares, and came mervailously fast together, and smote either other in the shields, but their speares and their course was so big that it bare downe horse and man, so that they lay both in a swowne ; but Balin was sore brused with the fall of his horse, for he was weary of travaile. And Balan the first that rose on foote, and drew his sword, and went toward

[1] *Aventred.*—To aventer was to place the spear in the position for striking an adversary.

Balin; and he arose and went against him, but Balan smote Balin first, and he put up his shield, and smote him through the shield, and brake his helme. Then Balin smote him againe with that unhappy sword, and wel nigh had feld his brother Balan, and so they fought there together till their breaths failed. Then Balin looked up to the castle, and saw the towers stand full of ladyes. So they went to battaile againe, and wounded each other grievously, and then they breathed oftentime, and so went to battaile, that all the place there as they fought was red of their blood. And at that time there was none of them both but they had smitten either other seaven great wounds, so that the least of them might have been the death of the mightiest giant in the world. Then they went to battaile againe so marvailously, that doubt it was to heare of that battaile for the great bloodsheding, and their hawberks unnailed, that naked they were on every side. At the last Balan, the younger brother, withdrew him a little and laid him down. Then said Balin le Savage, "What knight art thou? for or now I found never no knight that matched me." "My name is," said he, "Balan, brother to the good knight Balin." "Alas!" said Balin, "that ever I should see this day." And therewith he fel backward in a swowne. Then Balan went on all foure feete and hands, and put off the helme of his brother, and might not know him by the visage it was so full hewen and bebled; but when he awok he said, "O Balan my brother, thou hast slaine me, and I thee, wherefore all the wide world shall speake of us both."

"Alas!" said Balan, "that ever I saw this day, that through mishap I might not know you, for I espied well your two swords, but because yee had another shield, I deemed you had beene another knight." "Alas!" said Balin, "al that made an unhappy knight in the castle, for he caused me to leave mine owne shield to the destruction of us both; and if I might live, I would destroy that castle for the ill customes." "That were well done," said

Balan, "for I had never grace to depart from them sith that I came hither; for heere it happened me to slay a knight that kept this iland, and sith might I never depart; and no more should yee, brother, and ye might have slaine me, as ye have, and escaped your selfe with your life." Right so came the lady of the tower, with foure knights, and sixe ladyes, and six yeomen, unto them; and there she heard how they made their mone either to other, and said, "We came both out of one wombe, that is to say, mothers belly, and so shall we lye both in one pit." So Balan prayed the lady of her gentlenesse, for his true service, that shee would burie them both in that place there the battel was done. And she graunted them with weeping cheere, and said, "It should be done richly and in the best manner." " Now will ye send for a priest, that we may receive the sacrament and blessed body of our Lord Jesus Christ." " Yea," said the lady, " it shal be done." And so she sent for a priest, and gave them their rightes. "Now," said Balin, " when we are buried in one tombe, and the mention made over us how two brethren slew each other, there will never good knight nor good man see our tombe but they will pray for our soules." And so all the ladyes and gentlewomen wept for pittie. And anone Balan dyed; but Balin dyed not till the midnight after, and so were buried both; and the lady let make a mention[1] of Balan, how he was there slaine by the hands of his owne brother, but she knew not Balins name.

---

[1] It may, perhaps, be well to remark that the word *mention* is, here and in other passages, used in the sense of a monumental inscription.

CHAP. XLIV.—How Merlin buried Balin and Balan the two brethren in one tombe, and of Balins sword.

N the morrow came Merlin, and let write Balins name uppon the tombe with letters of gold: "Heere lyeth Balin le Savage, that was the knight with the two swords, and hee that smote the dolourous stroke." Merlin let make there also a bed, that there should never man lye in but he went out of his wit, yet Lancelot du Lake foredid[1] that bed through his noblenesse. And anon after, as Balin was dead, Merlin tooke his sword, and tooke off the pomel, and set on another pomell. Then Merlin bad a knight that stood afore him to handle that sword, and he assayed, but he could not handle it. Then Merlin laught. "Why laugh ye?" said the knight. "This is the cause," said Merlin; "there shal never no man handle this sword but the best knight of the world, and that shall bee sir Lancelot, or else Galahad his sonne; and Lancelot with this sword shal slay the man that in this world he loved best, that shall bee sir Gawayne." All this he let write in the pomell of the sword. Then Merlin let make a bridge of iron and of steele into that iland, and it was but halfe a foote broade, and there shall never man passe that bridge, nor have hardinesse to goe over, but if he were a passing good man and a good knight without trechery or vilany. Also the scabbard of Balins sword Merlin left it on this side the iland that Galahad should finde it. Also Merlin let make by his subtiltie and craft that Balins sword was put in marble ston, standing upright as great as a milstone, and the stone hoved alwayes above the water, and did many yeares, and so by adventure it swam downe the streame to the citie of

[1] *Foredid.*—Destroyed.

Camelot, that is in English, Winchester;[1] and that same day Galahad the haute prince came with king Arthur, and so Galahad brought with him the scabbard, and atchieved the sword that was there in the marble ston hoving upon the water. And on Whitsunday he atchieved the sword, as it is rehearsed in the booke of the sancgreall. Soone after this was done, Merlin came to king Arthur, and told him of the dolorous stroke that Balin gave to king Pellam, and how Balin and Balan fought together the marvailest battaile that ever was heard of, and how they were buried both in on tombe. "Alas!" said king Arthur, "this is the greatest pittie that ever I heard tell of two knights; for in the world I know not such two knights as they were." Thus endeth the tale of Balin and Balan, two brethren borne in Northumberland, good knights.

CHAP. XLV.—How king Arthur tooke and wedded Guenever unto his wife, which was daughter to Leodegraunce king of the land of Cameliard, with whom he had the round table.

N the beginning of king Arthur, after that hee was chosen king by adventure and by grace, for the most part of the barons knew not that he was Utherpendragons sonne, but as Merlin made it openly knowen. But yet many kings and lords made great war against him for that cause, but king Arthur full well overcame them all; for the most part of the dayes of his life he was much ruled by the counsaile of Merlin. So it befell on a time that king Arthur said unto Merlin: "My barons will let me have no rest, but needes they will have that I take a wife, and I will none take but by thy counsaile and by thine advise." "It is well done," said Merlin, "that ye take a wife, for a man of your

---

[1] *Winchester.*—An evident mistake of the compiler of this romance, see before, the note to p. 59.

bountie and noblenesse should not be without a wife. Now is there any faire lady that yee love better then another?" "Yea," said king Arthur, "I love Guenever,[1] the kings daughter Leodegrance of the land of Camelyard,[2] which Leodegrance holdeth in his house the table round that ye told he had of my father Uther. And this damosell is the most gentilest and fairest lady that I know living, or yet that ever I could find." "Sir," said Merlin, "as of her beautie and fairenesse she is one of the fairest that live; but and you loved her not so well as ye doe, I would finde you a damosell of beautie and of goodnesse that should like you, and please you, and your heart were not set. But there as a mans heart is set, he will be loth to returne." "That is truth," said king Arthur. But Merlin warned the king privily that Guenever was not wholesome for him to take to wife, for he warned him that Lancelot should love her and shee him againe; and so he turned his tale to the adventures of the sancgreall. Then Merlin desired of the king to have men with him that should enquire of Guenever. And so the king graunted him. And Merlin went forth to king Leodegrance of Cameliard, and told him of the desire of the king, that he would have to his wife Guenever his daughter. "That is to me," said king Leodegrance, "the best tidings that ever I heard, that so worthy a king of prowesse and of noblenesse will wed my daughter. And as for my lands I will give him, wisht[3] I that it might please him, but he hath lands enough, hee needeth none; but I shall send him a gift that shal please him much more, for I shal give him the table round, the which Uther-

[1] *Guenever.*—Geoffrey of Monmouth calls this clebrated heroine of romance, Guanhumara. Hist. Reg. Brit. ix. 9. See a former note, p. 41. According to some of the romances, it was Guenever who first became enamoured of king Arthur, on account of his gallant exploits, and she took care to show herself to the best advantage, in order to excite his passion.
[2] *Lodigrean of the land of Camelyard*, Caxton.
[3] *Wisht.*—i. e. wist, knew.

KING ARTHUR. 93

pendragon gave me; and when it is ful compleate, there is an hundred knights and fiftie, and as for an hundred good knights I have my selfe, but I lack fifty, for so many have beene slaine in my dayes." And so king Leodegrance delivered his daughter Guenever unto Merlin, and the table round with the hundred knights; and so they rode freshly with great royalty, what by water and what by land, till they came that night unto London.

CHAP. XLVI.—How the knights of the round table were ordained, and how their sieges[1] were blessed by the archbishop of Canterbury.

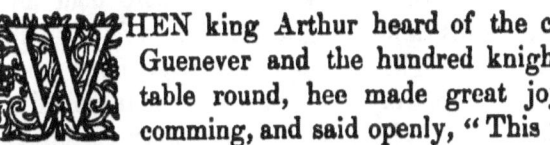HEN king Arthur heard of the comming of Guenever and the hundred knights with the table round, hee made great joy for their comming, and said openly, "This faire lady is passing welcome to me, for I loved her long, and therefore there is nothing so pleasing to me. And these knights with the round table please me more then right great riches." Then in all haste the king did ordaine for the mariage and the coronation in the most honourablest wise that could be devised. "Now, Merlin," said king Arthur, "goe thou and espie me in al this land fiftie knights that beene of most prowesse and worshippe." Within short time Merlin made the best speede he might, and found twenty eight good knights, but no more could hee find. Then the archbishop of Canterbury was sent for, and he blessed the sieges of his table round with great roialty and devotion, and there set the twenty eight knights in their sieges. And when this was done, Merlin said, "Faire sirs, ye must al arise and come unto king Arthur for to doe him homage, he will have the better wil to maintaine you." And so they arose, and did their homage. And when they were gone, Merlin found in the sieges letters of gold that

[1] *Sieges.*—Seats.

told the knights names that had sitten therein. But two sieges were void. And so anon came young Gawayne, and asked the king a gift. "Aske," said the king, "and I shall grant it you." " Sir, I aske that ye will make me knight the same day that ye shall wed faire Guenever." " I will doe it with a good will," said king Arthur, " and doe to you al the worship that I may, for I must so doe by reason you are my nephew and sisters sonne."

CHAP. XLVII.—How a poore man, riding upon a leane mare, desired king Arthur to make his sonne a knight.

FORTH withall there came a poore man into the court, and brought with him a faire young man of eighteene yeares of age, riding upon a leane mare. And the poore man asked al men that he met, "Where shall I find king Arthur?" " Yonder hee is," said the knights, " wilt thou any thing with him?" " Yea," said the poore man, " therefore I came hither." Anone as he came before the king he saluted him, and said, " O king Arthur, the floure of all knights and kings, I beseech Jesus save thee. Sir, it it was told me that at this time of your marriage ye would give any man the gift that he would aske, except it were unreasonable." " That is truth," said the king, " such cries I let make, and that wil I hold, so it appaire not my realme nor mine estate." " Yee say well and graciously," said the poore man. " Sir, I aske nothing else but that ye will make my sonne here a knight." " It is a great thing that thou askest of me," said the king. " What is thy name?" said the king to the poore man. " Sir, my name is Aries the cowheard."[1]

[1] *Aries the cowheard.*—This notion of noble blood irregularly grafted in a plebeian family, and showing itself by the warlike and aristocratic tendency of the youth who had sprung from the connection, was a favourite one in the Middle Ages, and is the subject of many romances and stories. It may be remarked that riding on a mare was not considered honourable in a knight.

"Whether commeth this of thee or of thy sonne?" said the king. "Nay, sir," said Aries, "this desire commeth of my sonne, and not of me. For I shall tel you I have thirteene sonnes, and all they will fall to what labour I put them to, and will bee right glad to doe labour, but this child will doe no labour for me, for any thing that my wife or I may do, but alwayes he wil be shooting or casting of darts, and glad to see battailes and to behold knights, and alwayes both day and night he desireth of me that hee might be made a knight." "What is thy name?" said the king unto the young man. "Sir, my name is Tor." The king beheld him fast, and saw he was passingly well visaged and passingly well made of his yeares. "Well," said king Arthur to Aries the cowheard, "fetch all thy sonnes afore me, that I may see them." And so the poore man did, and all were shapen much like the poore man, but Tor was not like none of them all in shape nor in countenance, for he was much more[1] than any of them. "Now," said king Arthur unto Aries the cowheard, "where is that sword that he shal be made knight withal?" "It is here," said Tor. "Take it out of the sheath," said the king, "and require me to make you a knight." Then Tor alight off his mare, and pulled out his sword kneeling, requiring the king that he would make him knight, and that he might be a knight of the table round. "As for a knight, I will make you;" and therewith smote him in the neck with the sword, saying, "Bee yee a good knight, and so I pray to God ye may be; and if ye be of prowesse and of worthynesse ye shal be a knight of the table round. Now, Merlin," said king Arthur, "say whether this Tor shal be a good knight or no." "Yea, sir, he ought to be a good knight, for he is come of as good a man as any is on live, and of kings blood." "How so, sir?" said the king. "I shall tell you," said Merlin; "this poore man Aries the cowheard is not his

[1] *More.*—Greater.

father, he is nothing like[1] to him, for king Pellinore is his father." "I suppose nay," said the cowheard. "Fetch thy wife afore me," said Merlin, "and she shall not say nay." Anon the wife was fet,[2] which was a faire houswife; and there she answered Merlin full womanly, and there she told the king and Merlin, that when she was a maide and went to milke kien, "ther met with me a sterne knight, and halfe by force he had my maidenhead, and at that time he begat my sonne Tor, and he tooke away from me my greyhound that I had that time with me, and said that he would keepe the greyhound for my love." "Ah," said the cowheard, "I wend not this, but I may beleeve it well, for hee had never no tatches[3] of me." "Sir," said Tor to Merlin, "dishonour not my mother." "Sir," said Merlin, "it is more for your worshippe then hurt, for your father is a good man and a king, and he may right well advance you and your mother, for ye were begotten or ever she was wedded." "That is truth," said the wife. "It is the lesse griefe to me," said the cowheard.

CHAP. XLVIII.—How sir Tor was knowen for the sonne of king Pellinore, and Gawayne was made knight.

SO on the morrow king Pellinore came to the court of king Arthur, which had great joy of him, and told him of Tor, how he was his sonne, and how he had made him knight at the request of the cowheard. When king Pellinore beheld Tor, hee pleased him much. So the king made Gawayne knight, but Tor was the first that he made at the feast. "What is the cause," said king Arthur, "that there bene two places void in the sieges?" "Sir," said Merlin, "there

[1] *Like.*—Caxton reads *syb*, i. e. akin, which is, no doubt, the more correct.
[2] *Fet.*—Fetched.
[3] *Tatches.*—Qualities or dispositions.

shall no man sit in those places but they that shall be of most worship. But in the siege perillous there shall no man sit therein but one, and if there be any so hardy to do it, he shall be destroyed, and he that shall sit there shall have no fellow." And therewith Merlin tooke king Pellinore by the hand, and, in the one hand next the two sieges and the siege perillous, he said in open audience, " This is your place, and best ye be worthy to sit therein of any that is here. Thereat had sir Gawayne great envy, and said to Gaheris his brother, " Yonder knight is put unto great worship, the which greveth me sore, for he slew our father king Lot, therefore I will slay him," said sir Gawaine, " with a sword that was sent me, which is passing trenchaint." " Ye shall not doe so," said Gaheris, " at this time; for at this time I am but a squier, and when I am made knight I will be avenged on him; and therefore, brother, it is best ye suffer till another time, that we may have him out of the court, for and wee did so now we should trouble this high feast." " I will well," said sir Gawayne, " as ye will."[1]

CHAP. XLIX.—How, at the feast of the wedding of king Arthur unto Guenever, a white hart came into the hall, and thirty couple of hounds, and how a brachet pinched the hart, the which was taken away.

HEN was the high feast made ready, and the king was wedded at Camelot unto dame Guenever in the church of Saint Stevens with great solemnitie; and as every man was set after his degree, Merlin went unto all the knights of the round table and bad them sit still, and that none should remove, " for

[1] It has been remarked by more than one writer, that the compiler of this romance of the Morte Arthur, whether Malory wrote it or merely translated it, labours always to depreciate the character of Gawaine, and speaks disparagingly of him, quite contrary to the spirit of the older romances, in which he is held forth as a pure example of the perfect knight.

ye shall see a strange and a marvelous adventure." Right
so as they sat, there came running in a white hart into the
hal, and a white brachet[1] next him, and thirtie couple of
black running hounds came after with a great crie, and
the hart went about the table round; as hee went by other
bordes,[2] the white brachet bote[3] him by the buttocke, and
pulled out a peece, wherethrough the hart leapt a great
leape, and overthrew a knight that sat at the bords side; and
therewith the knight arose, and tooke up the brachet, and
so went forth out of the hall, and took his horse and rode
his way with the brachet. Right so anone came in a lady
on a white palfrey, and cryed aloud to king Arthur, " Sir,
suffer me not to have this dispite, for the brachet was mine
that the knight lad away." "I may not doe therewith,"
said the king. With this there came a knight riding all
armed on a great horse, and tooke the lady away with him
by force, and she cried and made great moane. When she
was gone the king was glad, because she made such a noyse.
" Nay," said Merlin, " yee may not leave these adventures
so lightly, for these adventures must be brought againe, or
else it would be disworship to you and to your feast." "I
will," said the king, "that all be done by your advise."
" Then," said Merlin, " let call sir Gawayne, for he must
bring againe the white hart. Also, sir, ye must let cal
sir Tor, for he must bring againe the brachet and the
knight, or else slay him. Also let call king Pellinore, for
he must bring againe the lady and the knight, or else slay
him. And these three knights shall doe marvailous adventures or they come againe." Then were they called all
three, as it is rehearsed afore, and every each of them
tooke his charge, and armed them surely. But sir Gawayne had the first request, and therefore we will beginne
at him.

[1] *A brachet.*—A kind of small scenting hound.
[2] *Bordes.*—Tables.
[3] *Bote.*—Bit. The preterite of to bite.

CHAP. L.—How sir Gawayne rode for to fetch againe the hart, and how two brethren fought each againe other for the hart.

SIR Gawayne rode more then a pace, and Gaheres his brother rode with him, in stead of a squire, for to doe him service. So as they rode, they saw two knights fight on horseback passing sore; so sir Gawayne and his brother rode betweene them, and asked them for what cause they fought so. The one knight answered, and said, " We fight for a simple matter, for we two be two brethren, and borne and begotten of one man and of one woman." "Alas!" said sir Gawayne, " why doe ye so?" " Sir," said the elder, " there came a white hart this way this day, and many hounds chaced him, and a white brachet was alway next him, and we understood it was aventure made for the high feast of king Arthur, and therefore I would have gone after to have won me worship, and here my younger brother said he would go after the hart, for he was a better knight then I, and for this cause we fell at debat, and so we thought to prove which of us both was better knight." " This is a simple cause," said sir Gawayne, "uncouth[1] men ye should debate withall, and not brother with brother; therefore, and if ye wil doe by my counsell, I will have adoe with you, that is ye shall yeeld you unto me, and that ye goe unto king Arthur and yeeld you unto his grace." " Sir knight," said the two brethren, " we are for-foughten,[2] and much blood have we lost through our wilfulnesse, and therefore we would be loath to have adoe with you." " Then doe as I wil have you," said sir Gawayne. " We will agree to fullfill your wil, but by whom shall we say that we be thither sent?" " Yee may say by the knight that followeth the quest of the white hart. Now what is your names?" said sir Gawayne. " Sorlouse of the Forrest," said the elder.

[1] *Uncouth.*—Strange.
For-foughten.—Weary with fighting.

"And my name is," said the yonger, "Brian of the Forrest." And so they departed, and went to the kings court, and sir Gawayne went on his quest; and as sir Gawayne followed the hart by the crie of the hounds, even afore him ther was a great river, and the hart swam over, and as sir Gawaine would have followed after, there stood a knight on the other side and said, " Sir knight, come not over after the hart, but if thou wilt just with me." " I will not faile as for that," said sir Gawayne, " to follow the quest that I am in." And so he made his horse to swim over the water, and anon they gat their speares and ran together full hard, but sir Gawaine smote him off his horse, and then he turned his horse and bad him yeeld him. " Nay," said the knight, " not so, though thou have the better of me on horseback, I pray thee, valiant knight, alight on foot, and match we togither with swords." " What is your name?" said sir Gawayne. "Allardin of the Iles," said the other. Then either dressed their shields and smote together, but sir Gawaine smot him through the helme so hard that it went to the braines, and the knight fel down dead. " Ah," said Gaheris, " that was a mighty stroke of a yong knight."

CHAP. LI.—How the hart was chased into a castle and there slaine, and how sir Gawaine slew a lady.

THEN sir Gawayne and Gaheris rode more then a pace after the white hart, and let slip at the hart three couple of greyhounds, and so they chaced the hart into a castle, and in the chief place of the castle they slew the hart that sir Gawayne and Gaheris folowed after. Right so there came a knight out of a chamber with a sword in his hand, and slew two of the hounds even in the sight of sir Gawaine, and the remnant he chaced them with his sword out of the castle. And when hee came againe, he said, " O my white hart, me repenteth that thou art dead, for my soveraigne lady gave thee to me, and evil have I kept thee, and thy death shall be deare bought and I live." And anone he went into his chamber and armed him, and came out fiersly, and there he met with sir Gawaine. "Why have ye slaine my houndes?" said sir Gawaine; "for they did but their kind, and I had rather ye had worken your anger upon me then upon the dombe beasts." "Thou saist truth," said the knight; "I have avenged me on thy hounds, and so will I be on thee or thou goe." Then sir Gawayne alighted on foote, and dressed his shield and strooke mightily, and clave their shields, and stonyed their helmes, and brak their hawberks, that the blood ranne downe to their feete. At the last sir Gawaine smote the knight so hard that he fel to the earth; and then he cried mercy and yeelded him, and besought him as he was a knight and gentleman to save his life. "Thou shalt die," said sir Gawaine, "for slaying of my hounds." "I will make amends unto my power," said the knight. Sir Gawaine would no mercy have, but unlaced his helm to have striken of his head, right so came his lady out of her chamber and fell over him, and so he smote off her head by misadventure. "Alas," said Gaheris, "that is foule and shamefully done, that shame shall never from you. Also ye should give mercy unto them that aske mercy, for a knight without mercy is without worshippe." Sir Gawaine was so astonied at the death of this faire lady that hee wist not what hee did, and said to the knight, "Arise, I will give thee mercy." "Nay, nay," said the knight, "I take no force of[1] mercy now, for thou hast slain my love and my lady that I loved best of all earthly things." "Me repenteth it sore," said sir Gawaine, "for I thought to have striken at thee. But now thou shalt goe unto king Arthur, and tell him of thine adventures, and how thou art overcome by the knight that went in the quest of the white hart." "I take no force," said the knight, "whether I live or die." But for dread of death hee swore to goe unto king Arthur, and hee made him for to beare one greyhound before him upon his

---

[1] *I take no force of.*—I care nothing for.

horse, and another behind him also. "What is your name," said sir Gawaine, "or we depart?" "My name is," said the knight, "Ablemore of the Marise."[1] So he departed toward Camelot.

CHAP. LII.—How foure knights fought against sir Gawaine and Gaheris, and how they were overcome, and their lives saved at the request of foure damosels.

AND sir Gawaine went into the castle, and made him ready to lye there all night, and would have unarmed him. "What will ye doe?" said Gaheris; "will yee unarme you in this countrey? ye may well thinke that yee have many enemies here about." They had no sooner said that word but there came foure knights well armed, and assayled sir Gawaine hard, and said thus unto him: "Thou new-made knight, thou hast shamed thy knighthood, for a knight without mercy is dishonoured. Thou hast also slaine a faire lady, which is unto thee great shame for evermore, and doubt thou not thou shalt have great neede of mercy or thou depart from us." And therewith one of them smote sir Gawaine such a strooke that he had nigh felled him to the earth, and Gaheris smote him againe sore; and so they were on the one side and on the other that sir Gawaine and Gaheris were in great jeopardie of their lives, and one of them with a bowe, an archer, smote sir Gawaine through the arme, that it grieved him wondrous sore. And as they should have beene both slaine, there came foure ladyes and besought the knights of grace for sir Gawaine; and goodly at the request of the ladyes, they gave sir Gawaine and Gaheris their lives, and made them to yeeld them as prisoners. Then sir Gawaine and Gaheris made great mone. "Alas," said sir Gawaine, "mine arme grieveth me sore. I am like to be maimed;" and so made his complaint piteously. On

[1] *Marise.*—A marsh.

the morrow early came one of the foure ladyes to sir Gawaine, which had hard all his complaints, and said, "Sir knight, what cheare?" "Not good," said he. "It is your owne default," said the lady, "for ye have done a passing foule deede in the slaying of the lady, which will be great villany to you. But bee yee not of king Arthurs kinne?" said the lady. "Yes, truly," said sir Gawaine. "What is your name?" said the lady; "ye must tel it or that ye passe." "My name is Gawaine, king Lots sonne of Orkeney, and my mother in king Arthurs sister." "Ah, then yee are nephew unto king Arthur," said the lady, "and I shall so speake for you that yee shall have conduct to goe to king Arthur for his love." And so shee departed, and told the foure knights how their prisoner was king Arthurs nephew, "and his name is Gawaine, king Lots sonne of Orkeney." Then they gave him the head of the white hart, because it was in his quest.[1] Then anon they delivered sir Gawaine under this promise, that he should bare the dead lady with him in this maner:—her head was hanged about his necke, and the whole body of her lay before him upon the maine of his horse. And in this manner he rode forth towards Camelot. And anon as he was come to the court, Merlin desired of king Arthur that sir Gawayne should be sworne to tell of all his adventures, and so hee was, and shewed how he slew the lady, and how he would give no mercy to the knight, wherethrough the lady was vilanously slaine. Then the king and the queene were greatly displeased with sir Gawaine for the slaying of the lady; and there by the ordinance of the queene was set a quest[1] of ladys on sir Gawaine; and they judged him ever while he lived to be with al ladyes and to fight for their quarrels, and that he should ever be curteous, and never to refuse mercy to him that asketh mercy. Thus was sir Gawaine

---

[1] *Quest* occurs in this chapter in two different senses: first, in that of a search or chase, and secondly, in that of a committee of inquiry, or inquest.

sworne upon the foure evangelists that hee would never be against ladyes ne gentlewomen, but if he fought for a lady and his adversarie for another. And thus endeth the adventure of sir Gawaine, which he did at the marriage of king Arthur.

CHAP. LIII.—How sir Tor rode after the knight with the brachet, and of his adventures by the way.

THEN sir Tor was ready, and hee mounted on horseback, and rode forth his way a good pace after the knight with the brachet. And so as he rode he met with a dwarfe sodainely, which smote his horse on the head with a staffe that he went backward more then his speares length. "In what intent doest thou smite my horse?" said sir Tor. "For thou shalt not passe this way," said the dwarfe, "but that thou shalt first just with yonder knights that abide in yonder pavilions that thou seest." Then was sir Tor ware where two pavilions wer, and great speres stood out, and two shields hung on two trees by the pavilions. "I may not tarry," said sir Tor, "for I am in a quest which I must needs follow." "Thou shalt not passe," said the dwarfe, and therewith he blew his horne. Then there came one armed on horseback, and dressed his shield, and came fast toward sir Tor, and he dressed him against him, and so ranne together that sir Tor bare him from his horse. And anon the knight yeelded him to his mercy; "but sir, I have a fellow in yonder pavilion that wil have adoe with you anon." "He shall bee welcome," said sir Tor. Then was hee ware of another knight comming with great raundon,[1] and each of them dressed to other, that marvaile it was to see, but the knight smote sir Tor a great strooke in the middest of the shield, that his speare all to-shievered, and sir Tor smote him

[1] *Great raundon.*—*Raundon* or *random* meant, originally, force or impetuosity.

through the shield bylow, that it went through the side of the knight, but the strooke slew him not. And therewith sir Tor alight, and smote him upon the helme a great stroke, and therewith the knight yeelded him, and besought him of mercy. " I wil wel," said sir Tor, " but thou and thy fellow must goe unto king Arthur, and yeeld you prisoners to him." " By whom shall wee say that wee are thither sent?" " Yee shal say, 'by the knight that went in quest of the knight that went with the brachet.' Now, what be your two names?" said sir Tor. " My name is," said the one, " sir Felot of Langdock."[1] " And my name is," said the other, " sir Petipace of Winchelsee." " Now, goe ye forth," said sir Tor ; " God speede you and mee." Then came the dwarfe and said to sir Tor, " I pray you to give me a gift." " I wil wel," said sir Tor. " I aske no more," said the dwarfe, " but that yee will suffer mee to doe you service, for I will serve no more recreaunt knights." " Then take a horse anon," said sir Tor, " and come on and ride with me." " I wot ye ride after the knight with the white brachet ; I shall bring you there hee is," said the dwarfe. And so they rode through the forrest, and at the last they were ware of two pavilions by a priorie, with two shields, and the one shield was renewed[2] with white, and the other shield was red.

CHAP. LIV.—How sir Tor found the brachet with a lady, and how a knight assailed him for the said brachet.

HEREWITH sir Tor alighted, and tooke[3] the dwarfe his speare, and so came to the white pavilion and saw three damosels lye therein on a pallet sleeping. And then hee went unto that other pavilion, and there he found a faire lady sleeping.

[1] *Langdock.—Laugduk*, Caxton. Perhaps a corruption of Languedoc.
[2] *Renewed.*—Caxton reads *anewed.*
[3] *Tooke.*—i. e. Gave.

And there was the white brachet, that bayed[1] at her fast. And therewith anon the lady awoke, and went out of the pavilion, and all her damosels. But anon as sir Tor espied the white brachet, hee tooke her by force, and tooke her to the dwarfe. "What will ye doe," said the lady, "will yee take away my brachet from me?" "Yea," said sir Tor, "this brachet have I sought from king Arthurs court to this place." "Well," said the lady, "sir knight, ye shall not goe farre with her but that yee shall be met withall or it be long, and also evill handled." "I shall abide it what adventure soever commeth by the grace of God." And so mounted upon his horse, and passed forth on his way toward Camelot, but it was so neere night that he might not passe but little farther. "Know ye any lodging?" said sir Tor. "I know none," said the dwarfe; "but here beside is an hermitage, and there yee must take such lodging as ye find." And within a while they came to the hermitage, and tooke lodging. And there was grasse, otes, and bread for their horses; soone it was sped, and full hard was their supper; but there they rested them all the night til on the morrow, and heard a masse devoutly, and tooke their leave of the hermite, and sir Tor praied the hermite to pray for him. He said he would, and betooke[2] him to God, and so mounted on horsebacke and rode toward Camelot a long while. With that they heard a knight call lowd that came after them, and said, "Knight, abide, and yeeld my brachet that thou tookest from my lady." Sir Tor returned againe, and beheld him, and saw hee was a seemely knight, and well horsed and armed at all points. Then sir Tor dressed his shield, and tooke his speare in his hand, and the other came fiersly upon him, and smote each other that both horse and men fell to the earth. Anon they lightly arose, and drew their swords as egerly as two lyons, and put their shields afore them, and smote through their shields

---

[1] *Bayed.*—Barked. [2] *Betooke.*—Committed.

KING ARTHUR. 107

that the canteles[1] fel off on both parties, and also they brake their helmes[2] that the hot blood ranne out, and the thick mailes of their halbeards[3] they carved and rove in sunder, that the hot blood ranne downe to the ground, and they had both many great wounds, and were passing weary. But sir Tor espied that the other knight fainted,[4] and then he pursued fast upon him, and doubled his strookes, and made him fall to the ground on the on side. Then sir Tor bad him yeeld him. "That will I not," said Abellius, "while my life lasteth and the soule within my body, unlesse that thou wilt give mee the brachet." "That will I not doe," said sir Tor, "for it was my request[5] to bring againe the brachet and thee, or else slay thee."

CHAP. LV.—How sir Tor overcame the knight, and how he lost his head at the request of a lady.

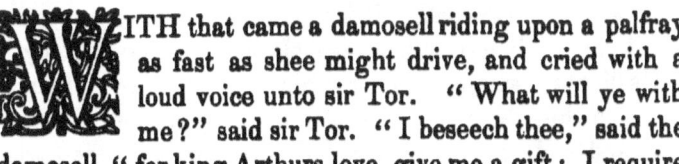ITH that came a damosell riding upon a palfray as fast as shee might drive, and cried with a loud voice unto sir Tor. "What will ye with me?" said sir Tor. "I beseech thee," said the damosell, "for king Arthurs love, give me a gift; I require thee, gentle knight, as thou art a gentleman." "Now," said sir Tor, "aske a gift, and I wil give it you." "Gramarcie!" said the damosell, "I aske the head of this false knight Abellius, for he is the most outragious knight that liveth and the greatest murderer." "I am right sorry and loth," sayd sir Tor, "of that gift which I have graunted you; let him make you amends in that which he hath trespassed against you." "He can not make amends," said

---

[1] *Canteles.*—Portions, fragments.
[2] *Helmes.*—Caxton's text has *tamyd their helmes*. To *tame*, meant to make a cut into.
[3] *Halbeards.*—*Hawberks*, Caxton. The printers of the edit. of 1634 perhaps mistook the meaning of the word.
[4] *Fainted*—i. e. was becoming weak.
[5] *Request.*—*Quest*, Caxton, and so all through the next chapter.

the damosell, "for hee hath slaine mine owne brother, which was a better knight then ever hee was, and he had no mercy upon him, in so much that I kneeled halfe an houre afore him in the myre for to save my brothers life, which had done him no dammage, but fought with him by adventure of armes, as knights adventurous doe; and for all that I could doe or say, he smote off my brothers head, wherefore I require thee as thou art a true knight to give me my gift, or else I shall shame thee in all the court of king Arthur, for he is the falsest knight living, and a great destroyer of good knights." Then when Abelleus heard this, he was sore aferd, and yeelded him and asked mercy. "I may not now," said sir Tor, "but if I should be found false of my promise, for when I would have taken you to mercy, ye would none aske, but if ye had the brachet again that was my request." And therewith he tooke off his helme, and he arose and fled, and sir Tor after him and smote off his head quite. "Now, sir," said the damosell, "it is neere night, I pray you come and lodge with me here at my place,[1] it is here fast by." "I will wel," said sir Tor; for his horse and hee had fared evil sith they departed from Camelot, and so he rode with her, and had passing good cheere with her, and shee had a passing faire old knight to her husband which made him passing good cheere, and well eased sir Tor and his horse. And on the morrow he heard masse, and brake his fast, and tooke his leave of the knight and of the lady, which besought him to tell them his name. "Truly," said he, "my name is sir Tor, that late was made knight, and this was the first request of armes that ever I did, to bring againe that this knight Abelleus tooke away from king Arthurs court. "Oh, knight," said the lady and her husband, "if ye come heere in our marches, come and see our poore lodging, and it shal be alwaies at your commandement." So sir Tor departed, and came to Camelot on the third day by noone; and the king and the queene and all the court was passing glad of

[1] *Place.*—A mansion, a dwelling-house.

his comming, and made great joy that he was come againe, for he went from the court with little succour, but that his father king Pellinore gave him an old courser, and king Arthur gave him armour and a sword, and else had hee none other succour, but rode so forth himselfe alone. And then the king and the queene, by Merlins advise, made him to sweare to tell of his adventures, and so he told and made proofes of his deedes as it is afore rehearsed, wherefore the king and the queene made great joy. "Nay," said Merlin, "these be but japes¹ to that he shal do; hee shal prove a noble knight of prowesse, as good as any is living, and gentle and curteous, and full of good parts, and passing true of his promise, and never shall doe outrage." Where, through Merlins words, king Arthur gave him an earledome of lands that fell unto him. And heere endeth the quest of sir Tor, king Pellinors sonne.

CHAP. LVI.—How king Pellinore rode after the lady and the knight that led her away, and how a lady desired helpe of him, and how hee fought with two knights for that lady, of whom he slew the one at the first strooke.

HEN king Pellinore armed him, and mounted upon his horse, and rode more then a pace after the lady that the knight led away. And so as hee rode in a forrest he saw in a valey a damosell sit by a well side, and a wounded knight betweene her armes, and sir Pellinore saluted her. And when shee was ware of him, shee cried over loud: "Helpe me, knight, for Christs sake." King Pellinore would not tarry, hee was so eger in his quest, and ever shee cried more then an hundred times after helpe. And when shee saw he would not abide, shee praied unto God for to send him as much neede of helpe as shee had, and that he might know it or he died. And as the booke telleth, the knight died that lay there

¹ *Japes.*—Jests.

wounded, wherefore the lady for pure sorrow slew her selfe with her loves sword. So as king Pellinore rode in that valey, hee met with a poore labouring man. " Sawest thou not," said king Pellinore, " a knight riding and leading away a lady?" " Yes," said the poore man, " I saw that knight and the lady that made great mone, and yonder beeneath in a valey there shall ye see two pavilions, and one of the knights of the pavilions chalenged that lady of that knight, and said shee was his neere cosen, wherefore he should lead her no farther; and so they waged battaile in that quarell, for the one said he would have her by force, and the other said he would have the rule of her because he was her kinsman, and would leade her to her friends. For this quarell I left them fighting, and if yee ride a pace ye shall find them yet fighting, and the lady is in keeping with the two squiers in the pavilions." " God thanke thee," said king Pellinore. Then he rode a gallop[1] till that he had a sight of the two pavilions, and the two knights fighting. Anone rode he to the two pavilions, and saw the lady that was his quest, and said to her: " Faire lady, yee must come with me unto king Arthurs court." " Sir knight," said the two squiers that were with her, " yonder be two knights that fight for this lady, goe thither and depart them, and be agreed with them, and then may ye have her at your owne pleasure." " Yee say well," said king Pellinore. And anone he rode betweene them, and parted them in sonder, and asked the cause why they fought. " Sir knight," said the one, " I shall tell you. This lady is my nigh kinswoman, mine aunts daughter, and when I heard her complaine that she was with him maugre her head, I waged battaile to fight with him." " Sir knight," said the other, whose name was Hontzlake of Wentland,[2] "this lady I gate by my prowesse of armes this day of king

---

[1] *A gallop.*—Caxton reads *a wallop.*
[2] *Wentland.*—Gwentland, the district in Monmouthshire of which Caer-Went (the Roman Venta Silurum) was the chief town.

Arthurs court." "That is truely¹ said," quoth king Pellinore, "for ye came in there all sodainely as we were at the high feast, and tooke away this lady or any man might make him ready; and therefore it was my request for to bring her againe and you also, or else the one of us to abide in field. Therefore the lady shall goe with me to king Arthur, or I shall die for it, for I have promised it unto him, and therefore fight no more for her, for none of you both shall have no part of her at this time; and if yee list to fight for her, fight with me, and I will defend her." "Well," said the knight, "make you ready, and wee shall assaile you with all our power." And as king Pellinore would have put his horse from them and alight on foote, sir Hontzlake runne his horse through with the sword, and said, "Now art thou on foote as wel as we." And when king Pellinore saw that his horse was so slaine, he was wroth, and then fiersly and lightly leapt from his horse, and in great hast drew out his sword, and put his shield afore him, and said, "Knight, keepe well thy head, for thou shalt have a buffet for the slaying of my horse." So king Pellinore gave him such a strooke upon the helme that he clove downe the head to the chin, and therewith he fell to the earth dead.

CHAP. LVII.—How king Pellinore gate the lady, and brought her to Camelot unto the court of king Arthur.

AND then he turned him to that other knight, that was sore wounded. But when hee had seene the buffet that the other had, hee would not fight, but kneeled downe and said, "Take my cosin the lady with you at your request, and I require you, as ye be a true knight, put her to no shame ne vilany."

¹ *Truely.*—Caxton has *untruly*, which is no doubt correct, for the knight did not obtain her by his prowess of arms at the court of king Arthur.

"What," said king Pellinore, "will ye not fight for her?" "No, sir," said the knight, " I wil not fight with a knight of prowes as ye be." "Wel," said king Pellinore, " ye say well, I promise you she shall have no vilany by me, as I am a true knight. But now I lack a horse," said king Pellinore; "I will have Hontzlakes horse." "Yee shall not neede," said the knight, "for I shall give you such a horse as shall please you, so that ye will lodge with me, for it is neere night." "I will well," said king Pellinore, "abide with you al night." And there he had with him right good cheere, and fared of the best, with passing good wine, and had merry rest that night. And on the morrow he heard a masse, and after dined,[1] and then was brought him a faire bay courser and king Pellinores saddle set upon him. "Now what shall I call you?" said the knight, "in as much as yee have my cosin at your desire of your quest." "Sir, I shall tell you, my name is Pellinore, king of the iles, and knight of the round table." "Now I am glad," said the knight, "that such a noble man as ye be shal have the rule of my cosin." "What is now your name?" said king Pellinore; "I pray you tell me." "Sir," said he, "my name is sir Meliot of Logurs, and this lady my cosin hight[2] Nimue, and the knight that is in that other pavilion is my sworne brother, a passing good knight, and his name is Brian of the Iles, and he is full loth to doe any wrong, and full loth to fight with any man or knight, but if he be sore sought upon, so that for shame he may not leave." "It is marvaile," said king Pellinore, "that he will not have adoe with me." "Sir, he will not have ado with no man but if it be at his request." "Bring him one of these dayes to the court of king Arthur," said king Pellinore. "Sir, we will come together." "Yee shal be greatly welcome there," said king Pellinore, "and also greatly alowed for

---

[1] *Dined.*—It has been before remarked that dinner was formerly a very early meal in the day. See p. 24.
[2] *Hight.*—Is called.

your coming." And so hee departed with the lady, and brought her to Camelot. So as they rode in a valey that was full of stones, the ladies horse stumbled and threw her down, wherwith her arme was sore brused, and neere she sowned for paine and anguish. "Alas! sir," said the lady, "mine arme is out of joynt, wherethrough I must needs rest me." "Ye shall doe well," said king Pellinore; and so he alighted under a faire tree, where as was faire grasse, and he put his horse thereto, and so laid him under the tree and slept till it was nigh night, and when he awoke hee would have riden. "Sir," said the lady, "it is so darke that ye may as well ride backward as forward." So they abode still, and made there their lodging. Then king Pellinore put off his armour, and then a litte before midnight they heard the troting of an horse. "Be ye still," said king Pellinore, "for we shall heare of some adventure."

CHAP. LVIII.—How king Pellinore heard two knights, as he lay by night in a valey, and of other adventures.

AND therewith he armed him. So right even afore him there met two knights, the one came from Camelot and the other from the north, and either saluted other. "What tidings at Camelot?" said the one. "By my head," said the other, "there have I beene, and espied the court of king Arthur, and there is such a fellowship that they may never be brok, and wel nigh al the world holdeth with king Arthur, for there is the floure of chivalry. Now for this cause I am riding into the north, to tel our chieftaines of the fellowship which is withholden with king Arthur." "As for that," said the other knight, "I have brought a remedy with me, that is the greatest poison that ever ye hard speake of, and to Camelot will I with it, for we have a friend right nigh king Arthur, and well cherished, that shall poyson king

VOL. I. I

Arthur; so he hath promised our chiefetaines, and hath received great gifts for to do it." "Beware," said the other knight, "of Merlin, for he knoweth all things by the divels craft." "Therefore will I not let[1] it," said the knight. And so they departed in sunder. Anone after king Pellinore made him ready, and his lady, and rode toward Camelot. And as they came by the well where as the wounded knight was and the lady, there he found the knight and the lady eaten with lions or wilde beasts all save the head, wherefore he made great mone and wept passing sore, and said, "Alas! her life I might have saved, but I was so fierce in my quest, therefore I would not abide." "Wherefore make ye such dole?" said the lady. "I wot not," said king Pellinore, "but my heart mourneth sore for the death of this lady, for shee was a passing faire lady and a young." "Now shall ye doe by mine advise," said the lady; "take this knight and let him be buried in an hermitage, and then take the ladyes head and beare it with you unto king Arthurs court." So king Pellinore tooke this dead knight on his shoulders, and had him to the hermitage, and charged the hermit with his corps, and that service should be done for the soule, "and take his harneis for your labour and paine." "It shall be done," said the hermit, "as I wil answere to God."

CHAP. LIX.—How king Pellinore, when he was come to Camelot, was sworne upon a booke to tell truth of his quest.

AND therewith they departed, and came whereas the head of the lady lay, with faire yellow haire, which grieved king Pellinore passing sore when he looked upon it, for much he cast his heart on the visage. And so by noone they came to Camelot, and king Arthur and the queene were passing glad of his comming to the court. And there he was made to swere

---

[1] *Let.*—Leave; abandon.

upon the four evangelists for to tel al the truth of his quest, from the begining unto the ending. "Ah, sir Pellinore," said the queene, "ye were greatly to blame that yee saved not the ladyes life." "Madam," said king Pellinore, "ye were greatly to blame and if ye would not save your owne life, and ye might; but, saving your honour, I was so furious in my quest that I would not abide, and that repenteth me, and shall doe all the dayes of my life." "Truely," said Merlin, "ye ought sore to repent it, for the lady was your owne daughter, begotten on the Lady of the Rule, and that knight that was dead was her love, and should have wedded her, and hee was a right good knight of a young man, and would have proved a good man, and to this court was hee comming, and his name was sir Miles of the Launds, and a knight came behind him and slew him with a speare, and his name is Loraine le Savage, a false knight and a very coward, and she for great sorrow slew her selfe with his sword, and her name was Eleine; and because ye would not abide and helpe her, ye shal se your best frind faile you when ye be in the greatest distresse that ever ye wer or shal be in, and that penance God hath ordeined you for that deede, that he that ye shall most trust to of any man alive, he shall leave you there as ye shal be slaine." "Me forethinketh," said king Pellinore. "that this shall betide mee, but God may well foredoe all destinies."

Thus when the quest was don of the white hart that sir Gawaine followed, and the quest of the brachet followed of sir Tor, son unto king Pellinore, and the quest of the lady that the knight tooke away, the which king Pellinore at that time followed, then king Arthur stablished all his knights, and gave them lands that were not rich of land, and charged them never to do outrage nor murder, and alway to flee treason; also by no meanes to be cruel, but to give mercy unto him that asked mercy, upon paine of forfeiture of their worship and lordship of king Arthur for evermore; and alway to doe ladies, damosels, and gentlewomen succour upon paine of death. Also that no man take no battailes in a wrong quarell for no law, nor for worldly goods. Unto this were all the knights sworne of the round table, both old and young. And every yeare they were sworne at the high feast of Penticost.

CHAP. LX.—How Merlin was assotted and doted on one of the ladies of the lake, and he was shut in a roche under a stone by a wood side, and there died.

THEN after these quests of sir Gawaine, of sir Tor, and of king Pellinore, Merlin fel in a dotage on the damosel that king Pellinore brought to the court with him, and she was one of the damosels of the lake which hight Nimue. But Merlin would let her have no rest, but alwayes he would be with her in every place. And ever she made Merlin good cheere, till she had learned of him all manner thing that shee desired; and hee was so sore assotted upon her that he might not be from her. So upon a time he told unto king Arthur that he should not endure long, and that for al his crafts he should be put in the earth quicke;[1] and so he told the king many things that should befall, but alwayes he warned king Arthur to keepe well his sword Excalibur and the scabbard, for he told him how the sword and the scabbard should be stolen by a woman from him that hee most trusted. Also he told king Arthur that he should misse him, "yet had yee rather then all your lands to have me againe." "Ah," said the king, "sith ye know of your adventure, purvey for it, and put away by your crafts that misadventure." "Nay," said Merlin, "it will not be." And then he departed from king Arthur. And within a while the damosell of the lake departed, and Merlin went evermore with her wheresoever she went. And oftentimes Merlin would have had her

[1] *Quicke.*—i. e. alive.

privily away by his subtile crafts, and then she made him to sweare that he should never do none enchauntment upon her if he would have his will, and so he swore. So she and Merlin went over the sea unto the land of Benwicke, where as king Ban was king, that had great warre against king Claudas, and there Merlin spake with king Bans wife, a faire lady and a good, and her name was Elein; and there he saw young Launcelot. There the queene made great sorrow for the mortall warre that king Claudas made on her lord and on her lands. "Take no heavinesse," said Merlin, "for this child within this twenty yeare shall revenge you on king Claudas, that all Christendome shall speake of it, and this same child shall be the most man of worship of this world, and I know well that his first name was Galahad, and sith ye have confirmed him Lancelot." "That is truth," said the queene, "his first name was Galahad. O Merlin," said the queene, "shall I live to see my sonne such a man of prowesse?" "Yea, lady, on my perill; ye shall see it, and live after many winters."[1] And then soone after the lady and Merlin departed; and by the way as they went Merlin shewed her many wonders, and came into Cornewaile. And alwaies Merlin lay about the lady for to have her maidenhead, and she was ever passing wery of him, and faine would have beene delivered of him, for she was afraid of him, because he was a divels sonne, and she could not put him away by no meanes.

And so upon a time it hapned that Merlin shewed to her in a roche where as was a great wonder, and wrought by enchauntment, which went under a stone.[2] So by her subtile

---

[1] *Winters.*—Our Anglo-Saxon forefathers reckoned the years by winters, not by summers.

[2] *Under a stone.*—The manner of Merlin's death is variously related. In the French romance it is a bush of hawthorn in which he was enclosed by the fairy Viviana, (the lady of the lake,) to whom he had communicated the charm. She tried it upon her lover to ascertain if what he told her were true, and was grieved when she found that he could not be extracted from his thorny coverture.

craft and working, she made Merlin to goe under that stone to let her wit[1] of the mervailes there, but she wrought so there for him, that he came never out, for all the craft that he could doe. And so she departed, and left Merlin.

CHAP. LXI.—How five kings came into this land to warre against king Arthur, and what counsaile king Arthur had against them.

AND then king Arthur rode to Camelot, and there he made a solemne feast with mirth and joy. So anon after he returned unto Cardoyle,[2] and there came to king Arthur new tidings that the king of Denmarke, and the king of Ireland his brother, and the king of the Vale, and the king of Soleyse, and the king of the isle of Longtainse,[3] all these five kings with a great hoast were entered into king Arthurs land, and burnt and slew all that they found afore them, both cities and castles, that it was great pittie to see. "Alas," said king Arthur, "yet had I never rest one moneth sith I was crowned king of this land. Now shall I never rest till I meete with those kings in a faire field, and to that I make mine avow; for my true liege people shall not be destroyed in my default, goe with me who will, and abide who will." Then the king let write unto king Pellinore, and praied him in all haste to make him ready with such people as he might lightliest reere,[4] and hie him after in al haste. Al the barons were priviely wroth that the king would depart so sodainely; but the king by no meanes would abide, but made writings unto them that were not there, and bad them hie after him such as were

[1] *Wit.*—For *wete*, know.
[2] *Cardoyle.*—Carlisle, which was so called by the Normans, apparently through a difficulty of pronunciation, as they called Lincoln, Nicole.
[3] *Longtainse.*—One might imagine this name to be made from *l'isle loigntaine*, the distant or remote island.
[4] *Reere.*—Raise.

not at that time in the court. Then the king came to queene Guenever, and said, "Lady, make you ready, for ye shall goe with me, for I may not long misse you, ye shall cause me to be the more hardier what adventure soever befall me. I will not wit[1] my lady to be in no jeopardie." "Sir," said she, I am at your command, and shall be ready what time soever ye be ready." So on the morrow the king and the queene departed, with such fellowship as they had, and came into the north into a forrest beside Humber, and there lodged them. When the tidings came to the five kings above said, that king Arthur was beside Humber in a forest, ther was a knight, brother unto one of the five kings, that gave them this counsaile: "Ye know wel that king Arthur hath with him the floure of chivalrie of the world, as it is proved by the great battaile that he did with the eleven kings, and therefore hie unto him night and day, till that we be nigh him, for the longer he tarieth the bigger he is, and we ever the weaker, and he is so couragious of himselfe that he is come to the field with little people, and therefore let us set upon him or it be day, and wee shall so slay of his knights that there shall not one escape."

CHAP. LXII.—How king Arthur overthrew and slew the five kings, and made the remnant to flee.

UNTO this counsaile the five kings assented, and so they passed forth with their hoast through Northwales, and came upon king Arthur by night, and set upon his hoast, he and his knights being in their pavilions, and king Arthur was unarmed, and had laid him to rest with the queene. "Sirs," said sir Kay, "it is not good that we be unarmed." "We shall have no neede," said sir Gawaine and sir Griflet, that lay

---

[1] *Wit*—Know.

in a little pavilion by the king. With that they hard a great noise, and many cried treason. "Alas!" said king Arthur, "we are al betraied. Unto armes, fellowes!" cried he then. So they were anon armed at all points. Then came there a wounded knight to king Arthur, and said to him, "Sir, save your selfe and my lady the queene, for our hoast is destroyed, and much people of ours slaine." So anon the king and the queene and three knights tooke their horses and rode toward Humber to passe over it, and the water was so rough that they were afeard to passe over. "Now may ye choose," said king Arthur, "whether ye will abide and take the adventure upon this side, for and ye be taken they will slay you." "It were me rather," said the queene, "to die in the water then for to fall into your enemies hands, and there to be slaine." And as they stood so talking, sir Kay saw the five kings comming on horseback by themselves alone, with their speares in their hand toward them. "Lo," said sir Kay, "yonder be the five kings, let us goe to them and match them." "That were folly," said sir Gawaine, "for we are but foure and they be five." "That is truth," said sir Griflet. "No force," said sir Kay, "I will undertake two of them, and then may ye three undertake the other three." And therewith sir Kay let his horse runne as fast as he might, and strooke one of them through the shield and the body of a fadom deepe, that the king fel to the earth starke dead. That saw sir Gawaine, and ran unto another king so hard, that he smote him through the body. And therewith king Arthur ran to another, and smote him through the body with a speare that he fell downe to the earth dead. Then sir Griflet ran to the fourth king, and gave him such a fall that he brake his necke. Anon sir Kay ran unto the fift king, and smote him so hard upon the helme that the strooke clave the helme and the head to the shoulders. "That was well stricken," said king Arthur, "and worshipfully haste thou holden thy promise, therefore I shall honour thee as long as I live." And therwith they set the queene in a barge in Humber, but alwayes queene Guenever praised sir Kay for his noble deedes, and said, "What lady that ye love, and she love you not againe, she were greatly to blame; and among ladies," said the queene, "I shall beare your noble fame, for ye spake a great word, and fulfilled it worshipfully." And therewith the queene departed. Then the king and the three knights rode into the forrest, for there they supposed to heare of them that were escaped, and there king Arthur found the most part of his people, and told them all how the five kings were dead, "and therefore let we hold us together till it be day, and when their hoast espie that their chiefetaines bee slaine they will make such sorrow that they shall not be able to helpe themselves." Right so as the king had said, so it was; for when they found the five kings dead, they made such sorrow that they fell downe from their horses. Therewith came king Arthur with a few people, and slew on the right hand and on the left, that well nigh there escaped no man, but all were slaine, to the number of thirtie thousand men. And when the battaile was all ended, king Arthur kneeled downe and thanked God full meekly. And then he sent for the queene, and she came anon, and made great joy for the victorie of that dangerous battaile.

CHAP. LXIII.—How the battaile was finished or that king Pellinore came, and how king Arthur founded an abbey where the battaile was.

THEREWITHALL came one to king Arthur, and told him that king Pellinore was within three mile with a great hoast, and said, "Goe unto him, and let him have knowledge how wee have sped." So within a while king Pellinore came with a great hoast, and saluted the people and the king. And there was great joy made on every side. Then king Arthur let search how much people of his party there was slaine. And there were found not past a two hundred men slaine, and eight knights of the round table in their pavilions. Then the king let reare and built in the same place there as the battaile was done a faire abbey, and endowed it with great livelihood, and let call it the abbey of Le Beaue Adventure. But when some of them came into their countries, there as the five kings were kings, and told them how they were slaine, there was made great sorrow. And when all king Arthurs enemies (as the king of Northwales and the king of the North) wist of the battaile, they were passing heavie. And so the king returned to Camelot in haste; and, when he was come to Camelot, he called king Pellinore unto him, and said : " Yee understand wel that we have lost eight good knights of the table round, and by your advise wee will choose eight againe of the best that we may find in this court." " Sir," said king Pellinore, " I shall counsaile you after my conceite the best. There are in your court right noble knights both old and young, and therefore by mine advise ye shal choose the one halfe of old, and the other halfe of young." " Which be the old?" said king Arthur. " Sir," said king Pellinore, " me seemeth that king Urience, that hath wedded your sister Morgan le Fay, and the king of the lake, and sir Hervise de Revel, a noble knight, and sir Galagars the fourth." " This is well devised," said king Arthur, " and right so shall it be. Now which are the foure young knights ?" said king Arthur. " Sir," said king Pellinore, " the first is sir Gawayne your nephew, that is as good a knight of his time as any in this land ; and the second as me seemeth is sir Griflet[1] le Fize de Deue, that is a good knight and full desirous in armes, and who may see him live he shal prove a good knight. And the third, as me seemeth, is well worthy sir Kay the seneshall, for many times he hath done full worshipfully, and now at your last battaile he did full

---

[1] *Sir Griflet.*—Caxton reads, *syre Gryflet le fyse the dene.*

honourably for to undertake to slay two kings." "By my head," said king Arthur, "he is best worthie to bee a knight of the round table of any that ye have rehearsed, and he had done no more prowesse all the dayes of my life."

CHAP. LXIV.—How sir Tor was made knight of the round table, and how Bagdemagus was displeased.

THEN said king Pellinore, "Now shal I put to you two knights, and ye shal choose which is most worthy, that is sir Bagdemagus[1] and sir Tor my sonne; but because sir Tor is my son, I may not praise him, but else and he were not my sonne, I durst say that of his age there is not in this land a better knight then he is, nor of better conditions, and loth to doe any wrong, and loth to take any wrong." "By my head," said king Arthur, "he is a passing good knight as any yee spake of this day, and that know I full well, for I have seene him proved, and he saith little, but he doth much more; for I know none in all this court and he were as well borne on his mothers side as he is on your side, that is like him of prowesse and of might, and therefore I will have him at this time, and leave sir Bagdemagus till another time." And when they were so chosen by the assent of al the barons, so were there found in their sieges every knights name as afore is rehearsed. And so were they set in their sieges, whereof sir Bagdemagus was wonderous wroth that sir Tor was so advanced afore him; and therefore sodainly he departed from the court of king Arthur, and tooke his squire with him, and rode long in a forrest, till they came to a crosse, and there he alighted and said his praiers devoutly. The meane while his squire found

[1] *Bagdemagus.*—This personage, called Baldemagus in the English metrical romance of Merlin, was the nephew of Urien.

written upon the crosse that Bagdemagus should never returne againe to the court till hee had wonne a knights body of the round table, body for body. "Lo, sir," said his squire, "heere I find written of you, therefore I bid you returne againe to the court." "That shall I never," said Bagdemagus, "til men speake of me great worship, and that I be worthie to bee a knight of the round table." And so he rode foorth, and by the way he found a branch of an holy hearbe, that was the signe of the sancgreall; and no knight found such tokens but he were a good liver. So as sir Bagdemagus rode to se many adventures, it happened him to come to the roche there as the lady of the lake had put Merlin under a stone, and there hee heard him make great mone, wherefore sir Bagdemagus would have holpen him, and went to the great stone, and it was so heavy that an hundred men might not lift it up. When Merlin wist that he was there, he bad him leave his labour, for all was in vaine, and he might never be holpen but by her that put him there. And so sir Bagdemagus departed, and did many adventures, and proved after a full good knight of prowesse, and came againe to the court of king Arthur, and was made knight of the round table. And so on the morrow there fell new tidings and other adventures.

CHAP. LXV.—How king Arthur, king Urience, and sir Accolon of Gaule, chased an hart, and of their marvailous adventures.

HEN it befell that king Arthur and many of his knights rode on hunting into a great forrest, and it happened king Arthur, king Urience, and sir Accolon of Gaule followed a great hart, for they three were well horsed, and they chased so fast that within a while they three were ten mile from their fellowship, and at the last they chaced so sore that they slew their horses under them. Then wer they al three on foot, and ever they saw the hart afore them passing weary and

embushed. "What will we doe?" said king Arthur, "we are hard bested." "Let us goe on foote," said king Urience, "till we may meete with some lodging." Then were they ware of the hart that lay on a great water-banck, and a brachet biting upon his throate, and many other hounds came after. Then king Arthur blew the price[1] and dight the hart there. Then king Arthur looked about him, and saw afore him in a great water a little ship al apparelled with silke downe to the water, and the ship came straight unto them, and landed[2] on the sands. Then king Arthur went to the banck and looked in, and saw none earthly creature therein. "Sirs," said the king, "come thence, and let us see what is in this ship." So they went in all three, and found it richly behanged with cloath of silk, and, by that time it was darke night, there suddainly were about them an hundred torches set on all the sides of the shippe bords, and gave a great light. And therewith came out twelve faire damosels, and saluted king Arthur on their knees, and called him by his name, and said he was welcome, and such cheere as they had he should have of the best. And the king thanked them faire. Therewith they led the king and his two fellowes into a faire chamber, and there was a cloth laid richly beseene of all that belonged to a table, and there they were served of all wines and meates that they could thinke of, that the king had great marvaile, for he fared never better in his life for one supper. And so when they had supped at their leasure, king Arthur was led into a chamber, a richer beseene chamber saw he never none, and so was king Urience served, and led into another chamber, and sir Accolon was led into the third chamber, passing rich and well beseene. And so were they laid in their beds right easily, and anon they fell on sleepe, and slept mervailously sore[3] all that night. And on the

[1] *Blew the price.*—The *prise* was the note blown on the death of the deer.
[2] *Landed.*—i. e. came to land.   [3] *Sore.*—Hard; soundly.

morrow king Urience was in Camelot abed in his wives armes, Morgan le Fay. And when he awok he had great mervaile how he came there, for on the even afore hee was about a two dayes journey from Camelot. And also when king Arthur awoke, he found himselfe in a darke prison, hearing about him many complaints of wofull knights.

CHAP. LXVI.—How king Arthur tooke upon him to fight for to be delivered out of prison, and also to deliver twentie knights that wer in prison.

THEN said king Arthur, "What are ye that so complaine?" "We are here twentie good knights prisoners," said they, "and some of us have lien here seaven yeere, and some more and som lesse." "For what cause?" said king Arthur. "We shall tell you," said the knights. "The lord of this castle is named sir Damas, and he is the falsest knight that liveth, and full of treason, and a very coward as any liveth, and hee hath a yonger brother, a good knight of prowesse, his name is sir Ontzlake, and this traitor Damas, the elder brother, wil give him no part of his livelihood but that sir Ontzlake keepeth through his prowesse, and so he keepeth from him a full faire mannor and a rich, and therin sir Ontzlake dwelleth worshipfully, and is well beloved of the people and comminalty. And this sir Damas our master is as evil beloved, for he is without mercy and he is a very coward, and great war hath bene betwen them both, but sir Ontzlake hath ever the better, and ever he proffereth sir Damas to fight for the livelihood,[1] body for body, but he will doe nothing; or else to find a knight to fight for him. Unto that sir Damas hath granted to find a knight, but he is so evill and hated that there is no knight that wil fight for him. And when sir Damas saw this,

---

[1] *For the livelihood* —i. e. for the property which sir Damas withheld from him.

that there was no knight that would fight for him, he hath dayly layen in a waite with many knights with him to take all the knights in this countrey to see and espie their adventures; he hath taken them by force and brought them into his prison, and so hee tooke us severally as wee rode on our adventures, and many good knights have died in this prison for hunger, to the number of eighteene knights, and if any of us al that is here or hath beene would have foughten with his brother Ontzlake, he would have delivered us; but because this sir Damas is so false and so full of treason, we would never fight for him to die for it. And we be so leane for hunger, that unnethes we may stand on our feete." "God deliver you for His mercy!". said king Arthur. Anon therewith came a damosell unto king Arthur, and asked him, "What cheere?" "I can not tel," said he. "Sir," quoth she, "and ye will fight for my lord, ye shall be delivered out of prison, or else ye shall never escape with your life." "Now," said king Arthur, "that is hard; yet had I rather to fight with a knight then to die in prison, if I may be delivered with this and all these prisoners," said king Arthur, "I will doe the battaile." "Yes," said the damosell. "I am ready," said king Arthur, "if I had a horse and armor." "Yee shal lacke none," said the damosell. "Me seemeth, damosell, I should have seene you in the court of king Arthur." "Nay," said the damosell, "I came never there, I am the lords daughter of this castle." Yet was shee false, for she was one of the damosels of Morgan le Fay. Anon shee went unto sir Damas, and told him how hee would doe battaile for him. And so he sent for king Arthur, and, when hee came, hee was well coloured and well made of his limbes, and that all the knights that saw him said it were pittie that such a knight should die in prison. So sir Damas and he were agreed that he should fight for him upon this covenant, that al the other knights should be delivered, and unto that was sir Damas sworne unto king Arthur, and also to doe this battaile to the uttermost. And with that all the twentie knights were brought out of the darke prison into the hall and delivered. And so they all abode to see the battaile.

CHAP. LXVII.—How sir Accolon found himselfe by a well, and he tooke upon him to doe battaile against king Arthur.

TURNE we unto sir Accolon of Gaule, that when he awoke he found himselfe by a deepe wel side within halfe a foote in great perill of death, and there came out of that fountaine a pipe of silver, and out of that pipe ranne water all on high in stone of marble. And when sir Accolon saw this, hee blessed him and said, "Jesus, save my lord king Arthur and king Urience! for these damosells in this ship have betraied us, they were divels and no women, and if I may escape this misadventure I shall destroy all where I may find these false damosels that use inchantments." And with that there came a dwarfe with a great mouth and flat nose, and saluted sir Accolon, and said how he came from queene Morgan le Fay, "and she greeteth you well, and biddeth you to bee strong of hart, for yee shall fight to morrow with a knight at the houre of prime, and therefore she hath sent you here Excalibur, king Arthurs sword, and the scabbard, and she desireth you, as you love her, that ye doe the battail to the uttermost without any mercy, like as ye have promised her when ye spake together in private; and what damosell that bringeth her the knights head that ye shall fight withall, shee wil make her a rich queene for ever." "Now I understand you well," said sir Accolon, "I shall hold that I have promised her, now I have the sword. When saw yee my lady queene Morgan?" "Right late," said the dwarfe. Then sir Accolon tooke him in his armes, and said, "Recommend me unto my lady queen Morgan, and tell her that all shall be done as I have promised her, or else I will die for it. Now, I suppose," said sir Accolon, "she hath made all these crafts and enchantments for this battel." "Yee may wel beleeve it," said the dwarfe. Right so came a knight and a lady with sixe squires, and saluted sir Accolon, and praied him to arise, and come and rest him at his manor. And so sir Accolon mounted upon a voide horse, and went with the knight unto a faire manor by a priorie, and there he had passing good cheere. Then sir Damas sent unto his brother sir Ontzlake, and bad him make him ready by to-morrow at the houre of prime, and to be in the field to fight with a good knight, for he had found a good knight that was ready to doo battaile at al points. When this word came unto sir Ontzlake, he was passing heavie, for he was wounded a little to-fore through both his thighes with a speare, and made great mone; but, for all hee was wounded, he would have taken the battell in hand. So it happened at that time by the meanes of Morgan le Fay, sir Accolon was lodged with sir Ontzlake, and when he heard of that battaile, and how sir Ontzlake was wounded, he said he would fight for him; because Morgan le Fay had sent him Excalibur and the scabbard for to fight with the knight on the morrow, this was the cause sir Accolon tooke the battaile in hand. Then sir Ontzlake was passing glad, and thanked sir Accolon hartily, that he would doe so much for him. And therewith sir Ontzlake sent word to his brother sir Damas, that he had a knight that for him should be ready in the field by the houre of prime. So on the morrow king Arthur was armed and well horsed, and asked sir Damas "When shall we goe to the field?" "Sir," said sir Damas, "ye shal heare masse." And when masse was doone, there came a squire on a great horse and asked sir Damas, if his knight were ready; "for our knight is ready in the field." Then king Arthur mounted on horsebacke, and there were al the knights and commons of the countrey, and so by al advises there were chosen twelve goodmen[1] of the countrey for to waite upon the two knights. And as king Arthur was upon horsebacke, there came a damosell from Morgan le Fay, and brought unto king Arthur a sword like unto Excalibur and the scabbard, and said unto king Arthur, " Morgan le Fay sendeth you here your sword for great love." And he thanked her, and wend it had beene so; but she was false, for the sword and the scabard was counterfeit, brittle, and false.

CHAP. LXVIII.—Of the battaile betweene king Arthur and sir Accolon.

AND then they dressed them on both parties of the field, and let their horses run so fast, that either smote other in the middest of their shields with their speares, that both horses and men went to the ground; and then they started up both and drew out their swords. And in the meane while that they were thus fighting came the damosel of the lake into the field, that had put Merlin under the stone, and she came thither for the love of king Arthur, for she knew how Morgan le Fay had so ordained that king Arthur should have beene slaine that day, and therefore she came to save his life. And so they went egerly to doe their battaile, and gave manie great strokes. But alway king Arthurs sword was not like sir Accolons sword, so that for the most part every strooke that sir Accolon gave wounded king Arthur sore, that it was marvaile that he stood, and alway his blood fell fast from him. When king Arthur beheld the ground so sore beblooded,[2] hee was dismaied, and then he

[1] *Goodmen.*—The term *good-men* (*boni homines*) was equivalent with freemen.
[2] *Beblooded.*—Covered with blood. The use of the prefix *be* in an intensitive or distributive sense is very common in this book, and it will be hardly necessary to point it out except in particular instances where the passage requires explanation.

deemed treason that his sword was changed, for his sword was not still¹ as it was wont to doe; therefore was he sore adread to be dead, for ever him seemed that the sword in sir Accolons hand was Excalibur, for at every strooke that sir Accolon strooke, he drew blood on king Arthur. "Now knight," said sir Accolon to king Arthur, "keepe thee well from me." But king Arthur answered not againe, and gave him such a buffet on the helme that he made him to stoope, nigh falling to the ground. Then sir Accolon withdrew him a little, and came on with Excalibur on high, and smote king Arthur such a buffet that he fell nigh to the earth. Then were they both wroth, and gave each other many sore strookes, but alwayes king Arthur lost so much blood that it was marvaile that he stood on his feete, but he was so full of knighthood that knightly he endured the paine. And sir Accolon lost not a drop of blood, therefore he waxed passing light; and king Arthur was passing feeble, and thought verily to have died. But for all that he made countenance as though he might endure, and held sir Accolon as short as he might, but sir Accolon was so bold because of Excalibur, that he waxed passing hardy. But al men that beheld them said they saw never knight fight so well as did king Arthur, considering the blood that he bled, and all the people were sory for him, but the two brethren would not accord. Then alway they fought together as fierce knights, and king Arthur withdrew him a little for to rest him, and sir Accolon called him to battaile, and said, "It is no time for me to suffer thee to rest." And therewith he came fiersly upon king Arthur, and king Arthur was wroth for the blood that he had lost, and smote sir Accolon upon the helme so mightily that hee made him nigh fall to the earth, and therewith king Arthurs sword

¹ *Was not still.*—An error of the printer of the edition of 1634. Caxton has, *boote not styl*, i. e. did not bite or cut into the steel as it used to do. See the explanation of the name, p. 18.

brak at the crosse¹ and fel in the grasse among the blood, and the pomell and the handle he held in his hand. When king Arthur saw that, he was greatly afeard to die, but alwayes he held up his shield, and lost no ground, no bated noe cheere.

CHAP. LXIX.—How king Arthurs sword that he fought with brake, and how he recovered of sir Accolon his owne sword Excalibur, and overcame his enemie.

THEN sir Accolon began to say thus with words of treason: "Knight, thou art overcome and maist no longer endure, and also thou art weaponlesse, and thou hast lost much of thy blood, and I am full loth to sley thee, therefore yeeld thee to mee as recreaunt." "Nay," said king Arthur, "I may not so, for I have promised to doe the battaile to the uttermost by the faith of my body while my life lasteth, and therefore I had rather to die with honour then to live with shame, and if it were possible for me to die an hundred times, I had rather so often die then to yeeld me to thee; for though I lacke weapon and am weaponlesse, yet shall I lacke no worship, and if thou sley me weaponlesse it shall be to thy shame." "Well," said sir Accolon, "as for the shame I wil not spare. Now keepe thee from me," said sir Accolon, "for thou art but a dead man." And therewith sir Accolon gave him such a strooke, that he fel nigh to the earth, and would have king Arthur to crie him mercy. But king Arthur pressed unto sir Accolon with his shield, and gave him with the pomell in his hand such a buffet that he went three strides back. When the damosell of the lake beheld king Arthur, how full of prowesse and worthinesse his body was, and the false treason that was wrought for him to have slaine him, she had great

¹ *Crosse.*—The piece of metal which crossed the sword above the handle, to guard the hand.

pittie that so good a knight and so noble a man of worship should be destroyed. And at the next strooke sir Accolon strooke him such a strooke, that by the damosels enchauntment the sword Excalibur fell out of sir Accolons hand to the earth. And therwith king Arthur lightly leapt to it, and quickly gate it in his hand, and forthwith he perceived clearely that it was his good sword Excalibur, and said, "Thou hast beene from me al too long, and much domage hast thou done me." And therewith he espied the scabbard hanging by sir Accolons side, and suddenly hee leapt to him, and pulled the scabbard from him, and anon threw it from him as farre as he might throw it. "O, knight," said king Arthur, "this day thou hast don me great domage with this sword. Now are ye come to your death, for I shall not warrant you but that ye shall be as well rewarded with this sword or we depart asunder as thou hast rewarded me, for much paine have yee made me to endure, and have lost much blood." And therewith king Arthur rushed upon him with all his might, and pulled him to the earth, and then rushed off his helme, and gave him such a buffet on the head that the blood came of his eares, nose, and mouth. "Now will I sley thee," said king Arthur. "Sley me yee may," said sir Accolon, "and it please you, for ye are the best knight that ever I found, and I see well that God is with you; but for I promised to doe this battaile," said sir Accolon, "to the uttermost, and never to be recreaunt while I lived, therefore shall I never yeeld me with my mouth, but God doe with my body what he wil." And then king Arthur remembred him, and thought he should have seene this knight. "Now tel me," said king Arthur, "or I will sley thee, of what countrey art thou? and of what court?" "Sir knight," quoth sir Accolon, "I am of the court of king Arthur, and my name is sir Accolon of Gaule." Then was king Arthur more dismaied then he was before, for then he remembred him of his sister Morgan le Fay, and of the enchantment of the ship. "Oh, sir knight," said he, "I pray thee tell me who gave thee this sword and by whom had ye it?"

CHAP. LXX.—How sir Accolon confessed the treason of Morgan le Fay, and how she would have caused her brother king Arthur to be slaine.

THEN sir Accolon bethought him, and said: "Woe worth this sword, for by it have I gotten my death." "It may wel be," said king Arthur. "Now sir," said sir Accolon, "I wil tel you. This sword hath beene in my keeping the most of these twelve monethes, and queene Morgan le Fay, king Urience wife, sent it me yesterday by a dwarfe to this intent, that I should sley king Arthur her brother, for ye shall understand that king Arthur is the man which shee most hateth in this world, because that he is the most of worship and of prowesse of any of her blood. Also she loveth me out of measure, as her paramoure, and I her againe. And if she might bring about for to sley king Arthur with her crafts, she would sley her husband king Urience lightly, and then had she me devised to be king in this land, and so for to raigne, and she to be my queene: but that is now done," said sir Accolon, "for I am sure of my death." "Well," said king Arthur, "I feele by you ye would have beene king in this land; it had beene great domage for to have destroyed your lord," said king Arthur. "It is truth," said sir Accolon, "but now have I told you the truth, wherefore I pray you that ye will tell me of whence ye are, and of what court?" "Oh, sir Accolon," said king Arthur, " now I let thee to wit that I am king Arthur, to whom thou hast done great domage." When sir Accolon heard that, he cried out aloud: "Oh, my gracious lord, have mercy on me, for I knew you not!" "Oh, sir Accolon," said king Arthur, "mercy shalt thou have, because I feele by thy words at this time thou knewest not my person. But I understand well by thy words that thou hast agreed to the death of my person, and therfore thou art a traitour. But I blame thee the lesse, for my sister Morgan le Fay, by her false crafts, made thee to agree and consent to her false lusts; but I shall so be avenged upon her and I live, that all Christendome shall speake of it. God knoweth, I have honoured her and worshiped her more then any of my kin, and more have I trusted her then mine owne wife and all my kin after." Then king Arthur called the keepers of the field, and said, " Sirs, come hither, for here we be two knights that have fought unto a great domage to us both, and like each one of us to have slaine other, if it had happened so ; and had any of us knowen other, here had beene no battaile nor stroke stricken." Then al aloud cried sir Accolon unto all the knights and men that there wer gathered together, and said to them in this manner wise: " Oh, my lords, this noble knight that I have fought withall, which me full sore repenteth, is the most man of prowesse, of manhood, and of worship that in all the world liveth, for it is himselfe king Arthur, our most soveraigne liege lord and king, and with great mishap and great misadventure have I done this battaile against my king and lord, that I am holded withall."

CHAP. LXXI.—How king Arthur accorded the two brethren, and delivered the twentie knights, and how sir Accolon died.

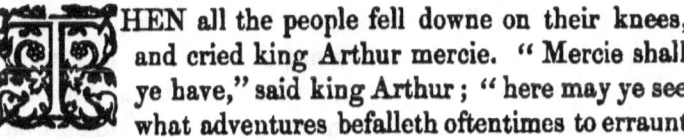HEN all the people fell downe on their knees, and cried king Arthur mercie. " Mercie shall ye have," said king Arthur ; " here may ye see what adventures befalleth oftentimes to erraunt knights ; how I have fought with one of mine owne knights to my great domage and his hurt. But, sirs, because I am sore hurt and he both, and haye great neede of a little rest, ye shall understand my opinion betweene you two brethren.

As to thee, sir Damas, for whom I have beene champion and won the field of this knight, yet will I judge because ye, sir Damas, are called a very proud knight and full of vilany, and nothing worth of prowesse of your deedes, therefore I will that ye give unto you brother all the whole manor with the appurtenance under this maner of forme, that sir Ontzlake hold the manor of you, and yearely to give you a palfrey to ride upon, for that will become you better to ride on then on a courser. Also, I charge thee, sir Damas, upon paine of death, that thou never distresse none erraunt knights that ride on their adventures. Also, that thou restore these twentie knights which thou hast long kept in prison of all their harneis, and that thou content them, and if any of them come to my court and complaine of thee, by my head thou shalt die therefore. Also, sir Ontzlake, as to you, because ye are named a good knight and ful of prowesse, and true and gentle in all your deedes, this shal be your charge. I will that in all goodly hast ye come to me and to my court, and ye shal be a knight of mine, and if your deedes be therafter, I shall so advance you by the grace of God that ye shall in short time be in case for to live as worshipfully as doth your brother sir Damas." "God thanke you of your largesse and of your great goodnesse," said sir Ontzlake, " and I promise you that from hencefoorth I shall be at all times at your commandement. For sir," said sir Ontzlake, " as God would I was hurt but late with an adventurous knight through both my thighes, which grieved me sore, and else I had done this battaile with you." "Would to God," said king Arthur, "it had been so, for then had not I beone hurt as I am, I shall tell you the cause why ; for I had not beene hurt as I am had not it beene mine owne sword that was stolen from me by treason, and this battaile was ordeined aforehand for to have slaine me, and so it was brought to the purpose by false engine,[1] and treason, and false enchantment." "Alas!"

[1] *Engine.*—Ingenuity; contrivance.

KING ARTHUR. 137

said sir Ontzlake, " that is great pittie that so noble a man as you are of your deedes and prowesse, that any man or woman might find in their hearts to work any treason against your person." " I shal reward them," said king Arthur, " in short space by the grace of God. Now tel me," said king Arthur, " how far am I from Camelot ?" " Sir, ye are two daies journey therfro." " I would fain be at some place of worship," said king Arthur, " that I might rest my selfe." " Sir," said sir Ontzlake, " heereby is a rich abbey of nuns of our[1] elders foundation, but three miles hence." So then the king tooke his leave of all the people, and mounted on horseback, and sir Accolon with him. And when they were come to the abbey, he let fetch surgions and leeches[2] for to search[3] his wounds, and sir Accolons both; but sir Accolon died within foure dayes after, for he had bled so much blood that hee might not live, but king Arthur was well recovered. And when sir Accolon was dead, he let send him on horsbacke with sixe knights to Camelot, and said, " Beare him to my sister Morgan le Fay, and say that I send him hir for a present, and tel her that I have my sword Excalibur and the scabbard." So they departed with the body.

CHAP. LXXII.—How Morgan le Fay would have slaine king Urience her husband, and how sir Ewaine her sonne saved him.

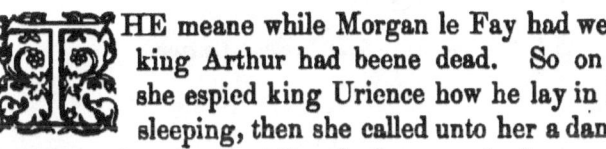HE meane while Morgan le Fay had wend that king Arthur had beene dead. So on a day she espied king Urience how he lay in his bed sleeping, then she called unto her a damosel of her counsell, and said, " Goe fetch me my lords sword, for I

---

[1] *Our.*—*Your*, Caxton.
[2] *Leeches.*—Physicians. *Surgions* is not found in Caxton's text; it was a word then in more common use.
[3] *To search.*—To probe; to examine.

saw never better time to sley him then now." "O madam," said the damosell, "and if ye sley my lord, ye can never escape." "Care not thou," said Morgan le Fay, "for now I see my time in the which it is best to doe it, and therefore hie thee fast and fetch me the sword." Then the damosel departed, and found sir Ewaine[1] sleeping upon a bed in another chamber; so she went unto sir Ewaine and wakned him, and bad him "arise and waite upon my lady your mother, for she will sley the king your father sleeping in his bed, for I goe to fetch her his sword." "Well," said sir Ewaine, "goe on your way, and let me deale." Anon the damosell brought the sword unto Morgan with quaking hands, and shee lightly tooke the sword and drew it out, and went boldly to the beds side, and awaited how and where she might sley him best. And as she lift up the sword for to smite, sir Ewaine lept unto his mother and caught her by the hand, and said, "Ah! fiend, what wilt thou doe? and thou were not my mother, with this sword I would smite off thy head. Ah," said sir Ewaine, "men say that Merlin was begotten of a divell, but I may say an earthly divell bare me." "Oh, faire sonne Ewaine," said Morgan, "have mercy upon me, I was tempted with a divell, wherefore I crie thee mercy, I wil never more doe so, and save my worship and discover me not." "On this covenant," said sir Ewaine, "I wil forgive you, so you wil never be about to do such deeds." "Nay, son," said she, "and therto I mak you assurance."

[1] *Sir Ewaine.—Syre Uwayne*, Caxton.

CHAP. LXXIII.—How Morgan le Fay made great sorrow for the death of sir Accolon, and how she stale away from king Arthur the scabbard.

THEN came tidings unto Morgan le Fay that sir Accolon was dead, and his body brought to the church, and how king Arthur had his sword againe. But when Morgan wist that sir Accolon was dead, she was so sorowful that neere her hart burst. But because she would not that it were knowen, she kept her countenance outward, and made no semblance of sorrow. But well she wist and if she abode till her brother Arthur came thither, there should no gold save her life. Then she went unto queene Guenever, and asked her leave to ride into the country. " Ye may abide," said queene Guenever, " til your brother the king come home." " I may not," said Morgan le Fay, " for I have such hastie tidings that I may not tarry." " Well," said queene Guenever, " ye may depart when ye will." So, early on the morrow or it was day, she tooke her horse and rode all that day and the most part of the night, and on the morrow by noone she came to the same abbey of nuns wher as king Arthur lay, and she knowing that he was there, she asked where he was. And they answered and said, " That he had laid him downe in his bed to sleepe, for he had had but little rest these three nights." " Well," said she, " I charge you that none of you awake him till I awake him my selfe." And then she alight from her horse, and thought to steale away Excalibur, his good sword, and so she went straight unto his chamber, and no man durst disobey her commandement, and there she found king Arthur asleepe in his bed, and Excalibur in his right hand naked. When she saw that, she was passing heavie that she might not come by the sword, without she had wakened him, and then she wist well that she had beene dead. Then she tooke the

scabbard, and went her way on horsebacke. When the king awoke and missed his scabbard, he was wonderous wroth, and asked who had beene there. And they said his sister queene Morgan had beene there, and had put the scabbard under her mantell, and was gone. "Alas!" said king Arthur, "falsely have ye watched me." "Sir," said they al, "we durst not disobey your sisters commandement." "Ah," said the king, "let fetch the best horse that may be found, and bid sir Ontzlake arme him in all haste, and take another good horse, and ride with me."

So anon the king and sir Ontzlake were well armed, and rode after this lady. And as they rode they came by a crosse, and found a cowheard, and they asked the poore man if there came any lady late riding that way. "Sir," said this poore man, "right late came a lady riding with fortie horses, and to yonder forrest she rode." Then they spurred their horses and followed fast after, and within a while king Arthur had a sight of her, that he chased as fast as he might. And when she espied him following her, she rode through the forrest a great pace till shee came to a plaine. And when she saw she might not escape, she rode unto a lake thereby, and said, "Whatsoever becommeth of me, my brother shall not have this scabbard." And then she let throw the scabbard in the deepest of the water, and it sunke, for it was so heavie of gold and precious stones. Then she rode into a valey where many great stones were. And when shee saw that shee must needes be overtaken, she shop[1] herself, horse and man, by enchantment, into a great marble stone. So anon king Arthur and sir Ontzlake came, wheras the king might know his sister and her men, and one knight from another. "Ah," said the king, "here may ye see the vengance of God, and now I am sorrie that this misadventure is befallen." And then he looked for the scabbard, but it could not be found. So he returned again to the

---

[1] *Shop.*—Shaped, i. e. transformed.

KING ARTHUR. 141

abbey that he came from. When king Arthur was gone, she turned all into the likenesse as she and they were before, and said, " Sirs, now may we goe wheresoever we will, for my brother Arthur is gone."

CHAP. LXXIV.—How Morgan le Fay saved a knight that should have beene drowned, and how king Arthur returned home againe to Camelot.

THEN said Morgan, " Saw ye my brother sir Arthur?" " Ye," said her knights, " right wel, and that ye should have found and we might have stirred from one steede, for by his armivestall[1] countenance he would have caused us to have fled." " I beleeve you wel," said Morgan. Anon after shee rode, she met with a knight leading another knight on his horse before him, bound hand and foote blindfold, to have drowned him in a fountaine. When shee saw that knight so bound, shee asked what hee would doe with that knight. " Lady," said he, " I will drowne him."

" For what cause?" said she. " For I found him with my wife, and she shal have the same death anon." " That were pittie," said Morgan. " Now what say you, ye knight, is it truth that he saith of you?" said she to the knight that should be drowned. " Nay truely, madam, he saith not right of me." " Of whence be yee?" said Morgan le Fay ; " and of what countrey?" " I am of the court of king Arthur, and my name is Manassen, cosin unto sir Accolon of Gaule." " Ye say well," said she, " and for the love of him ye shal be delivered, ye shall have your adversary in the same case that ye be in." And so Manassen was loosed, and the other knight bound. And anon Manassen unarmed him, and armed himselfe in his harneis, and so mounted on horseback, and the knight afore him, and so

---

[1] *Armivestall.*—warlike; fierce.

threw him into the fountaine and drowned him. And then
he rode to Morgan againe, and asked her if she would any-
thing unto king Arthur. " Tel him not that I rescewed
thee for the love of him, but for the love of sir Accolon, and
tel him that I feare him not while I can make me and them
that bee with me in likenesse of stones; and let him wit I
can doe much more when I see my time." And so she
departed and went into the countrey of Gore,[1] and there was
shee richly received, and made her castles and townes passing strong, for alwayes she dread much king Arthur. When
king Arthur had well rested him at that abbey, he rode to
Camelot, and found his queene and his barons right glad of
his comming. And when they heard of his strange adventures, as is afore rehearsed, they all had mervaile of the
falsehood of Morgan le Fay, and many knights wished her
brent. Then came Manassen to the court, and told the
king of his adventure. "Well," said the king, "she is a
kind sister; I shall so be avenged on her and I live, that
al Christendome shall speake of it." So on the morrow
there came a damosell from Morgan to the king, and shee
brought with her the richest mantell that ever was seene
in the court, for it was set as ful of precious stones as might
stand one by another, and there were the richest stones that
ever the king saw. And the damosell said, " Your sister
sendeth you this mantell, and desireth you that yee will
take this gift of her, and in what thing shee hath offended
you, she will amend it at your owne pleasure." When the
king beheld this mantell, it pleased him much, but he said
but little.

[1] *Gore.*—This country may perhaps be intended for the district
of Gower in North Wales.

CHAP. LXXV.—How the damosell of the lake saved king Arthur from a mantell which should have brent him.

AND with that came the damosel of the lake unto the king, and said, " Sir, I must speake with you in private." " Say on," said the king, " what ye will." " Sir," said the lady, " put not on you this mantell till ye have seene more, and in no wise let it not come upon you nor on no knight of yours till ye commaund the bringer thereof to put it upon her." " Well," said king Arthur, " it shall be done as ye counsaile me." And then he said unto the damosell that came from his sister, " Damosell, this mantell that ye have brought me, I will see it upon you." " Sir," said she, " it will not beseeme me to weare a knights[1] garment." " By my head," said king Arthur, " ye shall weare it or it come on my backe, or on any man that heere is ;" and so the king made it to be put upon her ; and foorthwith she fell downe dead, and never more spake word after, and was brent to coles.[2]

Then was the king wondrous wroth, more then he was afore, and said unto king Urience, " My sister, your wife, is alway about to betray me, and wel I wot either yee or my nephew your sonne is of counsaile with her to have me destroyed ; but as for you," said king Arthur to king Urience, " I deeme not greatly that ye be of her counsaile, for sir Accolon confessed to me with his owne mouth that she should have destroyed you as well as me, therefore I hold you excused ; but as for your sonne sir Ewaine, I hold him suspect, therefore I charge you put him out of my court." So sir Ewaine was charged. And when sir Gawaine[3] wist of

---

[1] *A kynges,* Caxton.
[2] *Coles.*—Coal, in the Middle Ages, meant always charcoal; the phrase here used is equivalent to, burnt to cinders.
[3] *Gawaine.*—The text of the edition of 1634 reads here *Ewaine,* but Caxton has correctly, *Syr Gawayne.*

it, he made him ready to goe with him, and said, "Who so banished my cosin Ewaine, shall banish me." So they two departed, and rode in a great forrest; and so they came to an abbey of monkes, and there were well lodged. But when the king wist that sir Gawaine was departed from the court, there was made great sorrow among all the states. "Now," said sir Gaheris, sir Gawaines brother, "we have lost two good knights for the love of one." So on the morrow they[1] hard masse in the abbey, and so they rode foorth till they came to a great forrest; then was sir Gawaine ware in a valey by a turret of twelve faire damosels, and two knights armed, upon two great horses, and the damosels went to and fro by a tree. And then was sir Gawaine ware how there hung a white shield on that tree, and ever as the damosels came by it, they spet upon it, and some threw mire upon it.

CHAP LXXVI.—How sir Gawaine and sir Ewaine met with twelve faire damosels, and how they complained upon sir Marhaus.

THEN sir Gawaine and sir Ewaine went and saluted them, and asked why they did that despite to the shield. "Sirs," said the damosels, "we shall tell you. There is a knight in this countrey that oweth[2] this white shield, and he is a passing good knight of his hands, but he hateth all ladies and gentlewomen, and therfore we doe all this despite to the white shield." "I shall say to you," said sir Gawaine to the ladies, "it beseemeth evill a good knight to despise all ladies and gentlewomen, and also peradventure, though he hate you, he hath some cause, and peradventure that he loveth in some other places good ladies and gentlewomen, and to be

[1] *They.*—i. e. Ewaine and Gawaine.
[2] *Oweth*—i. e. owneth.

loved againe, if he be such a man of prowesse as ye speake of; now what is his name?" "Sir," said they, "his name is Marhaus,[1] the kings sonne of Ireland." "I know him well," said sir Ewaine, "he is a passing good knight as any is living, for I saw him once prooved at a justing, where as many knights were gathered, and that time there might no man withstand him." "Ah," said sir Gawaine, "damosels, me thinketh ye are to blame, for it is to suppose that he that hung that shield ther, he wil not be long therefrom, and then may those knights match him on horsebacke, and that is more your worship then thus, for I will abide no longer to see a knights shield dishonoured." And therewith sir Ewaine and sir Gawaine departed a little from them, and then were they ware where sir Marhaus came riding upon a great horse strait toward them. And when the twelve damosels saw sir Marhaus, they fled into the turret as they had beene wilde, so that some of them fell by the way. Then the one of the knights of the turret dressed his shield, and said an high, "Sir Marhaus, defend thee;" and so they ran together that the knight brake his speare on sir Marhaus, and sir Marhaus smote him so hard that he brake his necke. That saw the other knight of the turret, and dressed him toward sir Marhaus, and they met so egerly together that the knight of the turret was soone smitten downe, horse and man, starke dead.

CHAP. LXXVII.—How sir Marhaus justed with sir Gawaine and sir Ewaine, and overthrew them both.

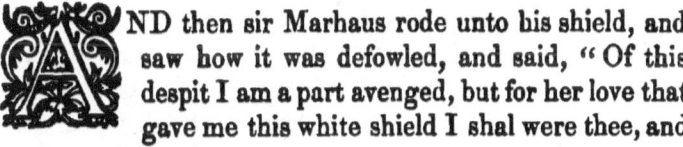ND then sir Marhaus rode unto his shield, and saw how it was defowled, and said, "Of this despit I am a part avenged, but for her love that gave me this white shield I shal were thee, and

[1] *Marhaus.*—Of this personage, who is called Morhoult in the French prose romance of sir Tristan, a further account will be found in the second part of the present work.

hang mine here in thy steed." And so hee hung it about his neck,[1] and then he rode straight to sir Gawaine and sir Ewaine, and asked them what they did there. They answered that they came from king Arthurs court for to seeke adventures. "Well," said Marhaus, "heere am I ready, a knight adventurous, that wil fulfill any adventure that yee will desire of me." And so departed from them to fetch his raunge. "Let him goe," said sir Ewaine to sir Gawaine, "for he is a passing good knight as any is living in this world; I would not by my will that any of us two should match with him. "Nay," said sir Gawaine, "not so; it were shame to us if hee were not assaied, were hee never so good a knight." "Well," said sir Ewaine, "I will assay him afore you, for I am more weaker then ye are, and if he smite me downe then may ye revenge me." So these two knights came together with great raundon, that sir Ewaine smote sir Marhaus that his speare burst in peeces on the shield, and sir Marhaus smote him so sore that horse and man he bare to the earth, and hurt sir Ewaine on the left side. Then sir Marhaus turned his horse, and rode toward sir Gawaine with his speare. And when sir Gawaine saw that, hee dressed his shield, and they adventred their speares, and they came together with all the might of their horses, that either knight smote other so hard in the middest of their two shields that sir Gawaines speare brake, and sir Marhaus speare held, and therewith sir Gawaine and his horse rushed downe to the earth, and lightly sir Gawaine arose upon his feete, and drew out his sword, and dressed him toward sir Marhaus on foote. And sir Marhaus saw that, and drew out his sword, and began to come to sir Gawaine on horsebacke. "Sir knight," said sir Gawaine, "alight on foote, or else I will sley thy horse." "Gramercy," said sir Marhaus, "of your gentilnesse ye teach me curtesie, for it is not according for one knight to bee on foote and the

[1] *About his neck.*—This was the usual manner of carrying the shield when not in actual use.

other on horsebacke." And therewith sir Marhaus set his speare against a tree, and alighted, and tied his horse to a tree, and dressed his shield, and either came to other egerly, and smot together with their swords that their shields flew in cantels, and they brused their helmes and their hawberkes, and wounded either other. But sir Gawaine, fro it passed nine of the clock, waxed ever stronger and stronger, for then it came to the houre of noone, and thrice his might was increased. All this espied sir Marhaus, and had great wonder how his might increased, and so they wounded each other passing sore. And when it was past noon and drew toward evensong time, sir Gawaines strength waxed passing faint, that unneth he might not endure any longer; and sir Marhaus waxed bigger and bigger. "Sir knight," said sir Marhaus, "I have well felt that ye are a passing good knight, and a marvailous man of might as ever I felt any, while it lasteth, and our quarrels are not great, and therefore it were pittie to do you hurt, for I perceive ye are passing feeble." "Ah," said sir Gawaine, "gentle knight, ye say the words that I should say." And therewith they tooke off their helmes, and either kissed other, and there they swore together either to love other as brethren. And sir Marhaus prayed sir Gawaine to lodge with him that night. And so they tooke their horses and rode toward sir Marhaus place. And as they rode by the way, sir Gawaine said, "Sir knight, I marvaile that so valiant a man as ye be love no ladies or gentlewomen." "Sir," said sir Marhaus, "they name me wrongfully that give me that name; but well I wot it is the damosels of the turret that so name me, and other such as they be. Now shall I tell you for what cause I hate them so. For they bee witches and enchauntresses the most part of them, and boe a knight never so good of his body and of prowesse as any man may bee, they will make him a coward for to have the better of him, and this is the principal cause that I hate them. And to all good ladies and gentlewomen I ow my service as a knight ought to doe." And as the French booke rehearseth, there were many knights that overmatched sir Gawaine, for al the thrice-might that he had; as sir Launcelot du Lake, sir Tristram, sir Bors de Gaule,[1] sir Percivale, and sir Marhaus, these five knights had the better of sir Gawaine. Then within a little while they came to sir Marhaus place, the which was in a little priorie, and there they alight, and ladies and damosels unarmed them and hastily looked to their hurts, for they were all three hurt. And so they had there good lodging with sir Marhaus, and good chere. For when he wist that they were king Arthurs sister sonnes, he made them all the cheere that lay in his power. And so they sojourned there about a seaven nights, and were right well eased of their wounds, and at the last departed. "Now," said sir Marhaus, " we will not depart so lightly, for I will bring you through the forrest;" and rode day by day well a seaven dayes or they found any adventure. At the last they came into a great forrest which was named the countrey and forrest of Arroy, and the countrey of strange adventures. "In this countrey," said sir Marhaus, "came never knight sithen it was christned,[2] but hee found strange adventures." So long they rode till they came into a deepe valey full of stones, and therby they saw a faire streame of water, and above thereby the head of the streme was a faire fountaine, and three damosels sitting thereby. And then they rode unto them, and either saluted other, and the eldest had a garland of gold about her head, and shee was threescore winters of age or more, and her haire was white under the garland. The second damosel was of thirtie winters of age, with a serklet[3] of gold about her head. The third damosell was but fifteene yeares of age, and she had a garland of flowers about her head. When these knights had well beholden them, they asked them the cause why they

---

[1] *Sir Bors de Gaule.*— Syr Bors de Ganys, Caxton.
[2] *Christned.*—i. e. made Christian; converted.
[3] *Serklet.*—A wreath, or band, for the head.

sate at that fountaine. "We be heere," said the damosels, "for this cause: if we may see any erraunt knights, to teach them unto strange adventures, and ye be three knights that seeken adventures, and we three damosels, and therefore each of you must choose one of us; and when ye have done so, we will leade you unto three high waies, and there each of you shall choose a way, and his damosell with him; and this day twelve monethes yee must meete heere againe and God spare you your lives, and thereto ye must plight your troth." "That is well said," said sir Marhaus.

CHAP. LXXVIII.—How sir Marhaus, sir Gawaine, and Ewaine met three damosels, and each of them tooke one.

HOW shall we choose every each of us a damosel?" "I shal tel you," said sir Ewaine; "I am the youngest and most weakest of you both, therefore I will have the eldest damosell, for she hath seene much and can helpe me best when I have neede, for I have most neede of helpe of you both." Then said sir Marhaus, "I will have the damosell of thirtie winters of age, for she falleth best to me." Then said sir Gawaine, "I thanke you, for ye have left me the youngest and the fairest, and she is most levest to me." Then every damosell tooke her knight by the raine of the bridle, and brought them to the three wayes, and there was their oath made to meete at the fountaine that day twelvemoneth and they lived. So they kist and departed, and each knight set his lady behind him. And sir Ewaine tooke the way that lay west, and sir Marhaus tooke the way that lay south, and sir Gawaine took the way that lay north. Now wil we begin at sir Gawaine, that held that way till he came to a faire mannor, where as dwelleth an old knight and a good housholder, and there sir Gawaine demanded of the old knight if he knew any adventures in that countrey. "I shall shew you some to-morrow," said the old knight, "and that marvailous." So on the morrow they rode into the forrest of adventures, til they came to a laund, and thereby they found a crosse, and as they stood and hoved,¹ there came by them the fairest knight and the seemeliest man that ever they saw, making the greatest moane that ever man made. And then he was ware of sir Gawaine, and saluted him, and prayed to God to send him much worship. " As to that," said sir Gawaine, " gramercy. Also I pray to God that he send to you honour and worship." " Ah," said the knight, " I may lay that on side, for sorrow and shame commeth to mee after worship."

CHAP. LXXIX.—How a knight and a dwarfe strove for a lady.

AND therewith he passed to that one side of the laund. And on that other side sir Gawaine saw ten knights that hoved still, and made them ready with their shields and spears against that one knight that came by sir Gawaine. Then this one knight adventred a great speare, and one of the ten knights encountred with him, but this wofull knight smote him so hard that he fel over the horse taile. So this dolorous knight served them all, and smote them downe horse and man, and all he did it with one speare. And when they were all ten on foote, they went to that one knight, and he stood ston stil and suffered them to pull him down off his horse, and bound him hand and foote, and tyed him under his horse belly, and so led him with them. " Oh, Jesus ! " said sir Gawaine, " this is a dolefull sight to see yonder knight so to be entreated, and it seemeth by the knight that he suffereth them to bind him so, for hee maketh no resistance." " No, verily," said his hoast, " that is truth, for and if that he would, they were all to weake so to doe to him." " Sir," said the damosell unto sir Gawaine, " me seemeth that it were your worship and honour to helpe that dolorous knight, for me thinketh he is one of the best knights that ever I

¹ *Hoved.*—Hovered ; halted.

saw." " I would be glad to doe for him," said sir Gawaine, "but it seemeth that he wil have no helpe." Then said the damosell, " Mee seemeth ye have no list to helpe him." Right thus as they talked, they saw a knight on that other side of the laund, all armed save the head. And on that other side of the laund came a dwarfe on horsebacke all armed save the head, with a great mouth and a short nose. And the dwarfe when hee came nigh to the knight and said, " Where is the lady that should meete us heere?" And therewithall she came foorth out of the wood. And then they began to strive for the lady; for the knight said he would have her, and the dwarfe said he would have her. " Wil ye doe wel?" said the dwarfe; " yonder is a knight at the crosse, let us put it to his judgement, and as he deemeth even so be it." " I will well," said the knight. And then they went all three unto sir Gawaine, and told him wherefore they two strove. " Well, sirs," said he, " will ye put the matter into my hand?" " Yea, sir," said they both. " Now, damosell," said sir Gawaine, " ye shall stand betweene them both, and whether ye list better to goe to, he shall have you." And so when the damosell was set betweene them both, she left the knight and went to the dwarfe. And the dwarfe tooke her, and went his way singing; and the knight went his way with great mourning. Then came there two knights all armed, and cried on high, " Sir Gawaine ! knight of king Arthur, make thee ready in all hast and just with me." So they ran together that either fell downe ; and then on foote they drew their swords and did full actually. In the meane while the other knight went unto the damosell, and asked her why she abode with that knight, and " if ye would abide with me, I wil be your faithfull knight." " And with you will I be," said the damosell, " for with sir Gawaine I may not find in mine hart to bee with him ; for now here was one knight that discomfited ten knights, and at the last hee was cowardly led away ; and therefore let us two goe our way while they fight." And sir Gawaine fought with that other knight long, but at the last they were both accorded; and then the knight prayed sir Gawaine to lodge with him that night. So as sir Gawaine went with this knight, he demaunded him: " What knight is he in this countrey that smot down the ten knights? for when he had done so manfully, he suffered them to bind him hand and foote, and so led him away." " Ah," said the knight, " that is the best knight I trow in the world, and the man most of prowesse, and he hath beene served so as he was even now more then ten times; and he is named sir Pelleas, and he loveth a great lady in this countrey, and her name is Ettarde, and so when hee loved her, there was cried in this countrey a great justes three daies; and all the knights of this countrey were there, and also the gentlewomen, and who that proved him the best knight should have a passing good sword and a serklet of gold, and the serklet the knight should give it to the fairest lady that was at those justes. And this knight sir Pelleas was the best knight that was there, and there were five hundred knights, but there was never man that ever sir Pelleas met withal, but that he strooke him downe, or else from his horse. And every day of the three dayes he strooke down twentie knights, therfore they gave him the price. And foorthwithall he went there as the lady Ettarde was, and gave her the serklet, and said openly that she was the fairest lady that was there, and that would he prove upon any knight that would say nay.

CHAP. LXXX.—How king Pelleas suffered himselfe to be taken prisoner because he would have a sight of his lady, and how sir Gawaine promised him for to get to him the love of his lady.

AND so he chose her for his soveraigne lady, and never to love other but her. But she was so proud that she had scorn of him, and said that she would never love him, though he would die for her. Wherefore al ladies and gentlewomen had scorne of her, because she was so proud, for there were fairer then she, and there was none that was there but, and sir Pelleas would have proffered them love, they would have loved him for his noble prowesse. And so this knight promised the lady Ettarde to follow her into this countrey, and never to leave her till she loved him. And thus he is here the most part nigh her, and lodgeth by a priorie, and every weeke she sendeth knights to fight with him; and when he hath put them to the worst, then will he suffer them wilfully to take him prisoner, because he would have a sight of this lady. And alway she doth him great dispite, for sometime she maketh her knights to tie him to the horse taile, and sometime binde him under the horse belly. Thus in the most shamefullest wise that she can thinke he is brought to her. And al this she doth for to cause him to leave this countrey, and to leave his loving; but all this cannot make him to leave, for and hee would have fought on foote hee might have had the better of the ten knights as well on foote as on horseback." "Alas!" said sir Gawaine, "it is great pittie of him, and after this night in the morning I will goe seeke him in the forrest, to doe him all the helpe that I can." So on the morrow sir Gawaine tooke his leave of his hoast sir Carodos, and rode into the forrest. And at the last hee met with sir Pelleas making great mone out of measure; so each of them saluted other, and asked him why he made such sorrow. And as it is above rehearsed, sir Pelleas told to sir Gawaine, "but alway I suffer her knights to fare so with me as ye saw yesterday, in trust at the last to winne her love, for she knoweth wel that al her knights should not lightly winne mee and mee list to fight with them to the uttermost. Wherefore, and I loved her not so sore, I had rather to die an hundred times, and I might die so often, rather then I would suffer, this great despite; but I trust she wil have pittie upon me at the last, for love causeth many a good knight to suffer, for to have his intent, but alas, I am unfortunate." And therewith he made so great mone and sorrow that unneth hee might hold him on horsback. "Now," said sir Gawaine, "leave off your mourning, and I shall promise you by the faith of my body to doe all that lieth in my power to get you the love of your lady, and thereto I will plight you my troth." "Ah, my good friend," said sir Pelleas, "of what court are ye; I pray you that you will tell me?" And then sir Gawaine said, "I am of the court of king Arthur, and am his sisters sonne; and king Lot of Orkeney was my father, and my name is sir Gawaine." And then hee said, "My name is sir Pelleas, born in the Isles, and of many isles I am lord, and never have I loved lady nor damosell till now in an unhappie time; and, sir knight, sith ye are so nigh cosin unto king Arthur and a kings sonne, therefore I pray thee betray me not, but helpe me, for I may never come by her but by the helpe of some good knight, for she is in a strong castle here fast by within this foure mile, and over all this countrey she is lady of. And so I may never come unto her presence but as I doe suffer her knights for to take me; and but if I did so, that I might have a sight of her, I had beene dead long afore this time, and yet had I never one faire word of her; but when I am brought before her she rebuketh me in the foulest manner that ever she may. And then her knights take me and my horse and my harneis, and put me out of the gates; and she will not suffer me to eate nor drinke, and alwayes I offer mee for to be her prisoner, but so she will not take me, for I would desire no more what paines soever I had, so that I might have a sight of her dayly." "Well," said sir Gawaine, "all this shall I amend, and ye will doe as I shall devise. I wil have your horse and your armour, and so will I ride to her castle, and tell her that I have slaine you, and so shal I come within to her to cause her to cherish me, and then I shall doe my true part, that yee shall not faile to have her love."

CHAP. LXXXI.—How sir Gawaine came to the lady Ettarde, and lay by her, and how sir Pelleas found them sleeping.

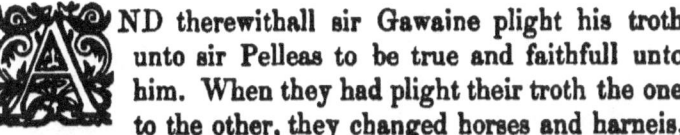ND therewithall sir Gawaine plight his troth unto sir Pelleas to be true and faithfull unto him. When they had plight their troth the one to the other, they changed horses and harneis, and sir Gawaine departed, and came to the castle where as stood the pavilions of this lady without the gate; and as soone as Ettarde had espied sir Gawaine, she fled toward the castle. Then sir Gawaine spake on high, and bad her abide, for he was not sir Pelleas, " I am another knight that hath slaine sir Pelleas." " Doe off your helme," said the lady Ettarde, "that I may behold your visage." And when she saw it was not sir Pelleas, she made him to alight, and led him unto her castle, and asked him faithfully whether he had slaine sir Pelleas. And he said, yea. And then sir Gawaine told her that his name was sir Gawaine, and of the court of king Arthur, and his sisters sonne. " Truely," said she, " that is great pittie, for hee was a passing good knight of his body, but of all men on live I hated him most, for I could never be quiet for him. And for that yee have slaine him, I shall bee your woman, and doe any thing that may please you." So shee made sir Gawaine good cheere. Then sir Gawaine said that he loved a lady, and by no meanes she would love him. " She is to blame," said Ettarde, " and she wil not love you, for that ye be so well borne a man and such a man of prowesse, there is no lady in this world too good for you." " Will ye," said sir Gawaine, " promise me to doe all that ye may doe by the faith of your body, to get me the love of my lady?" " Yea, sir," said she, " and that I promise you by the faith of my body." " Now," said sir Gawaine, " it is your selfe that I love so well, therefore I pray you hold your promise." " I may not choose," said the lady Ettarde, " but if I should be forsworne." And so she graunted to fulfill all his desire. And

then it was in the moneth of May, that she and sir Gawaine went out of the castle and supped in a pavilion, and there was a bed made, and there sir Gawaine and the lady Ettard went to bed together, and in another pavilion she layed her damosels, and in the third pavilion shee laid part of her knights; for then she had no dread nor feare of sir Pelleas. And there sir Gawaine lay with her, doing his pleasure in that pavilion two daies and two nights, against the faithfull promise that he made to sir Pelleas. And on the third day in the morning early sir Pelleas armed him, for he had not slept sith that sir Gawaine departed from him; for sir Gawaine had promised him by the faith of his body to come unto him to his pavilion by the priory within the space of a day and a night. Then sir Pelleas mounted on horsebacke, and came to the pavilions that stood without the castle, and found in the first pavilion three knights in their beds, and three squires lying at their feete. Then went he to the second pavilion, and found foure gentlewomen lying in foure beds. And then hee went to the third pavilion, and found sir Gawaine lying in a bed with his lady Ettard, and either clipping other in armes; and when he saw that, his heart almost brast for sorrow, and said, " Alas! that ever a knight should bee found so false." And then he tooke his horse, and might no longer abide for sorrow. And when he had ridden nigh halfe a mile, he turned againe and thought to sley them both, and when he saw them both lye so fast sleeping, unneth hee might hold him on horsebacke for sorrow, and said thus to himselfe, " Though this knight be never so false, I will not sley him sleeping, for I will never destroy the high order of knighthood." And therewith hee departed againe, and left them sleeping. And or hee had riden halfe a mile he returned againe, and thought then to sley them both, making the greatest sorrow that any man might make. And when he cam to the pavilions he tied his horse to a tree, and pulled out his sword naked in his hand, and went straight to them wher as they lay together, and yet he thought that it were great shame for him to sley them sleeping, and laid the naked sword overthwart both their throates, and then hee tooke his horse, and rod foorth his way, making great and wofull lamentation. And when sir Pelleas came to his pavilions, he told his knights and squires how he had sped, and said thus to them: "For your true and faithfull service that you have done to me, I shall give you all my goods, for I will goe unto my bed and never arise untill I be dead. And when I am dead, I charge you that ye take the heart of my body, and beare it unto her betweene two silver dishes, and tell her how I saw her lie in her pavilion with the false knight sir Gawaine." Right so sir Pelleas unarmed himselfe, and went to his bed, making the greatest sorrow that ever man heard. And then sir Gawaine and the lady Ettard wakned out of their sleepe, and found the naked sword overthwart both their throates. Then she knew wel that it was sir Pelleas sword. "Alas!" said she to sir Gawaine, "ye have betraied me and sir Pelleas also, for yee told me that yee had slaine him, and now I know well it is not so, he is on live. And if sir Pelleas had beene as uncourteous[1] to you as you have beene to him, ye had beene a dead knight, but ye have deceived me and betraied me falsly, that all ladies and damosels may beware by you and me." And therewith sir Gawaine made him ready, and went into the forrest. Then it hapned that the damosell of the lake, Nimue, met with a knight of sir Pelleas, which went on foote in the forrest making great mone, and she asked him the cause of his sorrow. Then the woful knight told her how that his master and lord was betraied through a knight and a lady, and how he would never arise out of his bed til he were dead. "Bring me to him anon, and I wil warrant his life, that he shall not die for love; and shee that hath caused him to love, she shall be in as evill a plite

---

[1] *Uncourteous.*—I have corrected this from Caxton's text. The edition of 1634 has *courteous.*

as he is now or it bee long, for it is no joy of such a presumptuous lady that wil have no mercy of such a valiant knight." Anon the knight brought her unto his lord and master. And when she saw him so lying in his bed, she thought shee had never seene so likely a knight. And therewith shee threw an enchantment upon him, and he fel on sleepe. And in the meane while she rode to the lady Ettard, and charged that no man should waken him til she came again. And so within two houres she brought the lady Ettard thither, and both the ladies found him on sleepe. "Loe," said the damosell of the lake, " ye ought to be ashamed to murder such a knight." And therewith she cast such an enchantment upon her, that shee loved him out of measure, that well nigh shee was out of her mind.[1] " Oh, Lord Jesus," said the lady Ettard, " how is it befallen me that I now love him which I before most hated of all men living ?" " This is the rightwise judgement of God," said the damosell of the lake. And then anon sir Pelleas awoke, and looked upon the lady Ettard. And when he saw her, he knew her, and then hee hated her more then any woman alive, and said, " Goe thy way hence, thou traitresse, come no more in my sight." And when she heard him say so, she wept, and made great sorow out of measure.

CHAP. LXXXII.—How sir Pelleas loved no more the lady Ettard by the meanes of the damosell of the lake, whom he loved ever after during his life.

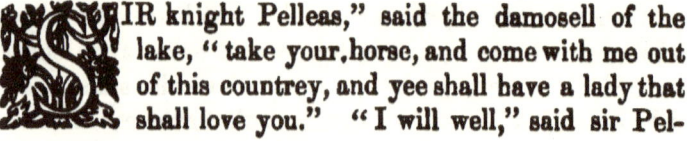"SIR knight Pelleas," said the damosell of the lake, " take your horse, and come with me out of this countrey, and yee shall have a lady that shall love you." " I will well," said sir Pel-

---

[1] *Out of her mind.*—This incident reminds us of a scene in Shakespeare's " Midsummer Night's Dream," the idea of which may perhaps have been suggested by it.

leas, "for the lady Ettard hath done me great dispite and shame." And there he told her the beginning, and how he had purposed never to have risen till that he had beene dead, "and now God hath sent me such grace that I hâte her as much as ever I loved her, thanked be our Lord God." "Thanke me," said the damosell of the lake. Anon sir Pelleas armed him, and tooke his horse, and commanded his men to bring after his pavilions and his stuff where as the damosell of the lake would assigne. So the lady Ettard died for sorrow, and the damosell of the lake rejoyced sir Pelleas, and loved together during their lives.

CHAP. LXXXIII.—How sir Marhaus rode with the damosell, and how he came to the duke of the South Marches.

NOW returne we unto sir Marhaus, that rode with the damosell of thirtie winters of age southward; and so they came into a deepe forrest, and by fortune they were nighted, and rode long in a deepe way, and at the last they came unto a courtlage, and there they demanded harbour.[1] But the man of the courtlage would not harbour them for no treating that they could treat, but thus much the good man said: "And ye wil tak the adventure of your lodging, I shall bring you there yee shall bee lodged." "What adventure is that, that I shall have for my lodging?" said sir Marhaus. "Yee shall wit when yee come there," said the good man. "What adventure so ever it bee, I require thee bring me thither," said sir Marhaus, "for I am weary, and my damosel, and my horse." So the good man went and opened the gate, and within an houre he brought him unto a faire castle. And then the poore man called the porter, and anon he was let into the castle, and forthwith hee shewed to the lord how hee

[1] *Harbour.*—i. e. a lodging. A *courtelage* was properly a courtyard, or the inclosure of a house.

had brought him a knight erraunt and a damosell that would bee lodged with him. "Let him come in," said the lord, "it may happen that they shall repent that they tooke their lodging here in this castle." So sir Marhaus was let in with torch light, and there was a goodly sight of young men that welcommed him. And then his horse was led into the stable, and he and his damosell were brought into the hall, and there stood a mightie duke and many goodly men about him. Then this lord asked him how he hight, and from whence he came, and with what man hee dwelled. "Sir," said he, "I am a knight of king Arthurs, and knight of the table round, and my name is sir Marhaus, and I am borne in Ireland." And then said the duke unto him, "That me sore repenteth, and the cause is this. I love not thy lord, nor none of all thy fellowes that be of the table round, and therfore ease thy selfe this night as well as thou mayest, for to morrow I and my sixe sonnes shall match with thee, if God will." "Is there none other remedy, but that I must have adoe with you and your sixe sonnes at once?" said sir Marhaus. "No," said the duke, "for this cause I made mine avow. Sir Gawaine slew my seaven sonnes in an encounter, and therefore I made mine avow, that there should never no knight of king Arthurs court lodge with me, or come there as I might have adoe with him, but that I should revenge the death of my seven sonnes." "Sir, I require you," said sir Marhaus, "that ye will tell me, if it please you, what your name is?" "Wit ye will that I am the duke of the Southmarches." "Ah," said sir Marhaus, "I have heard say that ye have beene a long time a great foe unto my lord king Arthur, and to his knights." "That shall ye feele to morrow," said the duke. "Shall I have adoe with you?" said sir Marhaus. "Yea," said the duke, "thereof thou shalt not choose, therefore take thee to thy chamber, where thou shalt have all that to thee belongeth." So sir Marhaus departed, and was led to a chamber, and his damosell was also led to her chamber.

KING ARTHUR. 161

And on the morrow the duke sent to sir Marhaus, that he should make him ready. And so sir Marhaus arose, and armed him, and then there was a masse sung afore him, and after brake his fast, and so mounted on horsebacke in the court of the castle where they should doe the battaile. So there was the duke all ready on horsebacke cleane armed, and his sixe sonnes by him, and every each had a speare in his hand, and so they encountred, whereas the duke and two of his sonnes brake their speares upon him, but sir Marhaus held up his speare, and touched none of them.

CHAP. LXXXIV.—How sir Marhaus fought with the duke and his sixe sonnes, and made them to yeeld them.

THEN came the foure sonnes of the duke by couples, and two of them brake their speares, and so did the other two. And all this while sir Marhaus did not touch them. Then sir Marhaus ranne to the duke, and so smote him with his speare, that horse and man fell to the earth, and so he served his sonnes. And then sir Marhaus alighted downe, and bad the duke yeeld him or else he would sley him. And then some of his sonnes recovered, and would have set upon sir Marhaus. Then said sir Marhaus to the duke, "Sease thy sonnes, or else I will doe the uttermost to you all." Then when the duke saw he might not escape death, hee cried to his sonnes, and charged them to yeeld them unto sir Marhaus. And they kneeled all downe, and put the pomels of their swords unto sir Marhaus, and he received them. And then they holpe their father; and there by a common assent promised unto sir Marhaus never to be foes unto king Arthur, and thereupon, at Penticost[1] after, he to come and his sixe sonnes and put them in the kings

[1] *Penticost.*—Caxton's text says, *Whytsontyde.*

grace. Then sir Marhaus departed, and within two daies his damosell brought him where as was a great turnament that the lady de Vause had cried, and who that did best should have a rich serklet of gold worth a thousand besaunts.[1] And there sir Marhaus did so nobly that hee was renowned to have smitten downe fortie knights, and so the serklet of gold was rewarded him. Then he departed from thence with great worship. And within seven dayes after, the damosell brought him to an earles place, whose name was called Fergus, which after was sir Tristrams knight. And this earle was but a young man and late come to his lands, and there was a giant fast by him that hight Taulurd, and he had a brother in Cornewaile that hight Taulas, that sir Tristram slew when he was out of his minde. So this earle made his complaint unto sir Marhaus, that there was a giant by him that destroyed all his lands, and how he durst no where ride nor goe for him. "Sir," said sir Marhaus, "useth he to fight on horsebacke or on foote?" "Nay," said the earle, "there may no horse beare him, he is so great." "Well," said sir Marhaus, "then will I fight with him on foote." So on the morrow sir Marhaus prayed the earle that one of his men might bring him where as the giant was, and so he was ware of him, for he saw him sit under an holy tree, and many clubbes of iron and gisarmes[2] about him. So sir Marhaus dressed him to the giant, putting his shield afore him, and the giant stert to a club of iron, and came against sir Marhaus as fast as he might drive; and at the first strooke he clave sir Marhaus shield all to peeces, and light on a stone and frushed[3] it into the earth, and there he was in great perill, for the giant was a wilely fighter; but at the last sir Marhaus smote

[1] *Besaunts.*—A gold coin, named from Byzantium, or Constantinople, of which it is understood to have been the coinage. Its value varied at different times.

[2] *Gisarmes.*—The gisarme was a sort of bill or battle-axe.

[3] *Frushed.*—Bruised or crushed. This incident of the stone is not found in Caxton.

KING ARTHUR.   163

off his right arme above the elbow. Then the giant fled, and the knight after him, and so hee drove him to a water; but the giant was so hie that he could not wade after him; and then sir Marhaus made the earle Fergus man to fetch stones, and with those stones he gave the giant many a sore knock, till at the last he made him to fall downe in the water, and so was he there drowned. Then sir Marhaus went to the giants castle, and there he delivered out of the giants prison twentie foure ladies, and twentie two[1] knights, and ther he had riches without number; so that all the dayes of his life he was never poore man after. Then he returned to the earle Fergus, which greatly thanked him, and would have given him halfe his lands, but he would take none. So sir Marhaus dwelled with the earle nigh halfe a yeere, for he was sore bruised with the giant, and at the last he tooke his leave. And as he rode by the way, he met with sir Gawaine and sir Ewaine; and so by adventure he met with foure knights of king Arthurs court, the first was sir Sagramore le Desirous, sir Osanna, sir Dodinas le Savage, and sir Felot of Listinoyse; and there sir Marhaus with one speare smote downe these foure knights, and hurt them sore. So hee departed, and met at his day afore set.

CHAP. LXXXV.—How sir Ewaine rode with the damosell of threescore yeeres of age, and how he gate the prise at a turney.

NOW turne we unto Ewaine, which rode westward with his damosell of threscore winters of age, and she brought him there as was a turneyment nigh the march of Wales. And at that turneyment sir Ewaine smote downe thirtie knights, wherfore the price was given him, and the price was a jerfawcon[2] and a white steede trapped with cloth of gold.

[1] *Twentie two.—Twelve*, Caxton.
[2] *Jerfawcon.*—The gerfalcon was the finest kind of hawk, procured chiefly from the north, but also, I believe, from Wales, and much prized.

So then sir Ewaine did many strange adventures by the meanes of the old damosell that went with him; and so she brought him unto a lady that was called the lady of the roche, which was a full curteous lady. So there were in that countrey two knights that were brethren, and they were called two perilous knights, the one hight sir Edward of the reed castle,[1] and the other hight sir Hue of the reed castle. And these two brethren had disherited the lady of the roch of a baroney of lands, by their extortion. And as sir Ewaine lodged with this lady, she made her complaint unto him of these two knights. "Madam," said sir Ewaine, " they are too blame,[2] for they doe against the high order of knighthood and the oath that they have made, and if it like you I will speake with them, because I am a knight of king Arthurs, and I will entreate them with fairenesse, and if they will not, I shall doe battaile with them in the defence of your right." "Gramercie," said the lady, " and there as I may not acquite you, God shall." So on the morrow, the two knights were sent for that they should come thither to speake with the lady of the roch. And wit it well, they failed not, for they cam with an hundred horses. But when the lady saw them in this maner so many, she would not suffer sir Ewaine to goe out unto them, neither upon suretie nor for faire language, but she made him to speake with them out of a towre. But finally these two brethren would not be entreated, and answered that they would keep that they had. "Wel," said sir Ewaine, " then wil I fight with one of you both, and prove upon your bodies that yee doe wrong and extortion unto this lady." "That will we not doe," said the two brethren. " For and we doe battaile, we two will fight with one knight at once; and therefore if ye will fight so, we will be ready at what houre

---

[1] *Reed castle.*—The red castle was Powis castle, still called in the Welsh language, " castle-coch," which has the same signification.

[2] *Too blame.*—On this phrase, see Nares's Glossary, under the word *blame.*

ye will assigne us. And if that yee winne us in plaine battaile, then the lady shall have her lands againe." "Yee say well," said sir Ewaine, "therefore make you ready, so that ye be heere to morrow in the defence of the ladyes right."

CHAP. LXXXVI.—How sir Ewaine fought with two knights, and overcame them.

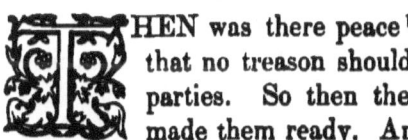HEN was there peace[1] made on both parties, that no treason should be wrought on neither parties. So then the knights departed, and made them ready. And that night sir Ewaine had great cheere. And on the morrow hee arose early, and heard masse, and brake his fast, and after rode unto the plaine without the gates, where hoved the two brethren biding him. Then rode they together passing sore, that sir Edward and sir Hue brake their speares upon sir Ewaine. And sir Ewaine smote sir Edward that he fell over his horse taile, and yet brake not his speare. And then hee spurred his horse and came upon sir Hue, and overthrew him; but they soone recovered and dressed their shields, and drew their swords, and bad sir Ewaine alight, and doe his battaile to the uttermost. Then sir Ewaine avoyded sodainely his horse, and put his shield afore him, and drew his sword, and so they dressed together, and either gave other great strookes. And there these two brethren wounded sir Ewaine passing sore, that the lady of the roche wend that he would have died. And thus fought they together five houres, as men enraged and without reason. And at the last sir Ewaine smote sir Edward upon the helme such a buffet that his sword karved him unto his canel bone,[2] and then sir Hue abated his courage. But sir Ewaine pressed

---

[1] *Peace.*—Caxton has *sykernesse*, i. e. surety.
[2] *Cunel bone.*—The collar-bone.

fast to have slaine him. And when sir Hue saw that, he kneeled downe and yeelded him unto sir Ewaine. And he of his gentlenesse received his sword, and tooke him by the hand, and went into the castle together. Then the lady of the roch was passing glad, and sir Hue made great mone for his brothers death. Then the lady was restored unto her lands, and sir Hue was commanded to be at the court of king Arthur at the next feast of Penticost. So sir Ewaine dwelled with the lady nigh halfe a yeare, for it was long or he might be whole of his great hurts. And then when it drew nigh the terme day that sir Gawaine should meete at the crosse way, then every knight drew him thither to hold his promise that they had made. And sir Marhaus and sir Ewaine brought their damosels with them; but sir Gawaine had lost his damosell, as it is afore rehearsed.

CHAP. LXXXVII.—How, at the yeares end, all the three knights with their three damosels met at the fountaine.

AND right at the twelve monethes end, they met all three knights at the fountaine, and their damosels. But the damosell that sir Gawaine had with him could say but little worship of him. So they departed from the damosels, and rode through a great forrest, and there they met with a messenger that came from king Arthur, which had sought them wel nigh a twelve moneth throughout all England, Wales, and Scotland, and was charged if that he might finde sir Gawaine and sir Ewaine, to bring them unto the court againe. And then were they all glad; and so they praied sir Marhaus to ride with them unto king Arthurs court. And so within twelve dayes they came to Camelot, and the king was passing glad of their comming, and so were al they of the court. Then king Arthur made them to sweare upon a booke, to tell him all their adventures that there had beene fallen them all the twelve monethes, and so they did. And there was sir Marhaus well knowen ; for there were knights that he had matched afore time, and hee was named one of the best knights then living. Against the feast of Penticost, came the damosell of the lake, and brought with her sir Pelleas. And at that high feast there was a great justing of knights, and, of all the knights that were at that justing, sir Pelleas had the prize, and sir Marhaus was named the next. But sir Pelleas was so strong, that there might but a few knights hit him a buffet with a speare. And at that feast sir Pelleas and sir Marhaus were made knights of the table round, for there were two sieges voide, for two knights had beene slaine in those twelve monethes ; and great joy had king Arthur of sir Pelleas and of sir Marhaus. But sir Pelleas loved never after sir Gawaine, but that he spared him for the love of king Arthur. But oftentimes, at the justs and turneyments, sir Pelleas quited sir Gawaine, for so it is rehearsed in the French booke. So sir Tristram[1] many dayes after that fought with sir Marhaus in an iland, and there they did a great battaile, but at the last sir Tristram slew him, and sir Tristram was sore wounded, that unneth hee might recover, and lay at a nunry halfe a yeare. And sir Pelleas was a worshipfull knight, and was one of the foure that atchieved the sancgreall. And the damosell of the lake made by her meanes that never he had adoe with sir Lancelot du Lake, for where as sir Lancelot was at any justs or turneyment, shee would not suffer him to bee there at that day, but if it were on sir Lancelots side.

[1] *Sir Tristram.*—The adventures of this celebrated hero will be found in a later part of this work.

CHAP. LXXXVIII.—How twelve aged men, embassadours of Rome, come to king Arthur for to demaund truage for the realme of Brittaine.[1]

WHEN king Arthur had rested a while after long war, and held a royall feast and table round, with his alies of kings, and princes, and noble knights, all of the round table, there came into his hall, he sitting in his throne royal, twelve ancient men, bearing each of them a branch of olive, in token they came as embassadours and messengers from the emperour Lucius,[2] which was called at that time dictatour or procuror of the publicke weale of Rome; which said messengers, after their entring and comming into the presence of king Arthur, did unto him their obeysance in making to him reverence, and said to him in this wise: "The high and mighty emperour Lucius sendeth unto thee, king of Brittaine, greeting, commanding thee to knowledge him for thy lord, and to send him the truage[3] due of this realme unto the empire, which thy father and other tofore thy predecessors have payed as it is of record, and thou as a rebell not knowing him as thy soveraigne withholdest and retainest, contrary to the statutes and decrees made by the noble Julius Cesar, conquerour of this realme and first emperour of Rome. And if thou refuse his demand and commandement, know thou for a certaine that he shal make strong warre against thee and thy realmes and lands, and shal chastise thee and thy subjects, that it shall bee an ensample perpetuall unto all kings and princes for to denie their tru-

---

[1] Here the romance returns to the narrative of Geoffrey of Monmouth, who (lib. ix, c. 15) describes the Roman embassy, and, in the chapters following, the war which arose out of it. It may be remarked that our romance omits entirely the pretended conquest of Gaul by king Arthur, which is related in Geoffrey of Monmouth, and is assumed in the following chapters of our romance.

[2] *Lucius.*—Geoffrey of Monmouth calls him Lucius Tiberius. Of course he is an imaginary emperor.

[3] *Truage.*—Fealty.

age unto that noble empire which dominereth[1] upon the universall world." Then when they had shewed the effect of their message, the king commanded them to withdraw them, and said hee should take advise of counsaile, and give to them an answere. Then some of the young knights, hearing their message, would have set upon them for to have slaine them, saying that it was a rebuke unto al the knights there being present to suffer them to say so to the king. Anon the king commanded that none of them upon paine of death to missay[2] them, ne doe to them any harme, and commanded a knight to bring them to their lodging, "and see that they have all that is necessary and requisite for them with the best cheere, and that no daintie be spared; for the Romaines beene great lords, and, though their message please me not, nor my court, yet I must remember mine honour." After this the king let call all his lords and knights of the round table to counsaile upon this matter, and desired them for to say their advise. Then sir Cador of Cornewaile spake first, and said, " Sir, this message liketh mee well, for wee have many dayes rested us, and have been idle, and now I hope ye shal make sharpe war on the Romaines, where I doubt not but wee shal get honour." " I beleeve well," said king Arthur, " that this matter pleaseth thee well, but these answers may not be answered, for the demand grieveth me sore, for truely I will never pay no truage to Rome, wherefore I pray you to counsaile me. I understand that Belinus and Brenius,[3] knights of Brittaine, have had the empire in their hands many dayes; and also Constantine, the sonne of queene Helaine; which is an open evidence that we owe no tribute to Rome, but of right we that bee descended of them have right to claime the title of the empire."

[1] *Dominereth.—Domyneth*, Caxton.
[2] *Missay.*—To say amiss; to abuse.
[3] *Belinus and Brenius.*—The allusion to these worthies is taken directly from Geoffrey of Monmouth.

CHAP. LXXXIX.—How the kings and lords promised unto king Arthur ayde and helpe against the Romaines.

THEN answered king Anguish of Scotland, " Sir, ye ought of right to be above all other kings, for unto you is none like ne pareile in al christendome of knighthood ne of dignity, and I counsaile you never to obey the Romaines ; for, when they reigned on us, they distressed our elders, and put this land to great extortions and tallages,[1] wherefore I make heere mine avow to avenge me on them, and, for to strength your quarrell, I shall furnish twentie thousand good men of warre, and wage them on my costs, which shal awaite on you with my selfe when it shall please you." And the king of little Brittaine granted him to the same thirtie thousand, wherefore king Arthur thanked them. And then every man agreed to make warre, and to ayde after their power; that is to wit, the lord of Westwales promised to bring thirtie thousand men, and sir Ewaine, sir Idres sonne, with their cosins, thirtie thousand men. Then sir Lancelot with al other in like wise promised every man a great multitude. And when king Arthur understood their courage and good will, he thanked them heartily, and after he let cal the embassadours that they should heare their answer. And in presence of all his noble lords and knights he said to them in this wise : " I will that yee returne unto your lord and procurour for the common weale for the Romaines, and say to him, of his demand and commandement I set nothing, and that I know of no truage ne tribute that I owe to him ne to none earthly creature nor prince christian nor heathen, but I pretend[2] to have and occupie the soveraintie of the empire, wherein I am entituled by the right of my predecessours, sometime kings of this land. And say to him that I am delivered[3] and fully concluded to goe with mine army

---

[1] *Tallages.*—Taxes. In French, *taillages.* [2] *Pretend.*—Claim.
[3] *Delivered.*—Resolved, deliberated.

with strength and power to Rome, by the grace of God to take possession in the empire, and subdue them that bee rebells; wherefore I command him and al them of Rome that incontinent they make to me their homage, and to knowledge me for their emperour and governour upon paine that shal ensue." And then he commanded his treasurer to give them great and large gifts, and to pay all their expences, and assigned sir Cador to convey them out of the land. And so they tooke their leave and departed for to goe toward their lord, and tooke their shipping at Sandwich, and passed foorth by Flaunders, Almaine,[1] the mountaines, and all Italy, untill they came to Lucius. And after the reverence made, they made relation of their answere, like as tofore ye have heard. When the emperour Lucius had well heard and understood their credence, hee was sore mooved as he had beene all enraged, and said: " I had supposed that Arthur would have obeyed my commandement, and have served me himselfe as him well beseemed or any other king so to doe." " O, sir," said one of the senatours, " let be such vaine words, for we doe you to wit that I and my fellowes were full sore afeard to behold his cheere and countenance; I feare me that yee have made a rod for your selfe, for hee intendeth to bee lord of this empire, which sore is to be doubted if he come, for he is an other maner of man than yee wist, and holdeth the most noble court of the world, all other kings nor princes may not compare unto his noble maintenance. On newyeares day we saw him in his great estate, which was the royallest that ever wee saw in our dayes, for he was served at the table with nine kings, and the noblest fellowship of other princes, lords, and knights that bee in all the world, and every knight approved and like a lord, and holdeth table round; and in his person the most manly man that liveth, and he is like to conquere al the world, for unto his courage it is all too little. Wherefore I advise you to keepe well your marches and

[1] *Almaine.*—Germany.

wayes in the mountaines, for certainely he is a lord to be redoubted." "Well," said Lucius, "before Easter I suppose to passe the mountaines, and so into France, and there bereave him of his lands with Genewayes[1] and other mighty warriours of Tuskaine and Lumberdy. And I shall send for all them that bee subject and alied to the empire of Rome to come unto mine ayde." And foorthwith sent old wise knights to these countries following: first to Ambage and Arrage, to Alexandrie, to Inde, to Hermony, where as the river of Euphrates runneth into Asie, to Affrike, and Europe, to Ertaine, and to Elamy, to Araby, to Egypt, and to Damaske, to Damiet, and to Cayer, to Capadoce, and to Tarce, to Turky, Pounce, and Pampoille, to Surry and Galacy. All these were subject to Rome, and many moe, as Greece, Cypres, and Macydone, Calabre, Cateland, Portingale, with many a thousand of Spaniards. Then all these kings, dukes, and admiralls assembled about Rome, with sixteene kings at once, with a wondrous great multitude of people. When the emperour understood their comming, hee made ready his Romaines and al the people betwen him and Flanders; and also he had gotten with him fiftie gyants, which had beene engendred of fiends, and they were ordained to keepe and garde his person, and to break the front of the battail of king Arthur. And thus he departed from Rome, and came downe the mountaines of Savoy for to destroy the lands that king Arthur had conquered, and came to Colaine[2] and besieged a castle thereby, and won it soone, and stuffed it well with two hundred Sarasins and infidels; and after destroyed many faire countries, which king Arthur had won of king Claudas. And thus Lucius came with all his hoast, which were disperpled[3] three score miles in bredth, and commanded them to meete with him in Burgoine, for hee supposed to destroy the realme of little Brittaine.

[1] *Genewayes.*—Genoese.   [2] *Colaine.*—Cologne.
[3] *Disperpled.*—Spread out; distributed.

CHAP. XC.—How king Arthur held a parliament at Yorke, and how hee ordeined in what maner the realme should bee governed in his absence.

OW leave wee off Lucius the emperour, and speake we of king Arthur, which commanded all them of his retinue to be ready at the utas[1] of Saint Hilary for to hold a parliament at Yorke. And at that parliament was concluded that all the navie of the land should bee arested,[2] and to bee ready within fifteene dayes at Sandwich, and there shewed hee unto all his army how he purposed to conquer the empire, which he ought to have of right. And there he ordeined two governours of the realme, that is to say, sir Bawdewaine of Brittaine for to counsaile to the best, and sir Constantine, sonne to sir Cador of Cornewaile, which after the death of king Arthur was king of this realme.[3] And in the presence of all his lords hee resigned the rule of the realme and Guenever his queene unto them; wherefore sir Launcelot was wroth, for he left sir Tristram with king Marke for the love of La beale Isoude. Then queene Guenever made great sorrow and lamentation for the departing of her lord and other, and swoned in such wise that the ladies bare her in her chamber. Thus the king with his great army departed, leaving the queene and the realme in the governance of sir Bawdewaine and sir Constantine. And when he was on his horse he said, with an hie voice, " If I die in that journey, I will that sir Constantine be mine heire and king crowned of this realme as next of my blood." And after departed and entred into the sea at Sandwich with all his army, with a great multitude of ships, gallies, cogges, and dromons,[4] sailing on the sea.

[1] *Utas.*—The octaves.

[2] *Arested.*—Alluding to the custom of the Middle Ages, when, in time of war, the shipping of the various seaports were seized temporarily for shipping the king's troops, or for other purposes of war.

[3] *King of this realme.*—According to Geoffrey of Monmouth, this Constantine was, as here stated, Arthur's immediate successor.

[4] *Cogges and dromons.*—The cog was a small vessel; the dromon, or dromond, was, on the contrary, a large ship of war.

CHAP XCI.—How king Arthur, being shipped and lying in his cabin, had a marvailous dreame, and of the exposition thereof.

AND as the king lay in his cabin in the ship, he fell into a slumbering sleepe, and dreamed a mervailous dreame; him seemed that a dreadful dragon devoured much of his people, and he came flying out of the west, and his head was enameled with azure, and his shoulders shined as gold, his belly like mailes of a mervailous hew, and his taile was full of tatters, his feete were full of fine sables, and his clawes like fine gold, and a hidious flame of fire flew out of his mouth, like as the land and water had flamed all on fire. After, him seemed that there came out of the orient a grimly bore all black in a cloud, and his pawes as big as a post; he was ruged looking roughly, he was the foulest beast that ever man saw; hee roared and romed[1] so hidiously that it was marveile to heare. Then the dreadful dragon advanced him and came in the winde like a faulcon, giving great strookes to the bore, and the bore hit him again with his grisly tuskes that his brest was all bloody, and that the hot blood made al the sea red of his blood. Then the dragon flew away all on an height, and came downe with such a might and smoote the boore on the ridge,[2] which was ten foote large from the head to the taile, and smote the boore all to powder, both flesh and bones, that it flittered all abroad on the sea. And therewith the king awoke, and was sore abashed of this dreame, and sent anon for a wise phylosopher, commanding him to tell him the signification of his dreame. "Sir," said the phylosopher, "the dragon that ye dreamed of betokeneth your owne person which saileth here, and the coulours of his wings be your realmes which yee have won, and his taile which is al to-tattered signifieth the noble knights of the round table; and the bore that the dragon

---

[1] *Romed.*—Growled.   [2] *Ridge.*—Back.

KING ARTHUR. 175

slew comming from the clouds betokeneth some tyrant that tormenteth the people, or else ye are like to fight with some gyant your selfe, being right horrible and abominable, whose peere ye saw never in your dayes; wherefore of this dreadfull dreame doubt nothing, but as a conquerer comfort your selfe." Then soone after this they had sight of land, and sayled till they arrived at Bireflet¹ in Flaunders; and when they were there, he found many of his great lords ready as they had beene commanded to waite upon him.

CHAP. XCII.—How a man of the countrey told him of a mervailous gyant,² and how he fought and conquered him.

THEN came to him an husbandman of the countrey, and told him how there was in the countrey of Constantine, beside Brittaine, a great gyant, which had slaine, murthered, and devoured much people of the countrey, and had beene sustained seaven yeares with the children of the commons of that land, " in so much that all the children be all slaine and destroyed ; and now late he hath taken the duchesse of Brittaine as she rode with her men, and had led her to his lodging which is in a mountaine, for to ravish her and lye by her to her lives end, and many people followed her, more then five hundred; but all they might not rescew her, but they left her shriking and crying lamentably, wherefore I suppose that hee hath slaine her in fullfiling his foule lust of lechery ; she was wife unto your cosin sir Howel, the which was full nigh of your blood. Now as ye are a rightfull king, have pittie on this lady, and revenge us all, as ye are a valiant

¹ *Bireflet.—Barflete*, Caxton.
² *A mervailous gyant.*—The fate of Helen of Britany, and Arthur's combat with the giant, are taken from Geoffrey of Monmouth, lib. x. c. 3. This legend appears to have been connected with Mount St. Michel in Normandy from an early period; and the supposed site of the adventure, formerly known by the name of Tombeleyne, was afterwards occupied by the church and monastery.

conquerer." "Alas!" said king Arthur, "this is a great mischiefe; I had rather then the best realme that I have that I had beene a furlong before him for to have rescewed that lady. Now, fellow," said king Arthur, "canst thou bring me there where as this gyant haunteth?" "Yea, sir," said the good man, "loe yonder wher as ye see the two great fires, there shall ye not faile to find him, and more treasure, as I suppose, then is in all the realme of Fraunce." When king Arthur had understood this pitious case, he returned into his tent, and called unto him sir Kay and sir Bedivere, and commanded them secretly to make ready horse and harneis for himselfe and for them twaine, for after evensong hee would ride on pilgrimage with them two onely, unto Saint Mighels mount.[1] And then anon they made them ready, and armed them at all points, and tooke their horses and their shields, and so they three departed thence, and rode forth as fast as they might till they came unto the furlong[2] of that mount, and there they alighted, and the king commanded them to tarry there, and said hee would himselfe goe up to that mount.

And so he ascended up the mount till hee came to a great fire, and there found hee a carefull[3] widow wringing her hands and making great sorrow, sitting by a grave new made. And then king Arthur saluted her, and demanded her wherefore she made such lamentation. Unto whom shee answered and said: "Sir knight, speake soft, for yonder is a divell, if he heare thee speake, he will come and destroy thee; I hold thee unhappy; what doest thou heare in this mountaine? for if yee were such fiftie as yee be, yee were not able to make resistance against this divel. Here lyeth

---

[1] *Saint Mighels mount.*—It is hardly necessary to state that Mount St. Michel of Normandy was, at a later period, a very celebrated object of pilgrimage; but our romance-writer is guilty of a great anachronism in making king Arthur go thither for that purpose.

[2] *Furlong.*—*Forbond of that mount*, Caxton. *Forbond* means, probably, the extreme boundary.

[3] *Carefull.*—Full of care; sorrowful.

a duchesse dead, which was the fairest lady of the world, wife unto sir Howell of Brittaine, he hath murthered her in forcing her, and hath slit her unto the navell." "Dame," said the king, " I come from the great conquerour king Arthur for to treat with that tyrant for his lyege people." " Fie upon such treties," said the widow, "hee setteth nought by the king, nor by no man else. But and if thou have brought king Arthurs wife, dame Guenever, he shal be gladder then if thou hadst given him halfe France. Beware, approach him not too nigh, for hee hath overcome and vanquished fifteene kings, and hath made him a coate full of precious stones, embrodred with their beards, which they sent him to have his love for salvation of their people this last Christmas, and if thou wilt speak with him, at yonder great fire he is at supper." "Wel," said king Arthur, "I wil accomplish my message for all your fearefull words;" and went forth by the creast of that hill, and saw wher he sate at supper, gnawing on a limbe of a man, beking[1] his broad limbes by the fire, and brichlesse, and three damosels turning three broches whereon was broached twelve young children late borne, like young birds. When king Arthur beheld that pitious sight, he had great compassion on them, so that his heart bled for sorrow, and hailed him, saying in this wise : " Hee that al the world weldeth, give thee short life and shameful death, and the divell have thy soule ! Why hast thou murthered these young innocent children, and this duchesse ? therefore arise and dresse thee, thou glutton ; for this day thou shalt die of my hands." Then anon the gyant start up, and took a great club in his hand, and smote at the king that his coronall fell to the earth. And king Arthur hit him againe that hee carved his belly and cut off his genitours, that his guts and entrailes fell downe to the ground. Then the gyant with great anguish threw away his club of iron, and caught the king in his armes that hee crushed his ribs. Then the thre damosels

---

[1] *Beking.*—Warming himself; basking.

kneeled downe and called unto our Lord Jesus Christ for helpe and comfort of the noble king Arthur. And then king Arthur weltred[1] and wrong that he was one while under and other while above. And so weltering and wallowing they roled downe the hill, till they came to the sea marke, and as they so tumbled and weltred, king Arthur smot him with his dagger; and it fortuned they came unto the place where as the two knights were that kept king Arthurs horse. Then when they saw the king fast in the gyants armes, they came and loosed him; and then king Arthur commanded sir Kay "to smite off the giants head, and to set it upon a truncheon of a speare, and beare it to sir Howell, and tel him that his enemy is slaine; and after let his head be bound to a barbican, that all the people may see and behold it; and goe ye two to the mountaine and fetch me my shield and my sword, and also the great club of iron, and as for the treasure take it to you, for yee shall find there goods without number, so that I have his kirtell and the club, I desire no more. This was the fiercest giant that ever I met with, save one in the mount of Araby which I overcame, but this was greater and fiercer." Then the knights fetched the club and the kirtell, and some of the treasure they tooke unto themselves, and returned againe to the hoost. And anon this was knowen through all the countrey, wherefore the people came and thanked the king; and hee said againe, "Give the thankes to God, and part the goods among you." And after that, king Arthur commanded his cosin Howell that he should ordeine for a church to bee builded upon the same hill, in the worship of Saint Mighell. And on the morrow after, the noble king Arthur removed with his great hoast, and came into the countrey of Champaine in a valey, and there they pight their pavilions. And the king being set at his dinner, there came in two messengers, of whom the one was marshal of France, and said to the king that the emperour was entred into

---

[1] *Weltred.*—Rolled about.

KING ARTHUR. 179

France, and had destroyed a great part thereof, and was in Burgoine, and had destroyed and made a great slaughter of people, and burned townes and burrowes, " wherefore if thou come not hastily they must yeeld up their bodies and goods."

CHAP. XCIII.—How king Arthur sent sir Gawaine and others to Lucius the emperour, and how they were assailed, and escaped with worship.

HEN king Arthur did cal sir Gawaine, sir Bors, sir Lionel, and sir Bedivere, and commanded them to goe straight to Lucius the emperour, " and say to him that hastely he remove out of my land. And if he will not, bid him make him ready to battaile, and not distresse the poore people." Then anon these noble knights dressed them on horsebacke, and when they came to the greene wood they saw pight in a meddow many pavilions of silke and divers coulours beside a river, and the emperours pavilion was in the middle with an eagle displayed above, toward which pavilion our knights rode, and ordained sir Gawaine and sir Bors to doe the message, and left in ambushment sir Lionell and sir Bedivere. And then sir Gawaine and sir Bors did their message, and commanded Lucius in king Arthurs name to avoide his land, or else shortly to dresse him to battaile. To whom Lucius answered and said, " Ye shall returne to your lord and say to him that I shal subdue him and all his lands." Then sir Gawaine was sore angred, and said, " I had rather then all France I might fight against thee." " And so had I," said sir Bors, " rather then all Brittaine or Burgoine." Then a knight named sir Gainus, nigh cosin to the emperour, said " Loe how these Britons bee full of pride and boast, and they brag as though they bare up all the world." Then was sir Gawaine sore agrieved with these words, and drew out his sword and smote off sir Gainus head, and

anon therewith turned their horses and rode over waters and through woods till they came to their ambushment, wheras sir Lionell and sir Bedivere were hoving. The Romaines followed fast after on horsebacke and on foote, over a champaine unto a wood, and then sir Bors turned his horse and saw a knight come fast on, whom he smote through the body with a speare, that hee fell downe starke dead on the ground. Then came there Caliburc,[1] one of the strongest of Pavy, and smote downe many of king Arthurs knights. And when sir Bors saw him doe so much harme, he dressed him toward him, and smote him through the brest, that he fell downe dead to the ground. Then sir Feldenak thought to revenge the death of Gainus upon sir Gawaine, but sir Gawaine was anon ware thereof, and smote him on the head, which strooke stinted not untill it came to his brest. And then he returned and came unto his fellowes in the ambushment, and there was an encounter, for the ambushment brake on the Romaines, and slew and hewed downeright the Romaines, and forced the Romaines to returne and flee; whom our noble knights did chase unto their tents. Then the Romaines gathered more people, and also foote men came on, and there was a new battaile and so much people that sir Bors and sir Berel were taken. But when sir Gawaine saw that, hee tooke with him sir Idrus the good knight, and said he would never se king Arthur but if he rescewed them, and drew out Galatine[2] his good sword, and followed them that led those two knights away with them, and he smote him that led sir Bors, and tooke sir Bors from him and delivered him unto his fellowes. And sir Idrus in like wise rescewed sir Berell. Then began the battaile to be passing great, and our knights were in great jeopardy, wherefore sir Gawaine sent for succour unto king

[1] *Calibure.—Callyburne*, Caxton.
[2] *Galatine.*—The sword of Gawaine was celebrated in mediæval romance. A curious extract from a MS. printed in the notes to Fr. Michel's Tristan, vol. ii. p. 181, says it was made by the mythic smith Weland.

Arthur, and that he hye him, " for I am sore wounded and hurt, and that our prisoners must pay good[1] out of number." And the messenger came unto the king and shewed him the message. And anon the king did assemble his armie; but anon or hee departed, the prisoners were come, and sir Gawaine and his fellowes gate the field and put the Romaines to flight, and after returned and came with their fellowship in such wise that no man of worship was lost of them, save that sir Gawaine was sore hurt. Then the king did ransake his woundes, and comforted him. And thus was the beginning of the first journey of the Britons and the Romaines. And there were slaine of the Romaines part moe then ten thousand, and great joy and mirth was made that same night in the hoast of king Arthur. And on the morrow after, he sent all the prisoners into Paris, under the gard of sir Lancelot and sir Cador, with many other knights.

CHAP. XCIV.—How Lucius sent certaine spies into ambush for to have taken his knights, being prisoners, and how they were letted.

NOW turne wee to the emperour of Rome, which espied that these prisoners should be sent to Paris, and anon he sent to lye in ambush certaine knights and princes with threescore thousand men for to rescew his knights and lords that were prisoners. And so on the morrow as sir Lancelot and sir Cador, chiefetaines and governours of all them that conveied the prisoners, as they would passe through a wood, sir Lancelot sent certaine knights to espie if any were in the wood to let them. And when the said knights came into the wood, anon they espied and saw the great ambushment, and returned and told sir Lancelot that there lay in waite threescore thousand Romaines. And then sir

[1] *Pay good.*—i. e. pay heavy ransoms.

Lancelot with such knights as hee had and men of warre to the number of ten thousand, put them in goodly array, and went and met with them, and fought with them manfully, and slew and detrenched[1] many of the Romans, and slew many knights and admiralls.[2] Of the Romaines and Sarasins partie there was slaine the king of Lyly and three great lords, Aladuke, Herawd, and Heringdale. But sir Lancelot[3] fought so nobly that no man might endure a strooke of his hand, but whersoever he came he shewed his prowesse and his might, for he slew downe right on every side, and the Romaines and Sarasins fled from him as the sheepe from the wolfe, or from the lion, and put them all to flight that abode alive. And so long they fought that tydings came unto king Arthur, and anon bee apparraled him and came to the battail, and saw how his knights had vanquished the battaile; bee embraced them knight by knight in his armes, and said, "Yee be worthy to weld all your honour and worship; there was never no king that had so noble knights as I have." "Sir," said sir Cador, "there was none of us that failed other, but of the prowesse and manhood of sir Lancelot were more then wonder to tell, and also of his cosins which did this day many noble feates of warre." And also sir Cador told who of his knights were slaine, as sir Berell and other, sir Moris and sir Maurell, two good knights. Then the king wept and dried his eyes with a handkercher, and said, "Your courage had neere hand destroyed you, for though yee had returned againe, yee had

---

[1] *Detrenched.*—Cut up; cut to pieces.
[2] *Admiralls.*—This word is not here taken in its modern sense, but means an emir or Saracen chief.
[3] *Sir Lancelot.*—Lancelot was one of the most celebrated of the heroes of this cycle of romances, and was the subject of several separate poems and romances. He is represented as the son of king Ban of Britany; and on the death of his father was carried away, then an infant, by the lady of the lake, who fostered him. Hence he was called Lancelot du Lac. Many of sir Lancelot's adventures are related in the sequel of the present romance.

lost no worship, for I call it folly, knights to abide when they bee overmatched." "Nay," said sir Lancelot and the other, "for once shamed may never bee recovered."

CHAP. XCV.—How a senatour told to the emperour Lucius of their discomfiture, and also of the great battaile betweene king Arthur and Lucius.

NOW leave wee off the noble king Arthur and his noble knights, which had won the field, and had brought their prisoners to Paris, and speake we of a senatour that escaped from the battaile, and came to the emperour Lucius, and said to him, "Sir emperour, I advise thee to withdraw thee; what doest thou heere? thou shalt win nothing in these marches but great strookes out of measure, for this day one of king Arthurs knights was worth in the battaile an hundred of ours." "Fie on thee," said Lucius, "thou speakest cowardly; thy words grieve me more then all the losse that I have had this day." Then anon he sent foorth a king that hight sir Liomy, with a great army, and bad him hye him fast afore, and he would hastily follow after. Then was king Arthur privily warned, and sent his people to Soissons,[1] and tooke up the townes and castles from the Romaines. Then king Arthur commanded sir Cador to take the rereward, and to take with him certaine knights of the round table; "and sir Lancelot, sir Bors, and sir Key, sir Maroke, with sir Marhaus, shall waite on our person." Thus the noble king Arthur disperpled his hoast into divers parts, to the end that his enemies should not escape. When the emperour was entred into the vale of Soissons, he might see where king Arthur was embatailed and his banners displaied, and saw that he was beset round about with his enemies, that needs he must fight or yeeld him, for he might not flee, but said openly to the Romaines, "Sirs, I admonish

[1] *Soissons.*—*Sessoyne*, Caxton.

you that this day yee fight and acquite you as men, and remember how Rome dominereth and is chiefe and head over all the earth and universall world, and suffer not these Britons this day to abide against us." And hee therwith commanded his trumpets blow the bloody sounds, in such wise that the ground trembled and dindled.[1] Then the battaile approached, and shove and shouted on both sides, and great strooks wer smitten on both sides, many men were overthrowne, hurt, and slaine; and great valiances, prowesses, and feates of warre were that day shewed, which were over long to recount the noble feates of every man, for they should comprehend a whole volume; but in especiall of them king Arthur rode into the battaile, exhorting his knights to doe well. And he himself did as nobly with his hands as it were possible a man to doe; he drew out Excalibur, his good sword, and awaited ever where the Romaines were thickest and most grieved his people, anon hee dressed him on that part and hew and slew downe right, and rescewed his people; and there he slew a great gyant named Galapas, which was a man of mervailous quantitie and hight; he shortned him and smote off both his legs by the knees, saying, "Now art thou better of a sise to deale with then thou were," and after smote off his head, and the body slew six Sarasins in the falling downe. There sir Gawaine fought nobly, and slew three admiralls in that battaile. And all the knights of the round table did full nobly. Thus the battaile endured long betweene king Arthur and Lucius the emperour. Lucius had on his side many Sarasins that were slaine. And thus the battaile was great, and oftentimes that one partie was at a foredele and anon at an afterdele,[2] which endured long. At the last king Arthur espied where Lucius fought and did wonder with his owne hands, and anon he rode to him, and either

---

[1] *Dindled.*—Tottered; shook.
[2] *Foredele, afterdele.*—*Foredele* meant advantage, and *afterdele* disadvantage.

smote other fiersly, and at the last Lucius smote king Arthur overthwart the visage and gave him a large wound ; and when king Arthur felt himself hurt, anon hee smote him againe with Excalibur that it cleft his head from the somet of his helm, and stinted not till it came beneath the brest. And then the emperour fell downe dead, and there ended he his life. Then when it was knowne that the emperour was slaine, anon all the Romaines with all their armie put them to flight. And king Arthur with al his knights followed the chase, and slew downe right all them that they might attaine. And thus was the victory given unto the noble conquerour king Arthur. And there were slaine on the part of Lucius, moe then an hundred thousand. And after king Arthur did ransake their dead bodies, and doe bury them that were slaine of his retinue, every man according to the estate and degree that he was of. And those that were hurt hee caused the surgions to search all their hurts and wounds, and commanded to spare no salves nor medicines till they were whole. Then the king rode straight to the place where the emperour Lucius lay dead, and with him hee found slaine the sowdan of Surrey, the king of Egypt, and the king of Ethiope, which were two noble kings, with seventeene other kings of divers other regions, and also threescore senatours of Rome, all noble men, whom the noble king Arthur did embaulme and gumme with many good aromatike gummes, and after hee did ceere them in threescore fold of ceered cloth of sendale,[1] and then laid them in chests of lead, because they should not chase[2] nor savour;[3] and upon all these bodyes were set their shields with their armes and banners, to the end they should bee known of what countrey they were. And after hee found three senatours that were alive, unto whom hee said, "For to save your lives, I will that yee take these dead bodies,

[1] *Sendale.*— A sort of thin silk.
[2] *Chase.*— *Chauffe ne savoure*, Caxton. *Chafe*, used perhaps in the sense of to decompose, is probably the correct reading.
[3] *Savour.*— Smell.

and carry them with you unto great Rome, and present them to the potestate[1] on my behalfe, shewing him my letters, and tel him that I in my person shall hastily bee at Rome, and I suppose the Romaines shal bee ware how they shal demaund of me any tribute. And I command you that ye say, when ye shal come to Rome, unto the potestate and all the counsaile and senate, that I send unto them these dead bodies for the tribute that they have demanded. And if so be they be not content with these, I shall pay more at my comming, for other tribute owe I none, nor none other will I pay. And mee thinketh this should suffise for Brittaine, Ireland, and all Almaine with Germany. And furthermore I charge you to say to them, that I command them upon paine of their heads never to demand nor aske of me nor of my lands any tribute." Then with this charge and commandement the three senatours aforesaid departed with all the said dead bodies, the body of Lucius lying in a cart covered with the armes of the empire all alone, and after alway two bodies of kings in a chariot, and then the bodies of the senatours after them, and so went toward Rome, and shewed their legation and message to the potestate and senate, recounting the battaile done in France, and how the field was lost and most people and innumerable slaine, wherefore they advised them in no wise to move more warre against that noble conquerour king Arthur, " for his might and prowesse is most to be doubted, seeing the noble kings and great multitude of knights of the round table, to whome none earthly prince may compare."

[1] *Potestate.*—This word is no doubt intended to represent the Italian *podestà*, or chief municipal officer.

CHAP. XCVI.—How king Arthur, after that he had atchieved the battaile against the Romaines, entred into Almaine, and so into Italy.

NOW turne we unto king Arthur and his noble knights, which, after the great battaile atchieved against the Romaines, entred into Loraine, Braband, and Flaunders, and sithen returned into hie Almaine, and so over the mountaines into Lumbardy, and after into Tuskaine, wherein was a citie which in no manner of wise would yeeld themselves nor obey, wherefore the noble king Arthur besieged it, and lay full long about it, and gave many assaults to the citie. And they within defended them valiantly. Then on a time the king called sir Florence, a knight, and told him that they lacked vitaile, " and not farre from hence be great forrests and great woods, wherein be many of mine enemies with much bestiall. I will that thou make thee ready and goe thither in forcing,[1] and take with thee sir Gawaine my nephew, and sir Whichard, and sir Clegis, sir Clemond,[2] and also the captaine of Cardife, with many other moe, and bring with you all the beastes that yee may get there." And anon these knights made them ready, and rod over holts and hills, through forrests and woods, till they came to a faire meddowe full of faire floures and grasse, and there they rested them and their horses all that night; and in the springing of the day on the next morrow sir Gawaine tooke his horse and stale away from his fellowes to seeke some adventure. And anon he was ware of a knight armed, walking his horse easily by a woods side, and his shield laced unto his shoulder, sitting on a strong courser, without any man save onely a page bearing a mighty spear, and the knight bare in his shield three griffons of gold in sable carbuncle, the chiefe of silver. When sir Gawaine espied this

[1] *In forcing.*—In *foreyeng*, Caxton; i. e. foraying, or foraging.
[2] *Clemond.*—*Claremond*, Caxton.

gay knight he fewtred¹ his speare, and rode straight unto him, and demanded him of whence he was. That other answered and said he was a Tuskaine, and demanded of sir Gawaine, " Thou proud knight, what profferest thou me so boldly? heere getest thou no prey; thou mayest prove when thou wilt, for thou shalt be my prisoner or thou depart." Then said sir Gawaine, " Thou vauntest thee greatly, and speakest all too proud words; I counsaile thee, for al thy boast, that thou make thee ready and take thy geere to thee, tofore greater game fall to thee."

CHAP. XCVII.—Of the battaile done by sir Gawaine against a Sarasin, which after was taken and became Christian.

THEN they tooke their speares, and ranne each at other with al the might they had, and smote each other through their shields into their shoulders, wherefore anon they drew out their swords and smote great strookes so that the fire sprang out of their helmes. Then was sir Gawaine all abashed, and with Galautine his good sword he smote him through the shield and thicke hawberke made of thicke mailes, and al to-rushed² and brake the precious stones, and made him a large wound that men might see both liver and longes. Then that knight groned, and dressed him to sir Gawaine, and with an awke³ strook gave him a great wound, and cut a veine that grieved sir Gawaine sore, and he bled fast. Then said the knight to sir Gawaine: " Bind thy wound or thy blood change, for thou beebleedest⁴ all thy horse and thy faire armes, for all the leeches⁵ of Brittaine shall not stench thy blood, for whosoever is hurt with this blade hee shall never

---

¹ *Fewtred.*—To *fewter* was the term for putting the spear in the rest.
² *To-rushed.*—Bruised.
³ *Awke strook.*—A cross or oblique stroke.
⁴ *Beebleedest.*—Coverest with blood.
⁵ *Leeches.*—*Burbours*, Caxton.

bee stenched of bleeding." Then answered sir Gawaine: "It grieveth mee but little, thy great words shall not feare me ne lesse my courage, but thou shalt suffer teene[1] and sorrow or we depart; but tell me in haste who may stench my bleeding." "That may I doe," said the knight, "if I will; and so I will if thou wilt succour and aide me that I may be christned and beleeve on God, and thereof I require thee of thy manhood, and it shall be great merit for thy soule." "I am content," said sir Gawaine, "so God helpe me to accomplish all thy desire. But first tell mee what thou soughtest thus here alone, and of what land and legiance thou art." "Sir," said the knight, "my name is Priamus, and a great prince is my father, and he hath beene rebel unto Rome, and hath overridden many of their land; my father is lineally descended of Alexander and of Hector by right line; and duke Josue and Machabæus were of our linage. I am right inheritor of Alexandry and Affrike and of all the out isles, yet will I beleeve on the Lord that thou beleevest on, and for thy labour I shall give thee treasure enough. I was so elevated and taken[2] in my heart that I thought no man my peere ne to me semblable. I was sent to this warre with sevenscore knights, and now I have encountred with thee which hath given me of fighting my fill, wherefore, sir knight, I pray thee to tell me what thou art, and of thy being." "I am no knight," said sir Gawaine, "I have beene brought up many yeares in the gardrobe with the noble prince king Arthur, for to take heede to his armour and his other aray, and for to point his paultockes[3] that belongeth to him selfe. At Christmas last hee made me yeoman and gave mee horse and harneis and an hundred pound in money, and, if fortune be my friend, I doubt not but to be well advanced and holpen by my liege

[1] *Teene.*—Grief. [2] *Elate and hawteyn in my hert,* Caxton.
[3] *Paultockes.*—Doublets; long cloaks. It is perhaps hardly necessary to remark that this old word has been resuscitated among modern tailors.

lord." "Ah," said Priamus, "if his knaves bee so keene and fierce, then his knights be passing good. Now for the kings love of heaven, whether you be knight or knave, tell me thy name." "By God," said sir Gawaine, "now wil I tel the truth: my name is sir Gawaine, and knowen I am in his noble court and in his chamber, and on of the knights of the round table; he dubbed me a duke with his owne hands, therefore grudge not if his grace is to me fortune and common, it is the goodnesse of God that lent to me my strength." "Now am I better pleased," said Priamus, "then if thou hadst given mee all the province of Paris the rich; I had rather to be torne with wild horses then any varlet should have wonne such lots,[1] or any page or priker[2] should have had the price of me; but now, sir knight, I warne thee that hereby is a duke of Loraine with all his army, and hath the noblest men of armes of all Dolphine,[3] and lords of Lumberdy, with the garnison of Godard, and Sarasins of Southland, to the number of threescore thousand of good men of warre; wherefore but if wee flee and hie us fast from hence, it will doe harm to us both, for we be sore hurt and wounded, and never like to recover; but take heede to my page that he blow no horne, for if hee doe, there bee hoveing here fast by an hundred good knights waiting upon my person, and if they take thee once, there shall no ransome of gold nor silver acquit thee." Then sir Gawaine rode over a water for to save himselfe, and the knight followed after him, and so they rode forth till they came to his fellowes that were in the meddow, where as they had beene all the night. Anon as sir Whichard was ware of sir Gawaine, and saw that he was hurt, he ranne unto him sorrowfully weeping, and demanded of him who it was that had so hurt and wounded him. And sir Gawaine told how hee had fought with that man, and each of them had hurt other, and

---

[1] *Lots.*—Caxton has *loos;* i. e. praise.
[2] *Priker.*—A light horseman—not a knight.
[3] *Dolphine.*—Dauphiné.

how hee had salves to heale them, " but I can tell you other tidings, that soone we shall have adoe with many enemies." Then sir Priamus and sir Gawaine alighted, and let their horses grase in the medow, and foorthwith there they unarmed them, and then the hot blood ranne downe freshly from their wounds. And Priamus tooke from his page a viole full of the foure waters that came out of Paradise,[1] and with certaine balme nointed their woundes, and washed them with that water, and within an houre after they were both as whole as ever they were. And then with a trumpet they were all assembled unto counsaile, and there Priamus told them what lords and knights had sworne to rescew him, and that without faile they should be assailed with many a thousand, wherefore he counseled them to withdraw them. Then said sir Gawaine, " it were great shame to them to avoide without any strookes, wherefore I advise you to take our armes and to make us ready to meete with these Sarasins and misbeleeving men, and with the helpe of God wee shall overthrow them and have a faire day on them. And sir Florens shall abide still in this field to keepe the stall[2] as a noble knight, and wee shall not forsake yonder fellowes." "Now," said Priamus, " cease your words, for I warne you ye shall find in yonder woods many perilous knights ; they will put forth beasts to call you on ; they be out of number, and ye are not past seven hundred, which be over few to fight with so many." " Neverthelesse," said sir Gawaine, " we shall once encounter with them, and see what they can doe, and the best shall have the victorie."

[1] *Paradise.*—The four rivers of Paradise are named in the following lines of the old Scottish poet, sir David Lindsay:
"Four fludis flowing from one fountane fair,
As Tigris, Ganges, Euphrates, and Nile,
Quhilk in the eist transcurris mony ane myle."
[2] *Stall.—Stale,* Caxton ; used here in the sense of an ambush, or post.

CHAP. XCVIII.—How that the Sarasins came out of a wood for to rescew their beasts, and of a great battaile.

THEN sir Florence called to him sir Floridas, with an hundred knights, and drove foorth the heard of beasts. Then followed him seven hundred men of armes, and sir Ferraunt of Spaine on a faire steede came leaping out of the wood, and came to sir Florens and asked him wherefore he fled. Then sir Florens tooke his speare and rode against him, and smote him so hard that he brake his necke bone. Then all the other were moved, and thought to avenge the death of sir Ferrant, and smote in among them, and there was great fight and many slaine and laid downe upon the cold ground, and sir Florens with his hundred knights alwayes kept the stale, and fought right manfuly. Then when Priamus the good knight perceived the great fight, hee went to sir Gawaine, and bad him that hee should goe and succour his fellowship, which were sore bestead with their enemies. "Sir, grieve you not," said sir Gawaine, "for the griefe shal bee theirs; I shall not once move my horse toward them but if I see more then there bee, for they bee strong inough to match them." And with that he saw an earle called sir Ethelwold and the duke of Duchmen came leaping out of a wood with many a thousand, and Priamus knights, and came straight unto the battaile. Then sir Gawaine comforted his knights, and bad them not bee abashed, "for all shall be ours." Then they began to gallop and meet fiersly with their enemies; there were men slaine and overthrowne on every side. And then thrusted in among them the knights of the table round, and smote downe to the earth all them that withstood them, in so much that they made them to give back and flee. "By God," said sir Gawaine, "this gladdeth well my heart, for now be they lesse in number by twentie thousand." Then entred into the battell a gyant

named Juliance,[1] and fought and slew down right, and
distressed many of our knights, among whom was slaine sir
Gherard, a knight of Wales. Then our knights tooke heart
to them, and slew many Sarasins. And then came in sir
Priamus with his penon, and rode with the knights of the
round table, and fought so manfully that many of their enemies lost their lives; and there sir Priamus slew the mar-
ques of Moises land. And sir Gawaine with his fellows
quit them so well that they had the field; but in that combat
was sir Chastilaine,[2] a child and ward of sir Gawaine, slaine,
wherefore was made much sorrow, and his death was soone
avenged. Thus was the battell ended, and many lords and
knights of Lomberdy and Sarasins left dead in the field.
Then Sir Florens and sir Gawaine harbowred surely their
people, and tooke great plenty of beasts, of gold and silver,
and of great treasure and riches, and returned unto king
Arthur which lay still at the siege. And when they came
to the king they presented him their prisoners, and told to
him their adventures, and how they had vanquished their
enemies.

CHAP. XCIX.—How sir Gawaine returned to king Arthur with his
prisoners, and how the king wan a citie, and how he was crowned
emperour.

"NOW thanked be God," said king Arthur; "but
what manner man is he that standeth by himselfe? he seemeth no prisoner." "Sir," said
sir Gawaine, "this is a good man of armes; he
hath matched me, but he is beholden unto God and to me
for to become a Christian; had not hee beene, we should
never have returned; wherefore I pray you that he may be
baptized, for there liveth not a nobler man nor a better

[1] *Juliance.—Jubaunce,* Caxton.
[2] *Sir Chastelayne,* Caxton.—The words which follow are corrected
from Caxton; the text of 1634 has, *a child, and was slaine of sir
Gawaine.*

knight of his hands." Then anone the king let him bee baptized, and did call him by his first name Priamus, and made him a duke and knight of the round table.

And then anon the king did make assault to the citie, and there was rearing of ladders, breaking of walls, and the ditch filled, that men with little paine might enter into the citie. Then came out a duchesse and Clarisine the countesse, with many ladies and damosels, kneeling before the king and requiring him for the love of God to receive the citie, and not to take it by assault, for then should many giltlesse be slaine. Then the king availed[1] his viser with a meeke and noble countenance, and said: "Madam, there shall none of my subjects misdoe you nor none of your damosels, nor to none that to you belongeth, but the duke shall abide my judgement." Then anon the king commanded to leave the assault. And anon the dukes eldest sonne brought out the keyes, and kneeling downe delivered them to the king, and besought him of grace, and the king seased[2] the towne by assent of his lords, and tooke the duke and sent him to Dover, there to abide prisoner the terme of his life, and assigned certaine rents for the dowry of the duchesse and for her children. Then he made lords to rule those lands, and lawes as a lord ought to doe in his owne countrey. And after that he tooke his journey toward Rome, and sent sir Floris and sir Floridas tofore with five hundred men of armes; and they came to the citie of Urbine, and laide ambushment there as them seemed it was most best for them, and rode to the towne, where anon issued out much people and scermished with the fore-riders. Then brake out the ambushment, and so wan the bridge, and after they wan the towne, and set upon the walls the kings banner. Then came king Arthur upon a hie hill, and saw the citie and his banner displaied upon the walls, by the

---

[1] *To avail.*—Literally, to lower. It was the term for moving down the visor of the helmet so as to uncover the face.

[2] *Seased.*—Took into his own possession.

which hee knew that the citie was won and gotten. And anon hee sent a commandement that none of his liege men should defile nor lye by noe ladie, wife, nor maide. Then when he came into the citie, hee passed through and came to the castle, and there comforted them that were in heavinesse, and ordeined there a knight of his owne countrey to be captaine. And when they of Milane heard that the foresaid citie was won, they sent unto king Arthur great summes of money, and besought him as their soveraigne lord to have pittie upon them, promising him to be his true subjects for evermore, and yeeld to him homage and fealtie for the lands of Pleasance,[1] and of Pavie, Petersaint, and the poore of Tremble, and to give unto him yearely a million of gold during all his life time. Then king Arthur rode into Tuskane, and there hee won townes and castles, and wasted all that hee found in his way that to him would not so obey; and went to Spolute and to Viterbe; and from thence he rode into the vale of Vicecount, among the vines. And from thence he sent unto the senatours of Rome, for to wit whether they would know him for their lord and chiefe governour or not. But soone after, upon a Saturday, came unto king Arthur all the senatours that were left on live, and all the noblest cardinalls which at that time dwelled within the citie of Rome, and they all praied him of peace, and proffered him full largely of goods. And they all besought him as governour to give them lycence for seven weekes to assemble together all the barony of the Romaines, and then to crowne him as emperour with holy creme,[2] as it belongeth unto such an high and noble estate. "I assent unto you," said king Arthur, "as ye have devised; and at Christmas there to be crowned, and to hold my round table with my knights there as me liketh." And then the senatours made al things ready for his crownation. And then

---

[1] Most of these names will be recognized at once. *Pleasance* is, of course, Placenza; and *Petersaint*, probably Pietra-Santa in Tuscany.
[2] *Creme.*—The crism, or consecrated oil.

at the day appointed, as the Romaines tell, he came into Rome, and there he was crowned emperour by the popes owne hands with all the solemnitie that could be made, and sojourned there a certaine time, and established all his lands from Rome unto France, and hee gave lands and realmes unto his servants and knights, to every each after his deserving, in such wise that none of them complained, neither rich nor poore. And he gave unto sir Priamus the dutchye of Loraine. And he thanked him, and said that he would serve him and bee his true subject all the dayes of his life. And after that he made dukes and earles, and constituted his men unto great riches and honour. Then after this, all his lords and knights and all the great men of estate assembled them together afore the triumphant conquerour king Arthur, and said: "Noble emperour, blessed be the eternal God! your mortall warre is all finished, and your conquest is achieved, in so much that we know no man so great nor mightie that dare make any warre against you, wherefore wee beseech and heartily pray your noble grace for to returne homeward, and also we pray you to give us licence to goe home to our wives, from whom wee have beene a long season, and for to rest us, for your journey is finished with great honour and worship." Then said king Arthur unto them : "Yee say truth; and for to tempt God, it is no wisdome, and therfore in all haste make you ready and returne we into England." Then was there trussing of harneis and of other baggage, and had great cariage. And after that the licence was given, king Arthur returned, and commanded that no man upon paine of death should rob by the way, neither take vitaile nor none other thing, but that hee should truely pay therefore. And thus hee came over the sea, and landed at Sandwich, against whom came queene Guenever and met with him, and made great joy of his comming. And he was full nobly received of all his commons in every citie, towne, and burrough. And great gifts were presented unto him at his home comming, for to welcome him with.

CHAP. C.—How sir Launcelot and sir Lionell departed from the court for to seeke adventures, and how sir Lionell left sir Launcelot sleeping, and was taken.

ANON after that the noble and worthy king Arthur was come from Rome into England, all the knights of the round table resorted unto the king, and made many justs and tourneiments, and some ther were that were good knights, which encreased so in armes and worship that they passed all their fellowes in prowesse and noble deedes, and that was well proved on many, but especially it was proved on sir Launcelot du Lake. For in al tourneiments and justs and deeds of armes, both for life and death, he passed all knights, and at no time he was never overcome, but it were by treason or enchantment. Sir Lancelot encreased so mervailously in worshippe and honour, wherefore he is the first knight that the French booke maketh mention of, after that king Arthur came from Rome, wherefore queene Guenever had him in great favour above all other knights, and certainely he loved the queene againe above all other ladies and damosels all the daies of his life, and for her he did many great deedes of armes, and saved her from the fire through his noble chivalrie. Thus sir Launcelot rested him a long while with play and game; and then hee thought to prove himselfe in strange adventures. Then he bad his brother sir Lionell to make him ready, "for we two will seeke adventures." So they mounted upon their horses armed at al points, and rode into a deepe forrest; and after they came into a great plaine, and then the weather was hot about noone, and sir Launcelot had great list to sleepe. Then sir Lionell espied a great apple tree that stood by an hedge, and said: "Brother, yonder is a faire shadow, there may we rest us and our horses." "It is well said, faire brother," said sir Lancelot; "for of al this seven yeare I was not so sleepie as I am now." And so they alighted there, and tyed their horses unto sundry trees, and so sir Launcelot laide him downe under an apple tree, and laid his helme under his head; and sir Lionell waked while he slept. So sir Launcelot slept passing fast. And in the meane while there came three knights riding as fast flying as ever they might ride, and there followed after those three but one knight. And when sir Lionell beheld him, he thought that he had never seen so great a knight, nor so well faring a man, neither so well apparaled at all points. So within a while this strong knight had overtaken one of these three knights that fled, and there smot him down to the ground. And then hee rode unto the second knight, and smote him such a strooke that horse and man fel downe unto the earth. And then he rode straight unto the third knight, and hee smote him over his horse arse more then the length of his speare. And then hee alighted downe and reined his horse on the bridle, and bound al the three knights fast with the reines of their owne bridles. And when sir Lionell saw him doe thus, hee thought to assay him, and made him ready; and slily and privily hee tooke his horse, and thought not to waken his brother sir Launcelot. And so when he was mounted upon his horse, and had overtaken this strong knight, he bade him turne. And so hee turned him, and smote sir Lionell so hard that horse and man hee bare to the earth, and then he alighted and bound him fast, and threw him overthwart his owne horse, and so he served them al foure, and rode with them away to his owne castle. And when hee came there, he unarmed them and beate them with thornes all naked, and after put them in a deepe prison, where were many moe knight that made great moone.[1]

---

[1] *Moone.*—Moan; lament.

KING ARTHUR. 199

CHAP. CI.—How sir Ector de Maris followed to seeke sir Launcelot, and how he was taken by sir Torquine.

WHEN sir Ector de Maris wist that sir Launcelot was past out of the court to seeke adventures, hee was wroth with himselfe, and made him ready to seeke sir Launcelot; and as hee had ridden long in a great forrest, hee met with a man that was like a foster.[1] "Faire fellow," said sir Ector, " knowest thou in this countrey any adventures which bee here nigh hand?" " Sir," said the foster, " this countrey know I well, and here within this mile is a strong mannor and wel ditched, and by that mannor on of the left hand there is a faire fourd for horses to drinke, and over that fourd ther groweth a faire tree, and theron hangeth many faire shields that belonged sometime unto good knights, and at the hole[2] of the tree hangeth a bason of copper and latin,[3] and strike upon that bason with the end of the speare thrice, and soone after thou shalt heere new tidings, and else hast thou the fairest grace that many a yeare any knight had that passed through this forrest." "Gramercy," said sir Ector; and so hee departed, and came to the tree, and saw many faire shields, and among them he saw his brothers shield sir Lionell, and many moe that he knew that were his fellowes of the round table, the which grieved his heart, and there hee promised to revenge his brother sir Lionell. And anon sir Ector beate upon thee bason as hee were wood, and then hee gave his horse drink at the fourd. Anon there came a knight behind him, and bad him come out of that water and make him ready. And sir Ector anon turned him shortly, and shaked his speare, and smote the other knight a great buffet, that his horse turned thrice about. "This was well done," said the strong knight, " and full knightly thou hast stricken me." And therewith hee rushed his horse upon sir Ector,

---

[1] *Foster.*—The common name for a forester.
[2] *Hole*—I suppose, the hollow or fork of the tree.
[3] *Latin.*—See before, p. 76.

and caught him under his right arme, and bare him cleane
out of the saddell, and so rode with him away into his hal,
and threw him downe in the middle of the flore. The name
of this knight was sir Turquine. Then said he unto sir
Ector: " For thou hast done this day more unto me then
any knight did these twelve yeares, now will I graunt thee
thy life, so that thou wilt bee sworne to mee as my prisoner
all the dayes of thy life." " Nay," said sir Ector, " that
wil I never promise thee, but that I will doe mine avantage."
" That me repenteth," said sir Turquine ; and then he tooke
him and unarmed him, and beate him with sharpe thornes
al naked, and after put him downe into a deepe dungeon,
where he knew many of his fellowes ; but when sir Ector
saw sir Lionell, then made he great sorrow. " Alas, brother !" said sir Ector, "where is my brother sir Launcelot?"
" Faire brother, I left him asleepe when I went from him
under an apple tree, and what is beecome of him I can not
tell you." "Alas," said the knights, " but[1] sir Launcelot
helpe us, we may never bee delivered, for we know now no
knight that is able to match our maister sir Turquin."

CHAP. CII.—How foure queenes found sir Launcelot sleeping, and
how by enchauntment he was taken and led into a strong castle.

NOW leave we these knights prisoners, and speake
wee of sir Launcelot du Lake, that lieth under
the apple tree sleeping. Even about the noone
there came by hym foure queenes of great estate,
and for the heate of the sun should not nigh them, there
rode foure knights about them, and bare a canope of greene
silke on foure speares, betweene them and the sun, and the
queenes rode on foure white mules. Thus as they rode
they heard by them a great horse grimly ney, and then
were they ware of a sleeping knight that lay all armed
under an apple tree ; anon as these queenes looked on his
face, they knew that it was sir Launcelot. Then they

[1] *But.*—Used here in the sense of unless.

began to strive for that knight, and each of them said shee would have him unto her love. "Wee shall not strive," said Morgan le Fay, that was king Arthurs sister, "I shall put an enchauntment upon him that hee shall not awake sixe houres, and then I will leade him away unto my castle, and when he is surely within my hold, I shall take the enchantment from him, and then let him choose which of us he will have unto his paramour." So this enchauntment was cast upon sir Launcelot; and then they laid him upon his shield, and bare him so on horsebacke betweene two knights, and brought him unto the castle Chariot, and there they laid him in a cold chamber, and at night they sent unto him a faire damosell with his supper ready dight. By that the enchauntment was past. And when she came she saluted him, and asked him what cheere. "I can not tell, faire damosell," said sir Launcelot, "for I wot not how I came into this castle, unlesse it bee by enchauntment." "Sir," said the damosell, "yee must make good cheere, and if ye be such a knight as is said that yee bee, I shall tell you more to morrow by prime of the day." "Gramercy," said sir Launcelot, "of your good will I require you." And so shee departed, and there he lay all that night without comfort of any person. And in the morning early came these foure queenes passingly well beseene, all they bidding him good morrow, and he them againe. "Sir knight," said the foure queenes, "thou must understand that thou art our prisoner, and we heere know thee well, that thou art sir Launcelot du Lake, king Bans son. And because we understand your worthinesse that ye are the noblest knight that is now living; and as we know well there can noe lady have thy love but one, and that is queene Guenever, and now thou shalt loose her for ever, and shee thee; and therefore it behoveth thee now to choose one of us foure. I am queene Morgan le Fay, queene of the land of Gore, and heere is also the queene of Northgales, and the queene of Eastland, and the queene of the out iles; now choose ye one of us, which yee will have unto your paramour; if ye will not doe thus, heere shall ye abide in this prison till that yee die." "This is an hard case," said sir Launcelot, " that either I must die, or else choose one of you; yet had I rather to die in this prison with worship then to have one of you to my paramour, maugre my head. And therefore be ye answered, for I will have none of you, for ye bee false enchauntresses. And as for my lady dame Guenever, were I at my libertie as I was, I would prove it upon you or upon yours, that she is the truest lady living unto her lord." "Well," said the queenes, " is this your answere, that you will refuse us?" "Yea, upon my life," said sir Launcelot, " refused yee bee of me." So they departed, and left him there alone that made great sorrow.

CHAP. CIII.—How sir Launcelot was delivered by the meanes of a damosell.

RIGHT so at noone came the damosel to him, and brought him his dinner, and asked him what cheere. "Truely, faire damosel," said sir Launcelot, " in al my life-dayes never so ill." " Sir," said she, " that me repenteth; but and ye will be ruled by me, I shall helpe you out of this distresse, and yee shall have no shame nor vilany, so that ye hold me a promesse." "Faire damosel, that I will grant you, and sore I am afeard of these queenes witches, for they have destroyed many a good knight." "Sir," said shee, "that is sooth, and for the renowne and bounty they heare of you, they would have your love, and, sir, they say that your name is sir Launcelot du Lake, the floure of al the knights that been living, and they beene passing wroth with you that yee have refused them; but, sir, and ye would promise me for to helpe my father on Tuesday next comming, that hath made a turneyment beetweene him and the king of Northgales; for the Tuesday laste past my father lost the field through three knights of king Arthurs court, and if ye will be there upon Twesday next coming and helpe my father, to morrow or prime, by the grace of God, I shall deliver you cleane." "Faire maiden," said sir Launcelot, "tell mee what is your fathers name, and then shall I give you an answere." "Sir knight," said the damosell, "my father is king Bagdemagus, that was fouly rebuked at the last turneyment." "I know your father well," said sir Launcelot, "for a noble king and a good knight, and by the faith of my body, yee shall have my body ready to doe your father and you service at that day." "Sir," said the damosell, "gramercy, and to morrow awaite that ye be ready betimes, and I shall deliver you, and take you your armour and your horse, shield, and speare; and hereby within these ten miles is an abbey of white monkes, and there I pray you to abide, and thither shall I bring my father unto you." "All this shal be done," said sir Launcelot, "as I am a true knight." And so she departed, and came on the morrow early and found him ready. Then she brought him out of twelve lockes, and brought him unto his armour. And when he was all armed and arrayed, she brought him unto his owne horse, and lightly hee sadled him, and tooke a great speare in his hand, and so rode forth, and said, "Faire damosell, I shall not faile you, by the grace of God." And so he rode into a great forrest all that day, and in no wise could he find any high way, and so the night fell on him, and then was he ware in a slade[1] of a pavilion of reed sandall.[2] "By my faith," said sir Launcelot, "in that pavilion will I lodge all this night." And so there he alighted downe, and tied his horse to the pavilion, and there he unarmed him, and found there a rich bed and laid him therein, and anon he fell on sleepe.

[1] *A slade.*—A valley, or ravine.
[2] *Reed sandall.*—Red silk.

CHAP. CIV.—How a knight found sir Launcelot lying in his lemans bed, and how sir Launcelot fought with that knight.

THEN within an houre came the knight to whom belonged the pavilion, and he wend his lemman[1] had layen in that bed, and so he laid him downe beside sir Launcelot, and tooke him in his armes, and began to kisse him. And when sir Launcelot felt a rough beard kissing him, he started lightly out of the bed, and the other knight lept after him, and either of them gat their swords in their hands, and out of the pavilion dore went the knight of the pavilion, and sir Launcelot followed him, and there by a little slade sir Launcelot wounded him sore nigh unto the death, and then he yeelded him unto sir Launcelot. And sir Launcelot tooke him to his mercy, so that he would tell him why he came into the bed. "Sir," said the knight, "the pavilion is mine owne, and there this night I had assigned my love and lady to have slept with me, and now I am likely to die of this wound." "That me repenteth," said sir Launcelot, "of your hurt, but I was sore adred of treason, for I was lately beguiled; and therefore come on your way into your pavilion, and take your rest, and as I suppose I shall stench your blood." And so they went both into the pavilion, and anon sir Launcelot stenched his blood. Therewith came the knights lady, which was a passing faire lady. And when she espied that her lord sir Belleus was so sore wounded, she cried out on sir Launcelot, and made great moone out of measure. "Peace, my lady and my love," said sir Belleus, "for this knight is a very good man and a knight adventurous." And there he told her all the cause how he was wounded; "and when I yeelded me unto him, hee goodly left me and tooke me to his mercy, and hath stenched my blood." "Sir," said the lady, "I require you tell me what knight yee are, and what is your name?" "Faire lady," said

---

[1] *Lemman.*—A mistress, or concubine.

he, "my name is Launcelot du Lake." "So me thought by your speache," said the lady, "for I have seene you often times or this, and I know you better then ye wene. But now and ye would promise mee of your curtesie for the harmes that ye have done to mee and to my lord sir Belleus, that when he commeth to king Arthurs court to cause him to be made a knight of the round table; for hee is a passing good man of armes, and a mighty lord of lands of many out iles." "Faire lady," said sir Launcelot, "let him come unto the court the next high feast, and looke that yee come with him. And I shall doe all my power, and if ye prove you doughty or mightie of your hands, then shall ye have your desire." So thus within a while, as they stood thus talking, the night passed and the day appeared, and then sir Launcelot armed him and mounted upon his horse, and tooke his leave, and they shewed him the way towards the abbey, and thither they rode within the space of two houres.

CHAP. CV. How sir Launcelot was received of king Bagdemagus daughter, and how he made his complaint unto her father.

AS soone as sir Launcelot came within the abbey yard, king Bagdemagus daughter heard a great horse goe on the pavement. And then she arose and went unto a window, and there shee saw that it was sir Launcelot, and anon shee made men hastely to goe to him, which tooke his horse and led him into a stable, and himselfe was led into a faire chamber, and there he unarmed him, and the lady sent to him a long gowne, and anon she came her selfe. And then she made sir Launcelot passing good cheere, and she said he was the knight in the world that was most welcome to her. Then she in al the haste sent for her father king Bagdemagus, that was within twelve mile of that abbey, and afore even hee came with a faire fellowship of knights with him. And when the king was alighted from his horse, he went straight unto sir Launcelots chamber, and there found his daughter, and then the king embraced sir Launcelot in his armes, and either made other good cheere. Anon sir Launcelot made his complaint unto the king how hee was betraied, and how his brother sir Lionell was departed from him hee wist not whither, and how his daughter had delivered him out of prison, "wherefore I shall while I live doe her service and all her friends and kindred." " Then 'am I sure of your helpe," said the king, " now on Tuesday next comming?" " Ye, sir," said sir Launcelot, " I shal not faile you, for so have I promised unto my lady, your daughter. But, sir, what knights beene they of my lord king Arthurs that were with the king of Northgales?" And the king said, " It was sir Mador de la Port, and sir Mordred, and sir Gahalatine, that foule fared[1] with my knights, for against them three I nor my knights might bare no strength." " Sir," said sir Launcelot, " as I heare say, the turnement shall be within three mile of this abbey; yee shall send unto mee three knights of yours, such as ye trust best, and looke that these three knights have all white shields and I also, and no painting on the shields, and wee foure will come out of a little wood in the midest of both parties, and we shall fall in the front of our enemies and grieve them all that wee may; and so I shall not bee knowen what knight I am." So they tooke their rest that night, and this was on the Sunday. And so the king departed, and sent unto sir Launcelot three knights, with foure white shields. And on the Tuesday they lodged them in a little leved[2] wood besid wher the turnement should be. And ther wer scaffolds and holes, that lords and ladies might behold and give the prise. Then came into the field the king of Northgales with eight score helmes, and then the three knights of king Arthurs stood by themselves.

[1] *That al fur fared,* Caxton.
[2] *Leved.*—In leaf; a shady wood.

Then came into the field king Bagdemagus with fourescore helmes   And then they fewtred[1] their speares, and came together with an huge dash, and there were slaine of knights at the first oncounter twelve of king Bagdemagus part, and sixe of the king of Northgales part, and king Bagdemagus part was far set backe.

CHAP. CVI.—How sir Launcelot behaved him in a turneyment, and how hee met with Sir Turquine leading away sir Gaheris with him.

WITH that came sir Launcelot du Lake, and he thrust in with his speare in the thickest of the presse, and there he smote downe with one speare five knights, and of foure of them he brake their backes, and in that throng hee cast downe the king of Northgales, and brake his thigh with that fall. All this doing of sir Launcelot saw the three knights of king Arthurs court. "Yonder is a shrewd gest," said sir Mador de la Port, "therefore have heere once at him." So they encountred, and sir Launcelot bare him downe horse and man, so that his shoulder went out of joynt. "Now befalleth it to me to just," said sir Mordred, "for sir Mador hath a sore fall." Sir Launcelot was ware of him, and gat a great speare in his hand, and met him, and sir Mordred brake his speare upon him, and sir Launcelot gave him such a buffet that the arson of his saddle brake, and so he flew over his horse taile that his helme pight into the earth a foote and more, that nigh his neck was broken ; and there hee lay long in a sound.[2] Then came in sir Gahalatine with a spear, and sir Launcelot against him, with all the strength that they might drive, that both their speares all brake unto their hands, and then they drew out their swords and gave each other many grim strookes. Then was sir Launcelot wroth out of measure, and then hee smote sir Gahalatine on the helme that booth his nose and his mouth burst out on bleeding, and his eares also, and

[1] *Fewtred*—See before, p. 188.   [2] *A sound*—A swoon.

therewith his head hung low, and his horse ranne away with him, and he fell downe to the earth. Anon therewith sir Launcelot gat a great speare in his hand, and or ever that great speare brake hee bare downe to the ground sixteene knights, some horse and man, and some the man and not the horse, and ther was non but that he was hit surely, so that hee bare no armes that day. And then he gat another great speare, and smot downe twelve knights, and the most of them never throve after. And then the knights of the king of Northgales would just no more. And the game was given unto king Bagdemagus. Soe either partie departed unto his owne place, and sir Launcelot rode foorth with king Bagdemagus unto his castle, and there hee had passing good cheere both with the king and with his daughter, and they promised him great gifts. And on the morrow he tooke his leave, and told king Bagdemagus that hee would goe seeke his brother sir Lionel, that went from him when he slept. So he tooke his horse, and betooke him all to God, and there hee said unto the kings daughter, "If yee have neede at any time of my service, I pray you let me have knowledge thereof, and I shall not faile you as I am true knight." And so sir Launcelot departed, and by adventure came into the same forrest where as he was taken sleeping. And in the middest of an hie way hee met with a damosell riding upon a white palfrey, and there either saluted other. "Faire damosell," said sir Launcelot, "know yee in this countrey any adventures?" "Sir knight," said the damosell to sir Launcelot, "heere are adventures neere hand, and thou durst prove them." "Why should I not prove adventures?" said sir Launcelot, "as for that cause comé I hither." "Well," said the damosell, "thou seemest well to be a right good knight, and if thou dare meete with a good knight, I shall bring thee where as the best knight is and the mightiest that ever thou found, so that thou wilt tell mee what thy name is, and of what countrey and knight thou art?" "Damosell, as for to tell thee my name, I take no great force. Truely my name is sir Launcelot du Lake." "Sir, thou beseemest well, here be adventures that be fallen for thee, for hereby dwelleth a knight that will not bee overmatched for no man that I know, but ye overmatch him, and his name is sir Turquine, and, as I understond, hee hath in his prison of king Arthurs court good knights threescore and foure, that he hath won with his owne hands. But, when ye have done this jorney, ye shall promise me as ye are a true knight for to go with me and helpe me and other damosels that are distressed with a false knight." "All your intent and desire, damosell, I will fulfil, so that ye wil bring me to this knight." "Now, faire knight, come on your way." And so shee brought him unto the fourd and unto the tree whereon the bason hung. So sir Launcelot let his horse drinke, and after he beate on the bason with the end of his speare so hard and with such a might that he made the bottome fall out, and long he did so, but he saw nothing. Then he rode endlong[1] the gates of the mannor well nigh halfe an houre, and then was hee ware of a great knight that drove an horse afore him, and overthwart the horse lay an armed knight bound. And ever as they came neerer and neerer, sir Launcelot thought that he should know him, then sir Launcelot was ware that it was sir Gaheris, sir Gawaines brother, a knight of the table round. "Now, faire damosell," said sir Launcelot, "I see yonder comes a knight fast bound, which is a fellow of mine, and brother hee is unto sir Gawaine, and at the first beginning I promise you, by the leave of God, to rescew that knight, but if his maister set the better in the saddle; I shall deliver all the prisoners out of danger, for I am sure that he hath two brethren of mine prisoners with him." By that time that either had seene other, they tooke their speares unto them. "Now, faire knight," said sir Launcelot, "put that wounded knight from thy horse, and let him rest a while, and then

---

[1] *Endlong.*—Along by the side of.

let us two prove our strength together. For as it is enformed and shewed me, thou doest and hast done great dispite and shame unto the knights of the round table, and therefore defend thee now shortly." "And thou bee of the round table," said sir Turquine, "I defie thee and all thy fellowship." "That is over much said," said Sir Launcelot.

CHAP. CVII.—How sir Launcelot and Turquine fought together.

AND then they put their speares in their rests, and came together with their horses as fast as it was possible for them to runne, and either smote other in the middest of their shields, that both their horses backs burst under them, whereof the knights were both astonied; and as soone as they might avoide their horses, they tooke their shields afore them, and drew out their swords, and came together egerly, and either gave other many great strookes, for there might neither shields nor harneis hold their dints. And so within a while thay had both grimly[1] wounds, and bled passing grievously. Thus they fared two houres or more, trasing and rasing[2] either other where they might hit any bare place. At the last they were both brethlesse, and stood leaning on their swords. "Now, fellow," said sir Turquine, "hold thy hand a while and tell me what I shall aske thee." "Say on," said sir Launcelot. "Thou art," said sir Turquine, "the biggest man that ever I met withall, and the best breathed, and like one knight that I hate above all other knights, and that thou be not he, I will lightly accord with thee, and for thy love I will deliver all the prisoners that I have, that is threescore and foure, so that thou wilt tell mee thy name, and thou and I we will be fellowes together, and never faile thee while I live." "It is well said," quoth sir Launcelot, "but sithence it is so that I may have thy

[1] *Grimly.*—Ghastly; horrible.
[2] *Trasing and rasing.*—Dodging and striking.

friendship, what knight is he that thou so hatest above all other?" "Truely," said sir Turquine, "his name is Launcelot du Lake, for he slew my brother sir Carados at the dolorous towre, which was one of the best knights then living, and therefore him I except of all knights, for and I may once meet with him, that one of us shall make an end of another, and do that I make avow. And for sir Launcelots sake I have slaine an hundred good knights, and as many I have utterly maimed, that never after they might helpe themselves, and many have died in my prison, and yet I have threescore and foure, and all shal be delivered, so that thou wilt tell me thy name, and so it bee that thou be not sir Launcelot." "Now see I well," said sir Launcelot, "that such a man I might be I might have peace, and such a man I might be there should be betweene us two mortall warre; and now, sir knight, at thy request, I will that thou wit and know that I am sir Launcelot du Lake, king Bans son of Benwicke, and knight of the round table. And now I defie thee doe thy best." "Ah!" said sir Turquine, "Launcelot, thou art unto mee most welcome, as ever was any knight, for we shall never depart till the one of us bee dead." And then hurtled they together as two wild bulls, rashing and lashing with their shields and swords, that sometime they fell both on their noses. Thus they fought still two houres and more, and never would rest, and sir Turquine gave sir Launcelot many wounds that all the ground there as they fought was all besprinkled with blood.

CHAP. CVIII.—How sir Turquine was slaine, and how sir Launcelot bad sir Gaheris deliver all the prisoners.

THEN at the last sir Turquine waxed very faint, and gave somewhat backe, and bare his shield full low for wearinesse. That soone espied sir Launcelot, and then lept upon him fiersly as a lyon, and got him by the banour of his helmet, and so he plucked him downe on his knees, and anon he rased[1] off his helme, and then hee smote his neck asunder. And when sir Launcelot had done this, he went unto the damosell and said to her, "Damosell, I am ready to goe with you where ye will have me, but I have no horse." "Faire sir," said the damosell, "take yee this wounded knights horse, and send ye him into this mannor, and command him to goe and deliver all the prisoners." And so sir Launcelot went unto sir Gaheris, and prayed him not to be greeved for to lend him his horse. "Nay, faire lord," said sir Gaheris, "I will that ye take my horse at your owne command, for ye have both saved me and my horse, and this day I say yee are the best knight in the world, for ye have slaine this day in my sight the mightiest man and the best knight (except your selfe) that ever I saw. Faire sir," said sir Gaheris, "I pray you tel me your name?" "Sir, my name is sir Launcelot du Lake, which ought to helpe you of right for king Arthurs sake, and in especiall for my lord sir Gawaines sake, your dear brother, and when ye come within yonder mannor, I am sure that yee shall finde there many noble knights of the round table, for I have seene many of their shields that I know; on yonder tree there is sir Kaies shield, and sir Brandels shield, and sir Marhaus shield, and sir Galinds, and sir Brian de Listinoise shield, and sir Alidukes shield, with many moe that I am not now advised of, and also my two brethrens shields, sir Ector de Maris and sir Lionell; wherefore I pray you greete them all from me, and say to them that I bid them take there such stuffe as they find, and that in any wise my brethren goe unto the court and abide there till I come thither; for by the high feast of Penticost I thinke to bee there, for as at this time I must ride with this damosell for to save my promisse." And so he departed from sir Gaheris; and sir Gaheris went into the mannor, and there hee found a yeoman porter keeping many keies. And forthwith sir Gaheris threw the porter against the ground that his eyes start

[1] *Rased*—Tore off.

out of his head, and tooke the keyes and opened the prison, and there he let out all the prisoners, and every each loosed other of their bands. And when they saw sir Gaheris they all thanked him, for they wend because he was wounded that he had slaine sir Turquine. "Not so," said Gaheris, "it was sir Launcelot that slew him worshipfully with his owne hands; I saw it with mine eyes. And he greeteth you all well, and prayeth you to haste you to the court, and as unto sir Lionell and sir Ector de Maris, he praieth you to abide him at the court."

"That shall wee not doe," said his brethren, "wee wil find him and wee may live." "So shall I," said Sir Key, "find him or I come at the court, as I am true knight." Then al the knights sought the house where as the armour was, and then they armed them, and every knight found his owne horse, and all that belonged unto him. And when all this was done, there came a forrester with foure horses laden with venison. Anon sir Kay said, "Heere is good meate for us for one meale, for we had not many a day one good repast." And so that venison was rosted, baked, and sodden, and so after supper some abode there all night, but sir Lionell, and sir Ector de Maris, and sir Kay rode after sir Launcelot for to finde him if they might.

CHAP. CIX.—How sir Launcelot rode with the damosel and slew a knight that distressed all ladies, and a villain that kept the passage over a bridge.

NOW turne we unto sir Launcelot, that rode with the damosell in a faire high way. "Sir," said the damosell, "heere by this way haunteth a knight that distresseth all ladies and gentlewomen, and at the least he robeth them or lyeth by them." "What," said sir Launcelot, "is hee a thecfe and a knight and a ravisher of women? hee doth great shame unto the order of knighthood and contrary to his oath, it is pittie that he liveth. But faire damosell, yee shall ride your selfe alone before, and I will keepe my selfe in covert, and if hee trouble you or distresse you, I shall bee your rescew, and learne him to bee ruled as a knight." So the damosel rode on by the way a soft ambling pace. And within a while came that knight on horsebacke out of the wood, and his page with him, and there hee put the damosell from her horse, and then she cried. With that came sir Launcelot as fast as he might, till hee came to that knight, saying, "Oh! thou false knight and traitour unto knighthood, who learned thee to distresse ladies and gentlewomen?" When the knight saw sir Launcelot thus rebuking him, he answered not, but drew his sword and rode unto sir Launcelot. And sir Launcelot threw his speare from him, and drew out his sword, and strok him such a buffet on the helmet that he clave his head unto the throate. "Now hast thou thy payment that thou long hast deserved." "That is truth," said the damosell, "for like as Turquine watched to destroy knights, so did this knight attend to destroy and distresse ladies and gentlewomen, and his name was sir Peers du Forest Savage." "Now, damosell," said sir Launcelot, "will ye any more service of me?" "Nay, sir," said she, "at this time, but almighty God preserve you wheresoever yee goe or ride, for the curtiest[1] knight thou art and meekest unto al ladies and gentlewomen that now liveth. But, sir knight, one thing me thinketh that ye lacke, ye that are a knight wivelesse that ye will not love some maiden or gentlewoman, for I could never heare say that ever ye loved any of no mauer degree, and that is great pittie; but it is noysed that yee love queene Guenever, and that she hath ordained by enchauntment that ye never shal love none other but her, ne none other damosell nor lady shall rejoyce you; wherefore manie in this countrey of hie estate and low make great sorrow." "Faire damosell," said sir Launcelot, "I may not warne the people to speake of me, they may speake what soever it please them. But to bee a wedded man I

---

[1] *Curtiest.*—So Caxton, *curteyst*, i. e. most courteous.

thinke never to be, for if I were, then should I be bound to tarry with my wife, and leave armes and turnements, battells and adventures. And as for to say that I take my pleasure with paramours, that will I refuse, and principally for dread of God. For knights that bee advouturous[1] or letcherous shall not bee happy nor fortunate in the warres, for either they shall be overcome with a simpler knight then they bee themselves, or else they shall by unhappye and their cursednesse sley better men then they be themselves; and so who that useth paramours shall bee unhappie, and all things is unhappie that is about them." And so sir Launcelot and the damosell departed. And then rode hee into a deepe forrest two daies and more, and had straite lodging. So on the third day hee rode over a great long bridge, and there start upon him sodainly a passing foule churle, and he smote his horse on the nose that hee turned about, and asked him why hee rode over that bridge without his licence. "Why should not I ride this way?" said sir Launcelot, " I may not ride beside." "Thou shalt not choose," said the churle; and so lashed at him with a mighty great club ful of pinns of iron. Then sir Launcelot drew his sword and put the strooke backe, and clove his head unto the navell.[2] And at the end of the bridge was a faire village, and all the people came and cried on sir Launcelot, and said, " Sir, a worser deede diddest thou never for thy selfe, for thou hast slaine the chiefe porter of our castle." Sir Launcelot let them say what they would, and he went straight into the castle. And when hee came into the castle, he alighted and tied his horse to a ring in the wall, and there he saw a faire greene court, and thither he dressed him, for there hee thought was a faire place to fight in. So hee looked about, and saw much people in doores and windowes, that said, "Faire knight, thou art unhappie."[3]

[1] *Advouturous.*—Adulterous.
[2] *Navell.*—*Unto the pappys,* Caxton.
[3] *Thou art unhappie.*—Thou art unfortunate to have come here.

CHAP. CX.—How sir Launcelot slew two gyants, and made a castle free.

ANON therewith came upon him two **great gyants**, well armed al save the heads, with **two horrible clubs in their hands.** Sir Launcelot put his shield afore him, and put the strooke **away of the one gyant**, and with his sword he clove his head unto his pappes.[1] When his fellow saw that, hee ranne away as he were mad for feare of that horrible strooke; and sir Launcelot ranne after him as fast as he might, and smote him on the shoulder, and clove him to the foundament.[2] Then sir Launcelot went into the hall, and there came afore him threescore ladies and damosells, and al kneeled unto him, and thanked God and him for their deliverance. "For, sir," said they, "the most part of us have been here this seven yeare their prisoners, and we have here wrought all manner of silke workes for our meate, and we are all great gentlewomen borne; and blessed be the time that ever thou were borne, for thou hast done the most deede of worship that ever any knight did in this world, and thereof wil we beare record, and we all pray you to tel us your name that we may tell our friends who delivered us out of prison." "Faire damosells," said hee, "my name is Launcelot du Lake." "Ah, sir," said they, "wel maiest thou be he, for else save your selfe, as wee deemed, there might no knight have the better of these two gyants, for many faire and goodly knights have assaied it, and heere have ended their lives, and also many times have wee wished after you, and these two gyants dread never knight but you." "Now may yee say," said sir Launcelot, "unto your friends how and who hath delivered you, and greete them from mee; and

[1] *Clafe his hede asondre*, Caxton.
[2] *Clafe hym to the navel*, Caxton. The editor of the edition of 1634, from which the present text is printed, in revising it from the older edition, shows a great tendency to increase upon the intensity of the exploits of the heroes.

if I come into any of your marches, shew mee such cheere as yee have cause, and what treasure there is in this castle I give it you for a reward for your grieveance, and the lord that is the owner of this castle, I would that he received it as his right and apurtenance." "Faire sir," said they, "the name of this castle is Tintagill, and a duke ought it some time that had weded faire Igraine, and after Utherpendragon wedded her, and gat on her king Arthur." "Wel," said sir Launcelot, "I understand now to whom this castle belongeth;" and so hee departed from them and betooke them to God. And then hee mounted upon his horse, and rode into many strange and wilde countries, and through many waters and valleyes, and evill was hee lodged. And at the last by fortune it happened him against a night to come to a faire courtlage, and therein he found an old gentlewoman which lodged him with a good will; and there he and his horse were well cheared. And when time was, his hoast brought him to a faire garret over a gate to his bed. There sir Launcelot unarmed him, and set his harneis by him, and went to bed, and anon he fell on sleepe. So soone after there came one on horsebacke, and knocked at the gate in great haste; and when sir Launcelot heard this, he arose up and looked out at the window, and saw by the moone light three knights that came riding after that one man, and al three lashed upon him at once with their swords, and that one knight turned on them knightly againe and defended himselfe. "Truely," said sir Launcelot, "yonder one knight shall I helpe, for it were shame for mee to see three knights on one, and if he were slaine I should be partner of his death." And therewith hee tooke his harneis, and went out at a window by a sheete downe to the foure knights, and then sir Launcelot said all on high: "Turne you knights unto mee, and leave your fighting with that knight." And then they all three left sir Kay, and turned unto sir Launcelot, and there began a great battaile, for they alighted all three and strake many great strookes at sir

Launncelot, and assailed him on every side. Then sir Kay dressed him for to have holpen sir Launcelot. "Nay, sir," said he "I will none of your helpe, and therefore as ye wil have my helpe, let mee alone with them." Sir Kay for the pleasure of the knight he suffered him to have his will, and so stood aside. And then anon within sixe strookes sir Launcelot had striken them to the earth. And then they all three cried: " Sir knight, we yeeld us unto you as man of might." " As to that," said sir Launcelot, " I will not take your yeelding unto mee, but so that yee wil yeeld you unto sir Kay the seneshall; upon that covenant will I save your lives, and else not." " Faire knight," said they, " that were we loth to do, for as for sir Kay we chased him hither and had overcome him, had not ye beene, therefore to yeeld us unto him it were no reason." " Well, as to that," said sir Launcelot, " advise you well, for yee may choose whether yee will die or live, for and ye be holden, it shall be unto sir Kay, or else not." " Faire knight," said they, " then in saving of our lives we will doe as yee commaund us." " Then shall ye," said sir Launcelot, " upon Whitsunday next comming, goe unto the court of king Arthur, and there shal yee yeeld you unto queene Guenever, and put you al three in her grace and mercy, and say that sir Kay sent you thither for to bee her prisoners." " Sir," said they, " it shall bee done, by the faith of our bodies, if wee bee living." And there every knight swore upon their swords; and so sir Launcelot suffered them to depart. And then sir Launcelot knocked at the gate with the pummell of his sword, and with that came his hoast, and so in they entred sir Kay and he. " Sir," said his hoast, " I wend ye had beene in your bed." " So I was," said sir Launcelot, " but I arose and lept out at my chamber window to help an old fellow of mine." And so when they came in the light, sir Kay knew well that it was sir Launcelot, and therewith he kneeled downe and thanked him of his kindnesse that he had holpen him twice from death. " Sir," said he, " I have done nothing but that I ought to doe, and ye are welcome, and here shall ye take your rest." So when sir Kay was unarmed, hee asked after meate, and anon there was meate brought him, and hee eate strongly; and when hee had supped, they went to their bed, and were lodged together in one bed. On the morrow sir Launcelot arose early, and left sir Kay sleeping; and sir Launcelot tooke sir Kays armour and his shield, and armed him. And so he went to the stable and took his horse, and tooke leave of his hoast, and so departed. Then soone after arose sir Kay, and missed sir Launcelot; and then he espied that he had his armour and his horse. " Now, by my faith, I know wel that hee will grieve some of king Arthurs court; for on him knights will bee bold, and deeme that it is I, and that will beguile them; and because of his armour and shield, I am sure that I shal ride in peace." And then soone after departed sir Kay, and thanked his hoast.

CHAP. CXI.—How sir Launcelot disguised in sir Kays armour, and how hee smote downe a knight.

NOW turne we unto sir Launcelot, that had long riden in a great forrest, and at the last came into a low countrey full of faire rivers and medowes, and afore him hee saw a long bridge, and three pavilions stood thereon of silke and sendell of divers hew, and without the pavilions hung three white shields on truncheons of speares, and great long speares stood upright by the pavilions, and at every pavilions doore stood three fresh squires, and so sir Launcelot passed by them and spake not a word. When he was past, the three knights said that it was the proud Kay, " he weeneth no knight so good as he, and the contrary is oftentimes proved." " By my faith," said one of the knights, whose name was sir Gaunter, " I will ride after him, and assay him for all his pride, and ye may behold how I speed." So this knight sir Gaunter armed him, and hung his shield upon his shoulder, and mounted upon a great horse, and gat his speare in his hand, and galloped after sir Launcelot. Then when hee came nigh him, hee cried : " Abide, thou proud knight sir Kay, for thou shalt not passe quit." So sir Launcelot turned him, and either fewtred their speares and came together with al their might, and sir Gaunters speare brake, but sir Launcelot smote him downe horse and man. And when sir Gaunter was on the earth, his brethren said one to another: " Yonder knight is not sir Kay, for hee is bigger then hee." " I dare lay my head," said sir Gilmere, " yonder knight hath slaine sir Kay, and hath taken his horse and harneis." " Whether it bee so or no," said sir Raynold the third brother, " let us now goe mount upon our horses and rescew our brother sir Gaunter upon paine of death ; wee all shall have enough adoe to match that knight, for mee seemeth by his person it is sir Launcelot, or sir Tristram, or sir Pelleas." Anon they tooke their horses, and overtooke sir Launcelot; and sir Gilmere put forth his speare and ran to sir Launcelot, and sir Launcelot smote him downe that hee lay in a sound. " Sir knight," said sir Reynold, " thou art a strong man : and as I suppose thou hast slaine my two brethren, for the which my heart riseth sore against thee, and if I might with my worship I would not have to doe with thee, but needs must I take part as they doe, and therefore, knight," said he, " keepe thyselfe." And so they hurtled together with all their might, and all to-shivered [1] both their speares ; and then they drew their swords and lashed together eagerly. Anon therewith arose sir Gaunter and came unto his brother sir Gilmere, and bad him arise " and help we our brother sir Reynold, which full mervailously matcheth yonder good knight." Therewith they lept on their horses and hurtled unto sir Launcelot. And when hee saw them come, hee smote a sore strooke unto sir Reynold, that he fell off his horse to the

---

[1] *To-shivered.*—Split or broke to splinters.

ground; and then he strooke at the other two brethren, and at two strookes he strooke them downe to the earth. With that sir Raynold began to start up with his head al bloody, and came straight unto sir Launcelot. "Now let bee," said sir Launcelot; "I was not far from thee when thou wert made knight, sir Reynold, and also I know thou art a good knight, and loth I were to sley thee." "Gramercy," said sir Reynold, "for your goodnesse; and I daresay as for me and my brethren, wee will not be loth to yeeld us unto you, so that we know your name, for we know wel ye are not sir Kay." "As for that, be it as it may, for yee shall yeeld you unto dame Guenever; and looke that yee bee with her on Whitsunday, and yeeld you unto her as prisoners, and say that sir Kay sent you unto her." Then they swore it should be done. And so passed forth sir Launcelot, and the three brethren helped each other as well as they might.

CHAP. CXII.—How sir Launcelot justed against foure knights of the round table, and overthrew them.

SIR Launcelot rode into a deepe forrest, and there by a slade[1] he saw foure knights hoving[2] under an oke, and they were of king Arthurs court; that one was Sagramour le Desirous, sir Ector de Maris, sir Gawaine, and sir Ewaine.[3] Anon as these foure knights had spied sir Launcelot, they wend by his arms it had beene sir Kay. "Now, by my faith," said sir Sagramour, "I will prove sir Kayes might;" and gat his speare in his hand and came toward sir Launcelot. Thereof was sir Launcelot ware, and knew him well, and fewtred his speare against him, and smote sir Sagramour so sore that horse and man fel to the earth. "Loe, my fel-

[1] *Slade.*—A little valley, or dell. See before, p. 203.
[2] *Hoving.*—Halting, waiting, sauntering.
[3] *Sir Ewaine.*— *Sir Uwayne,* Caxton.

lowes," said sir Ector, " yonder you may see what a buffet he hath; that knight is much bigger[1] then ever was sir Kay. Now shall ye see what I may doe to him." So sir Ector gat his speare in his hand, and galloped toward sir Launcelot, and sir Launcelot smote him through the shield and shoulder, that horse and man went to the earth, and ever his speare held. " By my faith," said sir Ewaine, " that is a strong knight, and I am sure he hath slaine sir Kay; and I see by his great strength it will be hard to match him." And therewith sir Ewaine gat the spear in his hand, and rode toward sir Launcelot, and sir Launcelot knew him well, and so he met him on the plaine, and gave him such a buffet that of a great while hee wist not where hee was. " Now I well see," said sir Gawaine, " I must encounter with that knight." And so he dressed his shield, and got a good speare in his hand, and sir Launcelot knew him well; and then they let their horses run as fast as they might, and either smote other in the middest of their shields, but sir Gawaines speare brake, and sir Launcelot charged so sore upon him, that his horse reversed up and downe,[2] and much sorrow[3] had sir Gawaine to avoide his horse; and so sir Launcelot passed on a pace and smiled, and said : " God give him joy that this speare made, for there came never a better in my hand." Then the foure knights went each one to other, and comforted each other. " What say yee by this jest?" said sir Gawaine, " that one speare hath feld us foure." " Wee commaund him to the divell," said they all, " for he is a man of great might." " Yee may well say it," said sir Gawaine, " that he is a man of great might, for I dare lay my life it is sir Launcelot, I know it by his riding. Let him go," said sir Gawaine, " for as we come to the court then shall wee wit."[4] And then had they much sorrow to get their horses againe.

[1] *Bigger.*—Big was used in the sense of strong and lusty.
[2] *Up and downe.*—*Up-so-downe,* Caxton; i. e. topsy-turvy.
[3] *Sorrow.*—Grief, trouble.
[4] *Wit.*—Know.

KING ARTHUR. 223

.CHAP. CXIII.—How sir Launcelot followed a brachet into a castle, where as he found a dead knight, and how afterward he was required of a damosell for to heale her brother.

NOW let us speake of sir Launcelot, that rode a great while in a deepe forrest, where he saw a blacke brachet,[1] seeking in maner as it had beene in the fealtie[2] of an hurt deere, and therewith hee rode after the brachet; and hee saw lye on the ground a large feaute[2] of blood, and then sir Launcelot rode after, and ever the brachet looked behind her. And so shee went through a great marish,[3] and ever sir Launcelot followed; and then was he ware of an old mannor, and thither ran the brachet, and so over the bridge. So sir Launcelot rode over the bridge, that was old and feeble. And when he came into the middest of a great hall, there saw he lye a dead knight, that was a seemely man, and that brachet licked his wounds. And therewith came out a lady weeping and wringing her hands; and she said: "Oh, knight, too much sorrow hast thou brought to mee!" "Why say yee so?" said sir Launcelot; "I never did harme to this knight, for hither by feaut of blood this brachet brought me, and therefore faire lady be not displeased with me, for I am full sore agrieved of your grievance." "Truely, sir," said she; "I trow it be not ye that have slaine my husband, for he that did that deed is sore wounded and he never likely to recover, that I shall ensure him." "What is your husbands name?" said sir Launcelot. "Sir," said shee, "his name was sir Gilbert the Bastard, one of the best knights of the world, and he that hath slaine him I know not his name." "Now God send you better comfort," said sir Launcelot. And so he departed, and went into the forrest againe, and there he met with a damosell that knew him well, and shee said with a loud

[1] *Brachet.*—A scenting dog. See p. 98.
[2] *Fealtie.*—*Feaute*, Caxton, i. e. track, or trace.
[3] *Marish.* — Marsh, or bog.

voice: "Yee bee well found, my lord, and now I require you of your knighthood to helpe my brother, that is sore wounded and never stinteth bleeding, for this day fought hee with sir Gilbert the Bastard, and slew him in plaine battell, and there was my brother sore wounded; and there is a lady, a sorceresse, that dwelleth in a castle here beside, and this day shee told me that my brothers wounds should never be whole till that I could find a knight that would goe into the chappell perilous, and there he should find a sword and a bloody cloath that the wounded knight was lapped in, and a peece of the cloath and sword should helpe my brothers wounds, so that his wounds were searched with the sword and the cloath." "This is a mervailous thing," said sir Launcelot; "but what is your brothers name?" "Sir," said shee, "his name is sir Meliot de Logres." "That mee repenteth," said sir Launcelot, "for he is a fellow of the round table, and to his helpe I will doe my power." "Then, sir," said she, "follow this hie way, and it will bring you unto the chappell perilous, and here I shal abide till God send you hither againe, and, but if you speede, I know no knight living that may atchieve that adventure.

CHAP. CXIV.—How sir Launcelot came into the chappell perilous, and gat there of a dead corps a peece of the cloath and a sword.

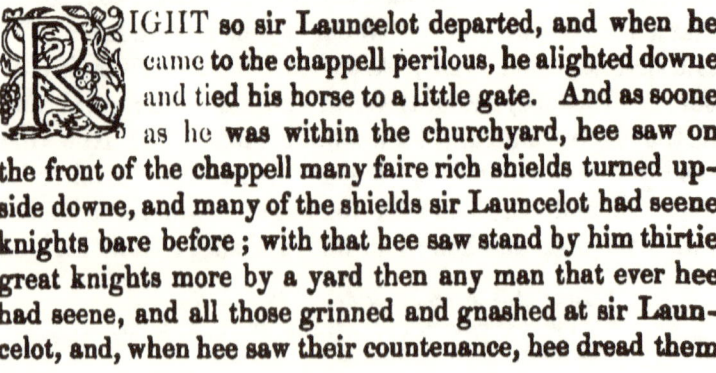

RIGHT so sir Launcelot departed, and when he came to the chappell perilous, he alighted downe and tied his horse to a little gate. And as soone as he was within the churchyard, hee saw on the front of the chappell many faire rich shields turned upside downe, and many of the shields sir Launcelot had seene knights bare before; with that hee saw stand by him thirtie great knights more by a yard then any man that ever hee had seene, and all those grinned and gnashed at sir Launcelot, and, when hee saw their countenance, hee dread them sore, and so put his shield afore him, and tooke his sword in his hand ready to doe battaile, and they were all armed in blacke harneis, ready with their shields and swords drawen. And when sir Launcelot would have gone through them, they scattered on every side of him, and gave him the way; and therewith hee waxed all bold, and entred into the chappell, and then hee saw no light but a dimme lampe burning, and then was he ware of a corps covered with a cloath of silke; then sir Launcelot stooped downe and cut a peece of that cloath away, and then it fared under him as the earth had quaked a little, whereof hee was afeard; and then hee saw a faire sword lye by the dead knight, and that he gat in his hand and hied him out of the chappell. As soone as hee was in the chappell yard, all the knights spake to him with a grimly voice, and said: " Knight sir Launcelot, lay that sword from thee, or else thou shalt die." " Whether I live or die," said sir Launcelot, " with no great words get yee it againe, therefore fight for it and yee list." Therewith he passed through them; and beyond the chappell yard there met him a faire damosell, and said, " Sir Launcelot, leave that sword behind thee or thou wilt die for it." " I will not leave it," said sir Launcelot, " for no treats."[1] " No," said she, " and ye did leave that sword, queene Guenever should ye never see." " Then were I a foole and I would leave this sword," said sir Launcelot. " Now, gentell knight," said the damosell, "I require thee to kisse mee once." " Nay," said sir Launcelot, " that God forbid." " Well, sir," said she, " and thou haddest kissed me, thy life dayes had beene done; but now, alas," said she, " I have lost all my labour, for I ordeined this chappell for thy sake, and for sir Gawaine; and once I had sir Gawaine within me, and at that time he fought with that knight which there lieth dead in yonder chappell, sir Gilbert the Bastard, and at that time hee smote off sir Gilbert the Bastards left hand. And so sir Launcelot, now I tell thee, that

---

[1] *Treats.*—Caxton has *treatys;* i. e. entreaties.

I have loved thee this seaven yeare, but there may no woman have thy love but queene Guenever; but sithen I may not rejoyce[1] thee to have thy body alive, I had kept no more joy in this world but to have had thy dead body, and I would have balmed it, and served, and so have kept it my life daies, and dayly I should have clipped thee and kissed thee in the despite of queene Guenever." "Yee say well," said sir Launcelot; "Jesus preserve me from your subtill crafts." And therewith hee tooke his horse, and departed from her. And as the booke saith, when sir Launcelot was departed, she tooke such sorrow that shee died within fifteene dayes,[2] and her name was Hellawes the sorceresse, lady of the castle Nigramus. Anon sir Launcelot met with the damosell sir Milliots sister. And when shee saw him shee clapped her hands and wept for joy; and then they rode to a castle thereby, where sir Meliot lay. Anon as sir Launcelot saw him he knew him; but he was pale as earth for bleeding. When sir Meliot saw sir Launcelot, hee kneeled on his knees and cried on hie: "Oh, lord sir Launcelot, helpe mee!" Anon sir Launcelot went unto him, and touched his wounds with sir Gilberts sword, and then he wiped his wounds with a part of the bloody cloath that sir Gilbert was wrapped in. Anon a wholer man in his life was he never. And then was there betweene them great joy; and they made sir Launcelot all the cheere that they might. And so on the morrow sir Launcelot tooke his leave, and sir Meliot to hie him to king Arthurs court, "for it draweth nigh to the feast of Pentecost, and there by the grace of God ye shall find me." And therewith they departed.

[1] *Rejoice.*—enjoy.
[2] *Fifteene dayes.*—*Within a fourten nights,* Caxton. The old Saxon custom of reckoning time by nights was becoming obsolete in the interval between Caxton's edition and that of 1634.

CHAP. CXV.—How sir Launcelot at the request of a lady recovered a fawcon, whereby he was deceived.

SO sir Launcelot rode through many strange countries, over marish and valies, til by fortune he came to a castle, and, as he passed beyond the castle, him thought hee heard two little bells ring, and then he was ware of a fawcon that came flying over his head toward an high elme, and long lines[1] about her feete ; and as shee flew unto the elme to take her perch, the lines overcaught a bough, and as she would have taken her flight she hung fast by the leggs, and sir Launcelot saw how she hung, and beheld the faire fawcon perigot,[2] and he was sorry for her. In the meane while came a lady out of a castle, and cried on hie : " Oh, Launcelot ! Launcelot ! as thou art floure of all knights of the world, helpe me to get my hawke, for, if my hawke be lost, my lord will destroy mee; for I kept the hawke, and she slipt away from me, and if my lord my husband know it, hee is so hastie that he will sley me." " What is your lords name ? " said sir Launcelot. " Sir," she said, " his name is sir Phelot, a knight that longeth to the king of Northgales." " Faire lady," said sir Launcelot, " sith that yee know my name and require me on my knighthood to helpe you, I will doe that I may to get your hawke, and yet, God knoweth, I am an il climer, and the tree is passing hie, and few boughs to helpe me withall." And therewith sir Launcelot alighted, and tied his horse to the same tree, and praied the lady to unarme him. And so when he was unarmed, hee put off all his clothes unto his shirt and breeches, and with might and force climbed up to the fawcon, and tied the lunes[3] to a great rotten branch, and threw the hawke downe with the

---

[1] *Lines.*—*Lunys,* Caxton. The *lunes* were long lines used for calling in hawks.
[2] *Perigot.*—Perhaps for *peregrine.*
[3] *Lunes.*—See the note above.

branch. Anon the lady gat the hawke with her hand. And therewithall came sir Phelot out of the groves[1] suddainely, that was her husband, al armed with his naked sword in his hand, and said: "Oh, knight sir Launcelot, now have I found thee as I would have thee," and stood at the bole of the tree to sley him. "Ah, lady!" said sir Launcelot, "why have ye betraied me?" "Shee hath done as I commanded her," said sir Phelot; "and therefore there is none other way but thine houre is come that thou must die." "That were shame," said sir Launcelot, "that an armed knight should sley a naked man by treason."

"Thou gettest none other grace," said sir Phelot. "Truely," said sir Launcelot, "that shall bee thy shame; but sith thou wilt doe none other wise, take mine harneis with thee, and hang my sword upon a bough that I may get it, and then doe thy best to sley me and thou canst." "Nay, nay," said sir Phelot, "for I know thee better then thou weenest, therefore thou gettest no weapon and I may keepe thee therefro." "Alas," said sir Launcelot, "that ever any knight should die weapenlesse." And therewithall hee looked above and under him, and over his head he saw a roundspike[2] on a big bough leavelesse, and brake it off by the body of the tree, and then hee came lower, and awaited[3] how his owne horse stood, and suddenly hee lept on the farther side of the horse from the knight. And then sir Phelot lashed at him egerly, weening to have slaine him, but sir Launcelot put away the strooke with the roundspike, and therewith he smote him on the side of the head that he fell in a sound to the ground. Then sir Launcelot tooke his sword out of his hand, and strooke his neck from the body. Then cried the lady, "Alas, why hast thou slaine my husband?" "I am not causer," said sir Launcelot, "for with falshood

---

[1] *Groves.—Grevys*, Caxton.
[2] *Roundspike.—A rounspyk, a bygge bough*, Caxton. *A rounespick*, or *rampick*, was a bough of a tree which had lesser branches growing out at its extremity.
[3] *Awaited.*—i. e. watched.

ye would have slaine me with treason, and now it is fallen on you both." And then she sounded[1] as though she would die. And therewithall sir Launcelot got all his armour as well as hee could, and put it on him for dread of more resort, for he dread that the knights castle was nigh. And as soone as hee might, hee tooke his horse and departed thence, and thanked our Lord God that he had escaped that adventure.

CHAP. CXVI.—How sir Launcelot overtooke a knight which chased his wife to have slaine her, and what he said to him.

SO sir Launcelot rode many wilde wayes, through maries and many other waies, and, as he rode in a valley, he saw a knight chasing a lady with a naked sword to have slaine her. And by fortune as this knight should have slaine this lady, shee cried on sir Launcelot, and prayed him to rescew her. When sir Launcelot saw that mischiefe, hee tooke his horse and rode betweene them, saying : " Knight, fie, for shame, why wilt thou sley this lady? thou doest shame to thee and al knights." " What hast thou to doe betweene me and my wife ? " said the knight; " I will sley her maugre thy head." " That shall ye not," said sir Launcelot, " for rather wee will have adoe together." " Sir Launcelot," said the knight, " thou doest not thy part, for this lady hath betraied me." " It is not so," said the lady ; " truely he saith wrong on me, and because I love and cherish my cosin germane, he is jelous betweene him and me, and, as I shall answere before God, there was never sinne betweene us. But sir," said the lady, " as thou art named the worshipfulest knight of the world, I require thee of thy true knighthood to keepe me and save me, for whatsomever ye say, he wil sley me, for he is without mercy." " Have ye no doubt," said sir Launcelot, " it shall not lie in his power." " Sir," said the knight, " in your sight I will be ruled as

[1] *Sounded.*—Swooned.

yee will have me." And so sir Launcelot rode on the one side and the lady on the other side. He had not ridden but a while, but that the knight bad sir Launcelot turne him, and looked behind him, and said, " Yonder come men of armes riding after us." And sir Launcelot turned him, and thought no treason. And therewith was the knight and the lady on one side, and suddainly hee strooke off the ladies head. And when sir Launcelot had espied what he had done, he called him traitour, and said, " Thou hast shamed me for ever." And suddainly sir Launcelot alighted from his horse, and drew out his sword to have slaine him. And therwith he fel flat to the earth, and caught sir Launcelot by the thighs, and cried him mercy. " Fie on thee," said sir Launcelot, " thou shamefull knight, thou mayest have no mercy, and therefore arise and fight with me." " Nay," said the knight, " I will not arise til ye graunt me mercy." " Now wil I proffer thee faire," said sir Launcelot. " I will unarme mee unto my shirt, and wil have nothing upon mee but my shirt, and my sword in my hand, and if thou canst sley me, quit bee thou for ever." " Nay, sir," said Pedivere, " that will I never doe." " Well," said sir Launcelot, " take this lady and the head, and beare it upon thee, and heere shalt thou sweare upon my sword to beare it alway upon thy backe, and never to rest, till thou come unto queene Guenever." " Sir," said hee, " that will I doe by the faith of my body." " Now," said sir Launcelot, " tell mee thy name?" " Sir, my name is Pedivere." " In a shamefull houre wert thou borne," said sir Launcelot. So Pedivere departed with the dead lady and the head, and found the queene with king Arthur at Winchester, and there hee told all the truth. " Sir knight," said the queene, " this is an horrible deede and a shameful, and a sore rebuke for sir Launcelot, but notwithstanding his worship is not knowen in divers countries ; but this shal I give you in pennance, make ye as good shift as you can, yee shall beare this lady with you on horsebacke unto the pope of Rome, and of him receive your pennance for your foule deedes, and ye shall never rest one night there as ye doe another, and if ye goe to any bed, the dead body shall lye with you." This oath hee made there, and so departed. And as the French booke saith, when hee came to Rome, the pope bad him goe againe to queene Guenever, and in Rome was his lady buried by the popes commandement. And after this sir Pedivere fell to great goodnesse, and was an holy man and an hermit.

CHAP. CXVII.—How sir Launcelot came unto king Arthurs court, and how there were recounted of his noble feates and acts.

NOW turne wee unto sir Launcelot, that came home two daies afore the feast of Penticost. And king Arthur and all the court were full glad of his comming. And when sir Gawaine, sir Ewaine, sir Sagramour, and sir Ector de Maris saw sir Launcelot in sir Kays armour, then they wist wel it was he that smot them down al with one spear. Then there was laughing and smiling among them. And ever now and then came all the knights home that sir Turquine had taken prisoners, and they all honoured and worshipped sir Launcelot. When sir Gaheris heard them speake, he said: "I saw al the battaile, from the beginning to the ending." And there hee told king Arthur all how it was, and how sir Turquine was the strongest knight that ever hee saw except sir Launcelot; there were many knights bare him record, nigh threescore. Then sir Kay told the king how sir Launcelot had rescewed him when hee was in danger to have beene slaine, and how "hee made the knights to yeeld them to me, and not to him." And there they were, all three, and bare record. "And by Jesus," said sir Kay, "because sir Launcelot tooke my harneis, and left me his, I rode in good peace, and no man would have to doe with me." Then anon therewithall came the three knights that fought with sir Launcelot at the long bridge, and there they yeelded them unto sir Kay, and sir Kay forsooke them, and said he fought never with them; "but I shall ease your hearts," said sir Kay, "yonder is sir Launcelot that overcame you." When they understood that, they were glad. Then sir Meliot de Logres came home, and told king Arthur how sir Launcelot had saved him from death, and all the deedes were knowen, how foure queenes, sorceresses, had him in prison, and how hee was delivered by the daughter of king Bagdemagus. Also, there were told all the great deedes of armes that sir Launcelot did betweene the two kings, that is to say, the king of Northgales and king Bagdemagus, all the truth sir Gahalatine told, and sir Mador de la Porte, and sir Mordred, for they three were at that turnemente. Then came in the lady that knew sir Launcelot when he wounded sir Belleus at that pavilion, and there, at the request of sir Launcelot, sir Belleus was made knight of the round table. And so at that time, sir Launcelot had the greatest name of any knight of the world, and most was hee honoured both of high and low.

CHAP. CXVIII.—How Beaumains came unto king Arthurs court, and demanded three petitions of king Arthur.

WHEN king Arthur held his round table most plenare, it fortuned that he commanded that the solemne and high feast of Pentecost should be holden at a citie and castle, which in those daies was called King-Kenedon,[1] upon the sands that marched nigh[2] Wales; so king Arthur had ever a custome that at the high feast of Pentecost, especially afore al other high feasts in the yeare, he would not goe that day to meat untill he had heard or seene some great adventure or mervaile. And for that custom all manner of strange adventures came before king Arthur at that feast afore all other feasts. And so sir Gawaine, a little before noone of the day of Pentecost,

[1] *King-Kenedon.*—Caxton has *Kynke-Kenadonne.*
[2] *Marched nigh.*—Bordered upon.

espied at a window three men on horsebacke, and a dwarfe on foote. And so the three men alighted, and the dwarfe kept their horses, and one of the three men was higher then the other twaine by a foote and a halfe. Then sir Gawaine went unto the king and said: " Sir, go to your meate, for here at hand commeth strange adventures." So king Arthur went to his meate, with many other kings. And there were all the knights of the round table, save those that were prisoners or slaine at an encounter. Then at the high feast evermore they should be fullfilled the whole number, an hundred and fiftie, for then was the round table fully accomplished. Right so came into the hall two men well beseene and richly, and upon their shoulders there leaned the goodliest young man and the fairest that ever they saw, and he was large, long, and broad in the shoulders, and well visaged, and the fairest and the largest hands[1] that ever man saw, but he fared as though he might not goe nor beare himselfe, but if bee leaned upon their shoulders. Anon, as king Arthur saw him, there was made silence and roome, and right so they went with him unto the hie dees,[2] without saying any word, and then this bigge young man drew him backe, and easily stretched up straight, saying to king Arthur, "God blesse you, and al your faire fellowship, and in especial the fellowship of the round table. And for this cause I am come hither, for to pray you to give me three gifts, and they shall not bee unreasonably asked, but that yee may worshipfully and honourably graunt them unto me, and to you no great hurt nor losse. And as for the first gift I will aske now, and the other two giftes I will aske at the same day twelve moneths wheresoever that ye hold your high feast." "Now aske," said king Arthur, "and yee shall have your petition." "Now, sir," said he, "this is my petition for this feast, that ye will give me meate and drinke sufficiently for

---

[1] *The largest hands.—The fayrest and the largest handed*, Caxton.
[2] *His dees.*—The high dais, or table at the head of the hall, where the persons of greatest dignity were seated.

these twelve-monethes, and at that day I will aske mine other two giftes." "My faire sonne," said king Arthur," "aske better, I counsaile thee, for this is but a simple asking, for my heart giveth mee to thee greatly that thou art come of men of worship, and greatly my conceit faileth me but thou shalt prove a man of right great worship." "Sir," said he, "as for that, be it as it may bee, I have asked that I will aske." "Well," said king Arthur, "yee shall have meate and drinke enough; I never defended that none, neither my friend nor foe. But what is thy name? I would faine know." "I can not tell you," said hee. "That have I marvaile of thee," said the king, "that thou knowest not thine owne name, and thou art one of the goodliest young men that ever I saw." Then the noble king Arthur betooke him unto the steward sir Kay, and charged him that hee should give him of all manner of meates and drinkes of the best, "and also that he have all manner of finding, as though hee were a lords sonne." "That shall little neede," said sir Kay, "to doe such cost upon him, for I dare well undertake that hee is a villaine[1] borne, and never will make man, for and hee had beene come of a gentleman, hee would have asked of you horse and harneis, but such as hee is he hath asked. And sithen hee hath no name, I shall give him a name, that shal be Beaumains, that is to say, faire hands; and into the kitchen I shall bring him, and there he shall have fat browesse[2] every day, that he shall bee as fat by the twelve-monethes end as a porke hog." Right so the two men that had brought him departed, and left him to sir Kay, that scorned and mocked him.

[1] *A villaine.*—i. e. a churl, or peasant; one of ignoble birth.
[2] *Browesse.*—Fat broth.

CHAP. CXIX.—How sir Launcelot and sir Gawaine were wroth because sir Kay mocked Beaumains, and of a damosell which desired a knight for to doe battaile for a lady.

HEREAT was sir Gawaine wroth, and especially sir Launcelot, for hee bad sir Kay leave his mocking, "for I dare lay my head he shall prove a man of great worship." "Let be," said sir Kay, "it cannot bee by reason; for as he is, so hath he asked." " Beware," said sir Launcelot, " so yee gave that good knight, sir Brewnor, sir Dinadans brother, a name, and ye cald him La-cot-male-taile, and that turned you to anger afterward." "As for that," said sir Kay, " this shall never prove no such, for sir Brewnore desired evermore worship, and this desireth bread and drinke; upon paine of my life he was brought up and fostred in some abbey,¹ and howsomever it was, they failed of meate and drinke, and so hither he is come for sustenance." And so sir Kay had got him a place, and sat downe to meate. So Beaumains went to the hall dore, and sat him downe among boyes and lads, and there hee eate sadly. And then sir Launcelot, after meate, bad him come to his chamber, and there hee should have meate and drinke enough. And so did sir Gawaine. But hee refused them all; hee would doe nothing but as sir Kay commanded him, for no profer. But as touching sir Gawaine, he had reason to proffer him lodging, meate, and drinke; for that proffer came of his blood, for hee was neerer kinne to him then hee wist. But that sir Launcelot did, was of his great gentlenesse and curtesie. So thus he was put into the kitchen, and lay every night as the boyes of the kitchen did; and so he endured al those twelve-monethes, and never displeased man nor

---

¹ *In some abbey.*—A satire upon the good living of the monasteries. Sir Kay intimates his belief that the main occupation of the monks was to fatten themselves.

child, but alwaies he was meeke and milde. But ever when hee knew of any justing of knights, that would he see and hee might. And ever sir Launcelot would give him gold to spend and cloathes, and so did sir Gawaine. And where as were any masteries[1] done, there would hee be; and there might none cast the barre or stone to him by two yards. Then would sir Kay say, " How like you my boy of the kitchen?" So it passed on till the feast of Pentecost, and at that time the king held it at Carlion, in the most royallest wise that might be, like as yearely hee did. But the king would eate no meate on the Whitsunday till hee had heard of some adventure. And then came there a squire to the king, and said: " Sir, yee may goe to your meate, for here commeth a damosell with some strange adventure." Then was the king glad, and set him downe. Right so there came in a damosell, and saluted the king, and praied him for succour. " For whom?" said the king: " what is the adventure?" " Sir, said she, " I have a lady of great worship and renown, and she is besieged with a tyrant, so that shee may not goe out of her castle, and because that heere in your court are called the noblest knights of the world, I come unto you and pray you for succour." " What call ye your lady, and where dwelleth she, and who is hee and what is his name that hath besieged her?" " Sir king," said shee, " as for my ladies name, that shall not bee knowne for me as at this time; but I let you wit shee is a lady of great worship, and of great lands. And as for the tyrant that besiegeth her and destroyeth her land, hee is called the red knight of the reede lands." " I know him not," said the king. " Sir," said sir Gawaine, " I know him well, for hee is one of the perilous knights of the world; men say that hee hath seaven mens strength, and from him I escaped once full hard with my life." " Faire damosell," said the king, " there bee knights heere that would doe their power to rescew your lady, but because ye wil not tell

---

[1] *Musteries.*—Trials of skill.

her name nor where she dwelleth, therefore none of my knights that be here now shall goe with you by my will." "Then must I speake further," said the damosell.

CHAP. CXX.—How Beaumains desired the battaile, and how it was graunted him, and how he desired to be made knight of sir Launcelot.

THEN with these words came before the king Beaumains, while the damosel was there; and thus he said: "Sir king, God thanke you, I have beene this twelve monethes in your kitchen, and have had my full sustenance, and now I will aske my two gifts that bee behind." "Aske upon my perrill," said the king. "Sir, these shal be my two gifts: first, that ye will grant mee to have this adventure of the damosell, for it belongeth to me." "Thou shalt have it," said the king; "I graunt it thee." "Then, sir, this is now the other gift; that ye shall bid sir Launcelot du Lake to make me a knight, for of him I will bee made knight, and else of none; and when I am past, I pray you let him ride after mee, and make mee knight when I require him." "All this shall be done," said the king. "Fie on thee," said the damosell; "shal I have none but one that is your kitchen page?" Then was shee wroth, and tooke her horse and departed. And with that there came one to Beaumains, and told him that his horse and armour was come for him, and there was a dwarfe come with al things that him needed in the richest manner. Thereat all the court had much marvaile from whence came all that geare. So when hee was armed, there was none but few so goodly a man as hee was. And right so he came into the hall, and tooke his leave of king Arthur and of sir Gawaine, and of sir Launcelot, and prayed him that he would hie after him; and so departed and rode after the damosell.

CHAP. CXXI.—How Beaumains departed, and how he got of sir Kay a speare and a shield, and how he justed and fought with sir Launcelot.

BUT there went many after to behold how well he was horsed and trapped in cloth of gold, but hee had neither shield nor speare. Then sir Kay said openly in the hall: "I will ride after my boy of the kitching, for to wit whether hee will know mee for his better." Sir Lancelot and sir Gawaine said, "yet abide at home." So sir Kay made him ready, and tooke his horse and his speare, and rode after him. And right as Beaumains overtooke the damosell, so came sir Kay, and said: "What, sir Beaumains, know yee not mee?" Then hee turned his horse, and knew that it was sir Kay, which had done him all the despite that yee have heard afore. "Yee," said Beaumains, "I know you for an ungentle knight of the court, and therefore beware of me." Therewith sir Kay put his speare in the rest, and runne straight to him, and Beaumains came as fast upon him with his sword in his hand; and so hee put away the speare with his sword, and with a foyne thrust him through the side, that sir Kay fell downe as hee had beene dead; and he alight downe, and tooke sir Kays shield and his speare, and start upon his owne horse and rode his way. All that saw sir Lancelot, and so did the damosell. And then he bad his dwarfe start upon sir Kays horse, and so he did. By that sir Lancelot was come. Then he profered sir Lancelot to just, and either made them ready, and came together so fiercely that either bare downe other to the earth, and sore were they brused. Then sir Lancelot arose, and helped him to avoyd his horse. And then Beaumains put his shield before him, and profered to fight with sir Lancelot on foote, and so they rashed together like two wild bores, trasing, rasing, and foyning to the mountenance of an houre; and sir Lancelot felt him so big, that hee mervailed of his strength, for hee fought more like a gyant then a knight, and that his fighting was durable and passing perilous; for sir Lancelot had much adoe with him, that hee dread himselfe to bee ashamed, and said: "Beaumains, fight not so sore; your quarrell and mine is not so great but wee may leave off." "Truly that is truth," said Beaumains, "but it doth mee good to feele your might, and yet, my lord, I have not shewed the uttermost."

CHAP. CXXII.—How Beanmains told his name to sir Lancelot, and how hee was dubbed knight of sir Lancelot, and after overtooke the damosell.

"IN Gods name," said sir Lancelot, "for I promise you by the faith of my body I had as much to doe as I might to save my selfe from you unshamed, and therefore have no doubt of none earthly knight." "Hope yee that I may any while stand a proved knight," said sir Beaumains. "Yea," said sir Launcelot, "doe yee as yee have done, and I shall bee your warrant." "Then I pray you," said Beaumains, "give mee the order of knighthood." "Then must yee tell mee your name," said sir Lancelot, "and of what kinne yee bee borne." "Sir, so that you will not discover me, I shall tell you," said Beaumains. "Nay," said sir Launcelot, "and that I promise you by the faith of my body, until it be openly knowne." "Then, sir," said hee, "my name is Gareth of Orkeney, and brother unto sir Gawaine of father and mother." "Ah, sir," said sir Lancelot, "I am now more gladder of you then I was, for ever mee thought yee should bee of a great blood, and that yee came not to the court for meate nor drinke." And then sir Lancelot gave him the order of knighthood. And then sir Gareth prayed him to depart and let him goe on his journey. So sir Lancelot departed from him, and came to sir Kay, and made him to bee borne upon his shield, and so he was healed hard with his life; and all men scorned sir Kay, and especially sir Gawaine, and also sir Lancelot said that it was not his part to rebuke no young man, for full little knew hee of what kinne hee is come, and for what cause he came unto this court. And so wee leave off sir Kay, and turne wee unto Beaumains. When he had overtaken the damosell, anone shee said: " What doest thou heere? thou stinkest all of the kitching; thy clothes bee all bawdy[1] of the grease and tallow that thou hast goten in king Arthurs kitching. Wenest thou," said shee, " that I alow thee for yonder knight that thou hast slaine? nay, truely, for thou slewest him unhappily and cowardly, therefore returne againe, bawdy kitching page. I know thee well, for sir Kay named thee Beaumains. What art thou but a luske[2] and a turner of broaches and a washer of dishes!" " Damosell," said sir Beaumains, " say to mee what ye list, I wil not goe from you whatsoever yee say, for I have undertaken of king Arthur for to atchieve your adventure, and I shall finish it to the end, or I shall die therefore." " Fie one thee, kitching knave. Wilt thou finish mine adventure? thou shalt anon bee met withall, that thou wouldest not, for all the broth that ever thou suppest, once looke him in the face." " I shall assay," said Beaumains. So as they thus rode in the wood, there came a man flying all that he might. " Whether wilt thou?" said Beaumains. " O lord," said he, " helpe mee, for hereby in a slade are six theeves which have taken my lord and bound him, and I am afraid least they will slay him." " Bring mee thither," said sir Beaumains. And so they rode together till they came there as the knight was bound, and then hee rode unto the theeves, and strake one at the first strooke to death, and then another, and at the third strooke hee slew the third thiefe; and then the other three fled, and hee rod after and overtooke them, and then those three

---

[1] *Bawdy.*—The original meaning of this word was dirty.
[2] *A Luske.*—A lazy lubber.

theeves turned againe and hard assailed sir Beaumains; but at the last hee slew them; and then returned and unbound the knight. And the knight thanked him, and prayed him to ride with him to his castle there a little beside, and he should worshipfully reward him for his good deedes. "Sir," said sir Beaumains, "I will no reward have; I was this day made knight of the noble sir Lancelot, and therefore I will have no reward, but God reward me. And also I must follow this damosell." And when hee came nigh her, shee bad him ride from her, "for thou smellest all of the kitching. Wenest thou that I have joy of thee? for all this deede that thou hast done, is but mishapned thee. But thou shalt see a sight that shall make thee to turne againe, and that lightly." Then the same knight which was rescued of the theeves rode after the damosell, and prayed her to lodge with him all that night. And because it was neere night, the damosell rode with him to his castle, and there they had great cheere. And at supper the knight set sir Beaumains before the damosell. "Fie, fie," said shee, "sir knight, yee are uncurteous for to set a kitching page before me; him beseemeth better to sticke a swine then to sit before a damosell of high parentage." Then the knight was ashamed of her words, and tooke him up and set before him at a side boord, and set himselfe before him. And so all that night they had good and merry rest.

CHAP. CXXIII.—How sir Beaumains fought and slew two knights at a passage.

SO on the morrow the damosell and he tooke their leave, and thanked the knight, and so departed, and rode one their way till they came to a great forrest, and there was a great river and but one passage, and there were redy two knights on the further side, to let them the passage. "What saist thou?" said the damosell; "wilt thou match yonder two knights, or wilt thou returne againe?" "Nay," said sir Beaumains, "I will not returne againe, and they were sixe moe." And therewith hee rashed[1] into the water, and in the midest of the water either brake their speares to their hands, and then they drew their swords and smote each at other egerly; and at the last, sir Beaumains smote the other upon the helme that his head was astonied,[2] and therewith hee fell downe into the water, and there was drowned. And then hee spurred his horse unto the land, where the other knight fell upon him and brake his speare, and so they drew their swords and fought long together. At the last sir Beaumains clove his helme and his head unto the shoulders. And then hee rode unto the damosell, and bad her ride forth on her way. "Alas," said shee, "that ever kitching page should have the fortune to destroy such two doughty knights! thou weenest thou hast done doughtily, and that is not so, for the first knights horse stumbled and there he was drowned in the water, and never it was by thy force and might; and the last knight by mishap thou camest behind him, and shamefully thou slewest him." "Damosell," said sir Beaumains, "yee may say what yee will, but with whomsoever I have adoe withall, I trust to God to serve him or hee depart, and therefore I reckon not what yee say, so that I may winne your lady." "Fie, fie, foule kitching knave; thou shalt see knights that shall abate thy boast." "Faire damosell, give mee faire language, and then my care is past, for what knights soever they be I care not, nor doubt[3] them not." "Also," said shee, "I say it for thine availe, yet mayst thou turne againe with thy worship, for if thou follow mee thou art but slaine, for I see all that ever thou doest is but by misadventure, and not by prownesse of thy hands." "Well, damosell, yee may say what yee will, but wheresoever that yee goe, I will follow you." So thus sir Beaumains rode with the damosell untill even-song, and ever shee chid

[1] *Rashed.*—Caxton, *Rasshyd.* Dashed; rushed.
[2] *Astonied.*—Stunned.
[3] *Doubt.*—Fear.

him and would not rest. And then they came to a blacke
laund, and there was a blacke hawthorne, and thereon hung
a blacke baner, and on the other side there hung a blacke
shield, and by it stood a black speare and a long, and a
greate blacke horse covered with silke, and a blacke stone
fast by it.

CHAP. CXXIV.—How sir Beaumains fought with the knight of the
blacke launds,[1] and he fought so long with him that the blacke
knight fell downe and dyed.

THERE sate a knight all armed in blacke harnies, and his name was the knight of the blacke laundes. When the damosell saw the blacke knight, shee bad sir Beaumains flee downe the valey, for his horse was not sadled. "I thanke you," said sir Beaumains, "for alwayes yee will have mee a coward." With that the blacke knight came to the damosell, and said, "Faire damosell, have yee brought this knight from king Arthurs court to be your champion?" "Nay, faire knight," said shee, "this is but a kitching knave, that hath beene fed in king Arthurs kitching for almes." "Wherefore commeth he in such aray?" said the knight, "it is great shame that he beareth you company." "Sir, I cannot bee delivered of him," said the damosell, "for with me hee rideth maugre mine head; would to God ye would put him from me, or else to sley him if ye may, for hee is an unhappie knave, and unhappie hath hee done to day through misadventure; for I saw him sley two knights at the passage of the water, and other deedes he did before right marvailous, and all through unhappinesse." "That marvaileth mee," said the blacke knight, "that any man the which is of worship will have to doo with him." "Sir, they know him not," said the damosell, "and because he

[1] *Launds.—Knight of the blak launde*, Caxton. The edition of 1634 has throughout printed *land* and *lands* for *launds* and *launds*.

rideth with me, they thinke he is some man of worship borne." "That may well be," said the blacke knight, "neverthelesse how be it you say that hee is no man of worship, yet he is a full likely person, and full like to bee a strong man; but thus much shall I graunt you," said the black knight, "I shall put him downe upon his feete, and his horse and his armour he shall leave with mee, for it were shame for mee to doe him any more harme." When sir Beaumains heard him say thus to her, hee said, "Sir knight, thou art full large[1] of my horse and my harneis; I let thee to wit it cost thee nought, and, whether it liketh thee or not, this laund will I passe maugre thine head, and horse nor harneis gettest thou none of me, but if thou winne them with thy hands; and therefore let mee see what thou canst doe." "Saiest thou that," said the blacke knight, "now yeeld thy lady from thee lightly, for it beseemeth not a kitchin knave to ride with such a lady." "Thou liest," said sir Beaumains, "I am a gentleman borne, and of more high linage then thou art, and that I will prove upon thy body." Then in great wrath they departed with their horses, and came together as it had beene thunder, and the blacke knights speare brake, and sir Beaumains thrust him through both his sides, and therewith his speare brake, and the truncheon stucke still in his side, but neverthelesse the blacke knight drew his sword, and smote many eager strookes and of great might, and hurt sir Beaumains full sore. But at the last the blacke knight within an houre and a halfe fell downe from his horse in a sound, and there died forthwith. And when sir Beaumains saw him so wel horsed and armed, he alighted down, and armed him in his armour, and so tooke his horse and rode after the damosell. When she saw him come nigh her, shee said to him, "Away, kitchen knave, goe out of the wind, for the smell of thy baudy cloathes grieveth me. Alas! that ever such a knave as thou art should by mishap sley so good a knight as thou

[1] *Large*—i. e. generous; liberal.

hast slaine, but all this is through thine unhappinesse. But hereby is a knight that shall pay thee all thy payment, and therefore yet I counsell thee to flee backe." "It may happen mee," said sir Beaumains, " to be beaten or slaine, but I warne you, faire damosell, I will not flee away for him, nor leave your company for all that ye can say; for ever ye say that they sley me or beat me, but how soever it happeneth I escape, and they lye on the ground, and therefore it were as good for you to hold you still, then thus to rebuke me all day, for away will I not till I feele the uttermost of this journey, or else I will bee slaine or truely beaten; therefore ride on your way, for follow you I will whatsoever happen."

CHAP. CXXV.—How the brother of the knight that was slaine met with sir Beaumains, and fought with sir Beaumains, which yeelded him at the last.

THUS as they rode together they saw a knight come driving by them all in greene, both his horse and his harneis, and when hee came nigh the damosell, hee asked of her, " Is that my brother the blacke knight that ye have brought with you?" "Nay, nay," said she, "this unhappie kitchin knave hath slaine your brother through unhappinesse." " Alas!" said the greene knight, " that is great pittie that so noble a knight as hee was should so unhappily be slaine, and namely of a knaves hand, as ye say he is. A! traitour," said the greene knight, " thou shalt die for slaying of my brother; he was a full noble knight, and his name was sir Pereard." " I defie thee," said sir Beaumains, " for I let thee to wit I slew him knightly, and not shamefully." There withall the greene knight rode unto an horne that was greene, and it hung upon a thorne, and there he blew three deadly notes,[1] and there came three[2] damosells that lightly[3] armed him.

[1] *Notes.—Motys*, Caxton.   [2] *Three.—Two*, Caxton.
[3] *Lightly.*—i. e. quickly.

And then tooke hee a great horse, and a greene shield, and a greene speare. And then they ranne together with all their might, and brake their speares to their hands. And then anon they drew out their swords and gave many sad strookes, and either of them wounded other full evill. And at the last at an overthwart sir Beaumains horse strooke the greene knights horse on the on side, that he fell to the ground. And then the greene knight lightly avoided his horse, and dressed him upon his feete. That saw sir Beaumains, and therewith he alighted, and they rashed together like two mightie champions[1] a long while, and they bled sore both. With that came the damosell, and said, "My lord the greene knight, for shame, why stand yee so long fighting with that kitchin knave? alas! it is shame that ever yee were made a knight, for to see such a stinking boy match such a valiant knight as ye bee." The greene knight hearing these words was ashamed, and incontinent he gave sir Beaumains a mightie strook and clove his shield throughout. When sir Beaumains saw his shield clove asunder, he was a little ashamed of that strooke and of the damosells language, and then hee gave him such a buffet upon the helme that hee fell on his knees, and suddenly sir Beaumains threw him downe on the ground groveling. And incontinent the greene knight cried sir Beaumains mercy, and yeelded him unto sir Beaumains, and praied him to grant him his life. "All this is in vaine," said sir Beaumains, "for thou shalt die but if this damosell which is come with me pray me to save thy life." And therewith hee unlaced his helme, like as hee would have slaine him. "Fie upon thee, thou kitchin page, I will never pray thee to save his life. For I will never bee so much in thy danger."[2] "Then shall hee die," said sir Beaumains. "Not so hardy, thou bawdy knave," said the damosell, "that thou sley

---

[1] *Champions.*—*Kempys,* Caxton. Both words have the same signification, and were formed from the same root.

[2] *In thy danger.*—i. e. under obligation to thee.

him." "Alas!" said the greene knight, "suffer me not to die, for a faire word may save my life. Oh, faire knight," said the greene knight, "save my life, and I will forgive the death of my brother, and for ever to become thy man, and thirtie knights that hold of mee for ever shall doe you service." "In the devills name," said the damosell, "that such a bawdy kitchin knave should have thee and thirtie knights service." "Sir knight," said sir Beaumains, "all this availeth not, but if my damosell speake with me for thy life." And therewithall he made resemblance to sley him. "Let be," said the damosell, "thou bawdy knave, sley him not, for if thou doe, thou shalt repent it." "Damosell," said sir Beaumains, "your charge is to mee a pleasure, and at your commaundement his life shall be saved, and else not." Then he said, "Sir knight with the greene armes, I release thee quit at this damosels request, for I wil not make her wroth, I will fulfil all that shee chargeth me." And then the green knight kneeled down and did him homage with his sword. Then said the damosell, "Me repenteth, greene knight, of your domage, and of your brothers death, the blacke knight, for of your helpe I had great neede, for I am sore adread to passe this great forrest." "Nay, dread ye not so sore," said the greene knight, "for yee shall lodge with me this night, and to morrow I shall helpe you through this forrest." So they tooke their horses and rode unto his mannor, which was fast there beside.

CHAP. CXXVI.—How the damosell alwayes rebuked sir Beaumains, and would not suffer him to sit at her table, but called him kitchin page.

AND alwayes the damosell rebuked sir Beaumains, and would not suffer him to sit at her table, but the greene knight tooke him up and set him at a side table. "Mee thinketh marvaile," said the greene knight to the damosell, "why that yee rebuke this noble knight as yee doe, for I warne you, damosell, hee is a full noble knight, and I know no knight able to match him; therefore ye doe great wrong to rebuke him, for he shall doe you right good service, for whatsoever he maketh him selfe, yee shall prove at the end that hee is come of noble blood, and of kings linage." "Fie, fie," said the damosell, "it is shame for you to say of him such worship." "Truely," said the greene knight, "it were shame for me to say of him any disworship, for he hath proved him selfe a better knight then I am, yet have I met with many knights in my dayes, and never or this time have I found no knight his match." And so that night they went unto their rest, and all the night the greene knight commanded thirtie knights privily to watch sir Beaumains for to keepe him from all treason. And so on the morrow they all arose, and heard their masse, and brake their fast, and then they tooke their horses and rode on their way, and the greene knight conveied them through the forrest, and then the greene knight said, "My lord sir Beaumains, I and my thirtie knights shall bee alway at your command, both early and late, at your calling, and where soever yee will send us." "It is well said," quoth sir Beaumains, "and when I cal upon you we must yeeld you and al your knights unto king Arthur." "If ye so commaund us, we shall be ready at all times," said the greene knight. "Fie, fie upon thee, in the divels name," said the damosel, "that any good knight should be obedient unto a kitchin knave." Then departed the greene knight and the damosell. And then she said to sir Beaumains, "Why followest thou me, thou kitchin boy? cast away thy shield and thy speare, I counsaile thee yet, and flee away betimes, or thou shalt say soone alas! for were thou as mightie as ever was Wade,[1] or

[1] *Wade.*—This is a curious allusion to one of the personages of Northern mythology, the romance of whom, as it existed in our island, seems to be lost. Some incidents in it are alluded to by Chaucer, and by one or two other old writers. The northern account of him is given in the Wilkina Saga. The notices of this hero are collected in a pamphlet entitled, "Wade; Lettre à M. Henri Ternaux-Compans,—par Fr. Michel, Paris, 1837."

KING ARTHUR. 249

sir Launcelot, sir Tristram, or the good knight sir Lamorake, thou shalt not passe a pace heereby, that is called the pace perilous."[1] "Damosell," said sir Beaumains, "who is afeard, let him flee, for it were shame to turne againe, sith I have ridden so long with you." "Well," said the damosell, "thou shalt see soone whether thou wilt or not."

CHAP. CXXVII.—How the third brother, called the red knight, justed and fought against sir Beaumains, and how sir Beaumains overcame him.

O within a while they saw a tower as white as any snow, well matchcold[2] all about, and double ditched; and over the tower gate there hung fiftie shields of divers coulours. And under that tower there was a faire medow, and therein were many knights and squires in pavilions and upon scaffolds to behold, for there on the morrow should bee a great turnement at that castle, and the lord of that tower was in his castle, and looked out at a window, and there he saw a damosel and a page, and a knight armed at all points. "So God mee helpe," said the lord, "with that knight will I just, for I see that he is a knight arraunt." And so anon he armed him, and tooke his horse hastily; and when he was on horseback with his shield and his speare, which was all red, both his horse and his harneis, and all that belonged unto him, and when he came nigh sir Beaumains, he wend he had beene his brother the blacke knight, and then hee cried aloud: "Brother, what doe yee heere in these marches?" "Nay, nay," said the damosell, "it is not your brother; this is but a kitchin knave, which hath beene brought up for almes in king Arthurs court." "Neverthelesse," said the red knight, "I will speake with him or he depart."

[1] *Pace perilous.*—The perilous pass.
[2] *Matchcold.—Machicolated.* A well-known term in the military architecture of the Middle Ages.

"Ah," said the damosell, "this unhapie knave hath slaine your brother, and sir Kay named him Beaumains, and this horse and harneis was your brothers the blacke knight. Also I saw him overcome your brother the greene knight, with his owne hands. Now may yee bee revenged upon him, for I cannot bee quit of him." And with this, both the knights departed asunder, and they came together with all their might, and either of their horses fell to the earth, and lightly they avoided their horses and put their shields afore them, and drew their swords, and either gave to other many sad strookes, as now heere and now there, rasing, trasing, foyning, and hurling like two boores, the space of three houres. And then the damosell cried out on high unto the red knight: "Alas, thou noble red knight, thinke what worship hath followed thee; let never a kitchin knave endure thee so long as he doth." Then the red knight waxed wroth and doubled his strookes, and hurt sir Beaumains wondrous sore, so that the blood ranne downe to the ground, and great mervaile was it to behold that strong battaile. Yet at the last sir Beaumains strooke him to the earth; and as hee would have slaine the red knight, he cried mercy, saying: "Noble knight, sley me not, and I shal yeeld me unto thee with fiftie knights that be at my command; and I forgive thee all the despite that thou hast done to me, and the death of my brother the blacke knight." "All this availeth thee not," said sir Beaumains, "but if my damosell pray me to save thy life." And therewith he made resemblance to strik off his head. "Let be, thou Beaumains, sley him not, for he is a noble knight, and not so hardy upon thine head but that thou save him." Then sir Beaumains bad the red knight stand up, "and thanke yee now the damosell for your life." Then the red knight prayed him to see his castle, and to be there all that night; and so the damosell granted him, and there they had merry cheere. But alwaies the damosell spake many foule words unto sir Beaumains, whereof the red knight had great marvaile; and all that night the red knight made threescore knights to watch sir Beaumains, that hee should have no shame nor villany. And on the morrow they heard masse, and brake their fast; and the red knight came before sir Beaumains with his threescore knights, and there he proffered him his homage and feaultie at al times hee and his knights to doe him service. "I thanke you," said sir Beaumains, "but this ye shall graunt mee, when I call upon you, to come afore my lord king Arthur, and yeeld you unto him to be his knight." "Sir," said the red knight, "I will bee ready with all my fellowship at your command." So sir Beaumains and the damosell departed, and ever she rode chiding him in the foulest manner.

CHAP. CXXVIII.—How sir Beaumains suffered great rebukes of the damosell, and he suffered it patiently.

"DAMOSELL," said sir Beaumains, "yee are uncurteous so to rebuke me as ye doe, for me seemeth I have done you great service, and ever ye threaten me for I shal be beaten with knights that we meete, but ever for all your best they lye in the dust or in the myre, and therefore I pray you rebuke mee no more, and when ye see mee beaten or yeelden recreaunt, then may yee bid me goe from you shamefully; but first I let you to wit I wil not depart from you, for I were worse then a foole if I would depart from you all the while I winne worship." "Well," said she, "right soone there shall meete with thee a knight that shall pay thee all thy wages, for he is the man of the most worship in the world, except king Arthur." "I will it well," said sir Beaumains, "the more he is of worship, the more shall it be my worshippe to have adoe with him." Then anon within a while they were ware where as was before them a faire citie, and betweene them and the citie a mile and a halfe there was a faire medow that was new mowen, and therein were many pavilions goodly to behold. "Loe," said the damosell, "yonder is a lord that oweth yonder citie, and his custome is such, that when the weather is faire he lieth in this medow for to just and turney, and ever there bee about him five hundred knights and all gentlemen of armes, and there be of al maner of games that any gentleman can devise or think." "That goodly lord," said sir Beaumains, "I would faine see." "Thou shalt see him time enough," said the damosell. And so as she rode neere shee espied the pavilion where he was. "Loe," said shee, "seest thou yonder pavilion that is all of the coulour of Inde,[1] and all manner thing that is about him, both men and women, and horses trapped, shields and speares, were all of the colour of Inde; and his name is sir Persaunt of Inde, the most lordliest knight that ever thou lookedst on." "It may well be," said sir Beaumains, "but be he never so stout a knight, in this field I shall abide till that I see him under his shield." "Ah! foole," said she, "thou were better to flee betime." "Why," said sir Beaumains, "and he be such a knight as ye make him, hee will not set upon mee with all his men, or with his five hundred knights at one bout; for if there come no more but one at once, I shall never fail him while my life lasteth." "Fie, fie," said the damosel, "that ever such a stinking knave should blow such a boast."

"Damosell," said sir Beaumains, "yee are to blame so to rebuke me, for I had rather to doe five battailes then so to be rebuked. Let him come, and then let him doe his worst." "Sir," said shee, "I marvaile what thou art, and of what kinne thou art come; boldly thou speakest, and boldly thou hast done, that have I wel seene; therefore I pray thee save thy selfe and thou maiest, for thine horse and thou have had great travaile, and I dread me we dwel overlong from the siege, for it is but seven mile hence, and all perilous pas-

---

[1] *Colour of Inde.*—A dark blue colour, often mentioned by the mediæval writers.

sages we are past, save all onely this passage, and here I dread me full sore, lest that ye shall catch some hurt or domage, and therefore I would ye were hence that ye were not bruised nor hurt with this strong knight; but I let you to wit that this sir Persaunt of Inde is nothing of might nor of strength unto the knight that hath laid the siege about my lady." "As for that," said sir Beaumains, " be it as it may, for sith I am come so nigh this good knight, I will prove his might or I depart from him. It were great shame to mee if I withdrew mee now from him, and therefore, damosell, have ye no doubt by the grace of God I shall so deale with this knight that within two houres after noone ye shall deliver him, and then shall wee come to the siege by day-light." " Oh, Jesus," said the damosell, "I have marvaile what manner of man ye be, for it may never be otherwise but that yee be come of a noble blood, for more fowler nor more shamefuller did never woman rule nor rebuke a knight as I have done to you, and ever curteously yee have suffered me, and that came never but of a gentle blood and linage." "Damosell," said sir Beaumains, "a knight may little doe that may not suffer a damosel; for what soever that ye said to me, I took no heed to your words, for the more ye said the more ye angred me, and my wrath I wreked upon them that I had adoe withal, and therfore all the missaying that ye missayed mee furthered me in my battailes, and caused mee to thinke to shew and prove my selfe at the end what I was; for peradventure though I had meate in king Arthurs kitchin, yet I might have had meat enough in other places ; but all that I did for to prove and to assay my friends, and that shall be knowne another day ; and whether I be a gentleman borne or no, I let you wit, faire damosell, I have done you gentlemans service, and peradventure better service yet will I doe you or I depart from you." "Alas," said shee, "faire sir Beaumains, forgive me all that I have missayed and misdone against you." "With all my heart," said sir Beaumains, " I forgive it you, for yee did nothing but as yee ought to doe, for all your evill words pleased mee; and, damosell," said sir Beaumains, "sith it liketh you to speake thus faire to mee, wit yee well it gladdeth greatly mine hart; and now me seemeth there is no knight living but I am able enough for him."

CHAP. CXXIX.—How sir Beaumains fought with sir Persaunt of Inde, and made him to be yeelden.

WITH this sir Persaunt of Inde[1] had espied them, as they hoved[2] in the field, and knightly hee sent to them to know whether hee came in warre or in peace. "Say unto thy lord," said sir Beaumains, "I take no force,[3] but whether as him list himselfe." So the messenger went againe unto sir Persaunt, and told him all his answere. "Well," said hee, "then will I have adoe with him to the uttermost;" and so he purveied him, and rode against him. And when sir Beaumains saw him, hee made him ready, and there they met with all the might that their horses might run, and brake their speares either in three peeces, and their horses rashed so together that both their horses fell dead to the earth; and lightly they avoyded their horses, and put their shields before them, and drew their swords, and gave each other many great strokes, that sometime they so hurled together that they fell both grovelling on the ground. Thus they fought two houres and more, that their shields and their hawberkes were all forhewen,[4] and in many places they were sore wounded. So at the last sir Beaumains smot him through the cost[5] of the body, and then he retrayed[6] him here and there, and knightly maintained his battaile long time. And at the last sir Beaumains smote sir Persaunt on the helme

[1] *Sir Persaunt of Inde.*—It must not be supposed that sir Persaunt was an Indian; but he was merely named from the colour he wore, like the black knight and the green knight. See before, p. 252.
[2] *Hoved.*—Loitered, hovered. [3] *No force.*—I care not.
[4] *Forhewen.*—Hewn to pieces. [5] *Cost.*—Side.
[6] *Retrayed.*—Drew back.

KING ARTHUR. 255

that hee fell grovelling to the earth, and then he lept overthwart[1] upon him, and unlaced his helme for to have slaine him. Then sir Persaunt yeelded him, and asked him mercy. With that came the damosell and prayed him to save his life. "I will well," said sir Beaumains, "for it were pittie that this noble knight should die." "Gramercie," said sir Persaunt, "gentle knight and damosell, for certainely now I know well it was you that slew the black knight my brother at the black thorne; hee was a full noble knight, his name was sir Periard. Also I am sure that yee are hee that wan mine other brother the greene knight; his name was sir Pertolope. Also yee wan the red knight my brother, sir Perimones. And now, sir, sith yee have won these knights, this shall I doe for to please you: yee shall have homage and feaultie of mee, and an hundred knights to bee alwayes at your command, to goe and ride where yee will command us." And so they went unto sir Persaunts pavilion, and there hee drank wine and eate spices. And afterward sir Persaunt made him to rest upon a bed till it was supper time, and after supper to bed againe. When sir Beaumains was abed, sir Persaunt had a daughter, a faire lady, of eighteene yeares of age; there hee called her unto him, and charged and commanded her upon his blessing to goe unto the knights bed, and lye downe by his side, "and make him no strange cheere, and take him in thine armes and kisse him, and looke that this bee done, I charge you, as yee will have my love and my good will." So sir Persaunts daughter did as her father bad her; and so shee went unto sir Beaumains bed, and privily shee dispoyled[2] her, and laid her downe by him. And then he awoke and saw her, and asked her what she was. "Sir," said shee, "I am sir Persaunts daughter, that by the commandement of my father am come hither." "Be yee a maide or a wife?" said hee. "Sir," said shee, "I am a cleane maide." "God defend," said hee, "that I should defoule you to doe sir Persaunt such a

---

[1] *Overthwart.*—Astride.   [2] *Dispoyled.*—Undressed.

shame; therefore, faire damosell, arise out of this bed, or else will I." "Sir," said shee, "I came not to you by mine owne will, but as I was commanded." "Alas," said sir Beaumains, "I were but a shamefull knight if I would doe your father any disworship." And so hee kissed her, and shee departed and came to sir Persaunt her father, and told him all how shee had sped. "Truly," said sir Persaunt, "whatsoever he be, he is extract of a noble blood." And so we leave him there till on the morrow.

CHAP. CXXX.—Of the goodly communication between sir Persaunt and sir Beaumains, and how he told him that his name was sir Gareth.

ON the morrow the damosell and sir Beaumains heard masse, and brake their fast, and so tooke their leave. "Faire damosell," said sir Persaunt, "whetherward are yee away leading this knight?" "Sir," said she, "this knight is going to the siege, that besiegeth my sister in the castle Dangerous." "Ah, ah," said Persaunt, "that is the knight of the red launds, which is the most perillous knight that I know now living, and a man that is without mercy, and men say that he hath seaven mens strength. God save you," said hee to sir Beaumains, "from that knight, for he doth great wrong to that lady, and that is great pittie, for shee is one of the fairest ladies of the world, and me seemeth that your lady is hir sister. Is not your name Linet?" said he. "Yea," said shee, "and my lady my sisters name is dame Lyones." "Now shall I tell you," said sir Persaunt, "this red knight of the red launds hath leyen long at the siege well nigh these two yeares, and many times hee might have had her and he had would, but he prolongeth the time to this intent, for to have sir Launcelot du Lake to doe battaile with him, or sir Tristram, or sir Lamoracke de Gales, or sir Gawain; and for this cause hee tarrieth so long at the siege." "Now my lord sir Persaunt," said the damosell Lynet, " I require you that yee will make this gentleman knight or ever he fight with the red knight." " I will with all my heart," said sir Persaunt, "and it please him to take the order of knighthood of so simple a man as I am." " Sir," said sir Beaumains, " I thanke you for your good will, for I am better sped, for certainely the noble knight sir Launcelot made mee knight." " Ah," said sir Persaunt, " of a more renowned knight might yee not bee made knight, for of all the knights in the world hee may bee called chiefe of all knighthood; and so all the world saith that betweene three knights is parted cleerely knighthood;[1] that is, sir Launcelot du Lake, sir Tristram de Lyones, and sir Lamoracke de Gales; these beare now the renowne. There be many other knights, as sir Palamides the Sarasin, and sir Safere his brother; also sir Bleoberis, and sir Blamore de Ganis his brother; also sir Bors de Ganis, and sir Ector de Maris, and sir Percivale de Galis; these and many moe be noble knights, but there be none that passe the three above said; therefore God speede you well," said sir Persaunt, " for and yee may match the red knight, yee shall bee called the fourth of the world." " Sir," said sir Beaumains, " I would faine have a good fame of knighthood, and I let you to wit I came of good men, for I dare say my father was a noble man, and so that yee will keepe it close and this damosell, I would tell you of what kinne I am." " Wee will not discover you," said they both, " till yee commaund us, by the faith that wee owe unto God." " Truely," said hee, " my name is sir Gareth of Orkeny, and king Lot was my father, and my mother is king Arthurs sister, whose name is dame Morgawse, and sir Gawaine is my brother, and sir Agravine and sir Gaheris, and I am the yongest of them all, and yet knoweth not king Arthur nor sir Gawaine what I am."

---

[1] *Knighthood.*—This word is here used in the sense of chivalry.

CHAP. CXXXI.—How the lady which was besieged had word from her sister how she had brought a knight to fight for her, and what battailes he had done.

SO the booke saith that the lady that was besieged had word of her sisters comming by the dwarfe, and brought a knight with her, and how hee had passed all the perilous passages. " What manner of man is hee?" said the lady dame Liones. " Hee is a noble knight, truely, madam," said the dwarfe, " and but a young man, but hee is as likely a man as ever yee saw any." " What is he?" said the lady ; " and of what kinne is he come? and of whom was hee made knight?" " Madam," said the dwarfe, " hee is the kings sonne of Orkeny, but his name I will not tel you at this time, but wit ye well that of sir Launcelot du Lake was hee made knight, for of none other would he be made knight, and sir Kay named him Beaumains."

" How escaped hee," said the lady, " from the brethren of sir Persaunt?" " Madame," said he, " as a noble knight should doe. First he slew two brethren at a passage of a water." " Ah!" said the lady, " they were very good knights, but they were strong murtherers, the one hight sir Gherard le Brewse, and that other was called sir Arnold le Brewse." " Then, madame, hee encountred with the blacke knight, and slew him in plaine battaile, and so he tooke his horse and his armour, and fought with the greene knight, and wan him in plaine battell. And in likewise he served the red knight, and after in the same wise hee served the blew knight, and won him in plaine battel." " Then," said the lady, " hee hath overcome sir Persaunt of Inde, one of the noblest knights of the world." And the dwarfe said, " He hath won all the foure brethren, and slaine the blacke knight. And yet hee did more, hee overthrew sir Kay and left him nigh dead upon the earth. Also he did great battaile with sir Launcelot, and there they departed on even

hands, and then sir Launcelot made him knight." The
lady said, "Dwarfe, I am glad of these tidings, therefore
goe thou in an hermitage of mine here beside, and thither
shalt thou beare with thee of my wine in two flagons of silver, they are of two gallons, and also two casts[1] of bread,
with fat venison baked, and daintie foules, and a cup of gold
heere I deliver thee that is rich and precious, and beare
all this to mine hermitage, and put it in the hermites
hands; and when thou hast thus done, goe to my sister and
greete her well, and recommend me unto that gentle knight,
and pray him to eate and drinke and make him strong, and
say yee to him that I thanke him of his curtesie and goodnesse that he would take upon him such labor for me that
never did him bounty nor curtesie. Also pray him that he
be of a good heart and good courage, for hee shall meete
with a full noble knight, but hee is neither of bountie,
curtesie, nor gentlenesse, for hee attendeth unto none other
thing but to murther, and that is the cause I cannot praise
him nor love him." So this dwarfe departed and came to
sir Persaunt, where hee found the damosell Lynet and sir
Beaumains, and there hee told them all as yee have heard;
and then they tooke their leave, but sir Persaunt tooke an
ambling hackney and conveied them on their way, and then
betooke them unto God. And so within a little while they
came unto the hermitage, and there they dranke the wine,
and eate the venison and the foules baken. And so when
they had repasted them well, the dwarfe returned with his
vessell unto the castle againe, and there met with him the
red knight of the red launds, and asked him from whence
hee came, and where hee had beene. "Sir," said the
dwarfe, "I have beene with my ladies sister of this castle,

[1] *Two casts.*—*Cast* was a term for a certain measure of bread. The
exact quantity is not known, but it has been conjectured to mean the
piece of several loaves attached together as it was drawn from the
oven. It may be remarked that most of the heroes of these romances
of chivalry were, as a rule, great eaters and drinkers, and few liked
to fight upon an empty stomach.

and she hath beene at king Arthurs court, and hath brought a knight with her." "Then I accompt her travaile lost, for though she had brought with her sir Launcelot, sir Tristram, sir Lamorake, and sir Gawaine, I would thinke my selfe good enough for them." "It may wel be," said the dwarfe, "but this knight hath passed all the perilous passages, and hath slaine the black knight and other two more, and hath won the greene knight, the red knight, and the blew knight." "Then is hee one of these foure that I have rehearsed." "He is none of those," said the dwarfe, "but he is a kings sonne." "What is his name?" said the red knight of the red launds. "That will I not tell you," said the dwarfe, "but sir Kay in scorne called him Beaumains." "I care not for him," said the red knight, "what knight soever he be, for I shall soone deliver him, and if so bee that I match him, hee shall have a shamefull death as many other have had." "That were pittie," said the dwarf, "and it is mervaile that yee make such a shamefull warre upon noble knights."

CHAP. CXXXII.—How the damosel and sir Beaumains came to the siege, and came to a sickamore tree, and there sir Beaumains blew an horne, and then the knight of the red launds came to fight with him.

NOW leave wee off the knight and the dwarfe, and speake we of sir Beaumains, that all night lay in the hermitage, and on the morrow hee and the damosell Lynet heard a masse and brake their fast. And then they tooke their horses and rode throughout a faire forrest, and then they came unto a plaine, and saw whereas were many pavilions and tents, and a faire castle, and there was much smoake and great noyse. And when they came neare the siege, sir Beaumains espied upon great trees, as hee rode, how there hung goodly armed knights by the neckes, and their shields about their neckes with their swords, and gilted spurres upon their heeles, and so there hung shamefully nigh forty knights with rich armes. Then sir Beaumains abated his countenaunce, and said, "What thing meaneth this?" "Faire sir," saith the damosell, "abate not your cheere for all this sight, for yee must encourage your selfe, or else yee bee all shent, for all these knights came hither unto this siege to rescue my sister dame Lyones, and when the red knight of the red launds had overcome them, hee put them to this shamefull death, without mercy and pittie, and in the same wise hee will serve you, but if yee quit you the better." "Now Jesu defend mee," said sir Beaumains, "from such a villaynous death and shenship[1] of armes! for rather then thus I should bee faren withall, I would rather bee slaine manfully in plaine battaile." "So were yee better," said the damosell, "trust not in him, for in him is no courtesie, but all goeth to the death or shamefull murther, and that is great pittie, for hee is a full likely man and well made of body, and a full noble knight of prowesse, and a lord of great lands and possessions." "Truely," said sir Beaumains, "hee may well bee a good knight, but hee useth shamefull customes, and it is great mervaile that hee endureth so long, that none of the noble knights of my lord king Arthurs court have not dealt with him." And then they rode unto the ditches,[2] and saw them double ditched with full strong wals, and there were lodged many great estates and lords nigh the wals, and there was great noyse of minstrels, and the sea beat upon the one side of the wals, where as were many ships and mariners noyse with hale and how.[3] And also there was fast by a sickamore tree, and thereon hung an horne, the greatest that ever they saw, of an olifants bone.[4] "And this knight of the red launds hath hanged it up there, that if there come any arraunt knight, he must

[1] *Shenship.*—Ruin; disgrace.
[2] *Ditches.*—i. e. the entrenchments which surrounded the camp of the besieging army.
[3] *Hale and how.*—Was the usual cry of the mariners at their work.
[4] *Olifants bone.*—Elephant's bone; i. e. ivory.

blow that horne, and then will he make him ready and come out unto him to doe battaile with him; but, sir, I pray you," said the damosell Lynet, " blow yee not the horne till it bee high noone, for now it is about prime, and now encreaseth his might, which as men say hee hath seaven mens strength." " Ah! fie for shame, faire damosell, say yee never so more to mee, for and he were as good a knight as ever was, I shall never faile him in his most might, for either will I worshipfully winne worship, or die knightly in the field." And therewith he spurred his horse unto the sycamore tree, and blew the horne so egerly, that all the siege and the castle rang thereof. And then knights lept there out of their tents and pavilions, and they that were within the castle looked over the wals and out at the windowes. Then the red knight of the red launds armed him hastily, and two barons set on his spurres upon his heeles, and all was blood red, his armour, speare, and shield, and an earle buckled his helme upon his head; and then they brought him a red speare and a steed, and so hee rode into a little vale under the castle, that all that were in the castle and at the siege might behold the battaile.

CHAP. CXXXIII.—How the two knights met together, and of their talking, and how they began their battaile.

"SIR," said the damosell Lynet unto sir Beaumains, " looke that yee be mery and light, for yonder is your deadly enemy, and at yonder window is my lady my sister dame Lyones." " Where?" said sir Beaumains. " Yonder," said the damosell, and pointed with her finger. " That is sooth," said sir Beaumains, " shee seemeth afarre the fairest lady that ever I looked upon, and truely," said hee, " I aske no better quarrell then now to doe battaile, for truely shee shall bee my lady, and for her will I fight." And ever hee looked up to the window with glad cheere. And the lady Liones made curtesie to him down to the ground, holding up her hands. With that the red knight of the red launds called to sir Beaumains, "Leave, sir knight, thy looking, and behold mee, I counsaile thee, for I warne thee well shee is my lady, and for her I have done many strong battailes." "If thou have so done," said sir Beaumains, "mee seemeth it but wast labour; for shee loveth none of thy fellowship, and thou to love that loveth not thee, it is a great folly; for if I understood that shee were not glad of my comming, I would be advised or I did battaile for her, but I understand by the besieging of this castle, shee may forbeare[1] thy company. And therefore wit thou well, thou red knight of the red launds, I love her and will rescew her, or else die in the quarrell." "Sayst thou that?" said the red knight; "me seemeth thou ought of reason to beware by yonder knights that thou sawest hang upon yonder great elmes." "Fie, fie, for shame," said sir Beaumains, "that ever thou shouldest say or doe so evill and such shamefulnesse, for in that thou shamest thy selfe and the order of knighthood, and thou mayst bee sure there will no lady love thee that knoweth thy detestable customs. And now thou weenest that the sight of these hanged knights should feare mee and make mee agast, nay truely not so, that shamefull sight causeth mee to have courage and hardinesse against thee, more then I would have had against thee and if thou bee a well ruled knight." "Make thee ready," said the red knight of the red launds, "and talke no longer with me." Then sir Beaumains bad the damosell goe from him, and then they put their speares in their rests, and came together with all the might they had, and either smote other in the mids of their shields, that the paytrels, sursengles, and crowpers[2] brast, and fell both to the ground with the raines of their

---

[1] *Forbeare.*—To do without.

[2] *Paytrels, sursengles, and crowpers.*—The *peytrel* was the breastplate of the horse; *surcingle*, the girth of the horse-cloth; and *crowper*, of course, the crupper.

bridles in their hands, and so they lay a great while sore astonied, and all they that were in the castle and at the siege wend their necks had beene broken, and then many a stranger and other said, that the strange knight was a big man and a noble juster, "for or now we saw never no knight match the red knight of the red launds;" thus they said both within the castle and without. Then they lightly avoided their horses and put their shields afore them, and drew their swords and ranne together like two fierce lyons, and either gave other such buffets upon their helmes that they reeled both backward two strides; and then they recovered both, and hewed great peeces from their harneis and their shields, that a great part fell in the fields.

CHAP. CXXXIV.—How, after long fighting, sir Beaumains overcame the knight, and would have slaine him, but at the request of the lords hee saved his life and made him to yeeld him to the lady.

AND thus still they fought till it was past noone and would not stint, till at the last they both lacked wind, and then they stood wagging, staggering, panting, blowing, and bleeding, so that all those that beheld them for the most part wept for pittie. And when they had rested them a while, they went to battaile againe, trasing, rasing, and foyning as two boores. And sometime they ranne the one against that other as it had beene two wild rams, and hurtled so togither that they fell to the ground groveling. And sometime they were so amased that either tooke others swords in steede of their owne. Thus they endured till even-song time, that there was none that there beheld them might know whether was likliest to winne the battaile; and their armour was so sore hewen that men might see their naked sides, and in other places they were naked, but ever the naked places they defended. And the red knight was a wily knight of warre, and his wily fighting taught sir Beaumains to be wise, but full sore he bought[1] it or he espied his fighting. And thus by assent of them both, they granted each other to rest a while, and so they set them downe upon two mole-hils there beside the fighting place, and either of them unlaced his helme and tooke the cold wind, for either of their pages were fast by them, to come when they called for them to unlace their harneis, and to set it on againe at their command. And then when sir Beaumains helme was off, he looked up unto the window, and there hee saw the faire lady dame Lyones. And shee made to him such countenance, that his heart was light and joyfull. And therewith he start up sudenly, and bad the red knight make him ready to doe the battaile to the uttermost." "I will well," said the red knight. And then they laced up their helmes, and their pages avoided,[2] and they stept togither and fought fiercely.[3] But the red knight of the red launds awaited him, and at an overthwart smote him within the hand, that his sword fell out of his hand. And yet hee gave him another buffet on the helme that he fell downe groveling to the earth, and the red knight fell over him for to hold him downe. Then cryed the damosell Lynet on high, "O, sir Beaumains, where is thy courage become? alas! my lady my sister beholdeth thee, and shee sobbeth and weepeth, so that it maketh my heart heavy." And when sir Beaumains heard her say so, hee arose up with a great might, and gate him upon his feete, and lightly hee lept to his sword and caught it in his hand, and doubled his pace unto the red knight, and there they fought together a new battaile. But sir Beaumains then doubled his strookes and smote so thicke, that he smote the sword out of the red knights hand, and then hee smote him upon the helme, that he fell to the ground, and sir Beaumains fell upon him and unlaced his helme for to have slaine him.

[1] *Bought.—He aboughte hit*, Caxton.
[2] *Avoided.—*Went from them, or aside.
[3] *Fiercely.—Fresshely*, Caxton.

And then the red knight yeelded him, and asked mercy, and said with a loud voice, " Oh, noble knight, I yeeld mee unto thy mercy!" Then sir Beaumains bethought him upon the knights that he had made to be hanged so shamefully, and then he said, "I may not with my worship save thy life, for the shamefull deathes that thou hast caused so many good knights to die." " Sir," said the red knight of the red launds, " hold ye your hands, and ye shall know the cause why I put them to so shamefull a death." " Say on," said sir Beaumains. " Sir, I loved once a lady, a faire damosell, and shee had her brother slaine, and shee said it was sir Launcelot du Lake, or sir Gawaine, and shee prayed mee that, as I loved her heartily, that I would make her a promise by the faith of my knighthood, for to labour dayly in armes unto the time that I had met with one of them, and all that I might overcome, that I should put them to a villainous death ; and this is the cause that I have put all these good knights to death, and so I ensured her to doe all this villanie unto king Arthurs knights, and that I should take vengance upon al his knights. And, sir, now I will tell thee that every day my strength encreaseth til noone, and al this time have I seven mens strength."

CHAP. CXXXV.—How the knight yeelded him, and how sir Beaumains made him to goe unto king Arthurs court, and to crie sir Launcelot mercy.

THEN came there many earles and barons and noble knights, and prayed sir Beaumains to save his life and to take him prisoner, and all they fell upon their knees and prayed him of mercy, and that hee would save his life. " And, sir," they said all, " it were better to take homage and fealtie of him, and let him hold his lands of you, then to slay him, for by his death ye shall have none advantage, and his misdeedes that bee done may not bee undone ; and therefore he shall make amends to all parties, and wee all bee heere will become your men, and doe you homage and feaultie." "Faire lords," said sir Beaumains, "wit you well I am full loth to slay this knight, neverthelesse hee hath done passing ill and shamefully. But insomuch as all that hee did was at a ladies request, I blame him the lesse, and for your sakes I will release him, and he shal have his life upon this covenant, that hee goe within the castle and yeeld him there to the lady, and, if shee will forgive and quite him, I wil well with that hee make her amends of all the trespasses hee hath done against her and her landes. And also, when that is done, that hee goe unto the court of king Arthur, and there that hee aske sir Launcelot and sir Gawaine, for the evill will that hee hath had against them." " Sir," said the red knight of the red launds, " all this will I doe as yee command, and siker assurance and borowes[1] ye shall have." And then, when the assurance was made, hee made his homage and feaultie, and all those earles and barons with him. And then the damosell Lynet came unto sir Beaumains, and unarmed him, and searched his wounds, and stinted his blood, and in like wise she did to the red knight of the red launds. And so they sojourned ten days in their tents. And the red knight made his lords and servants to doe al the pleasure that they might unto sir Beaumains. And within a while after, the red knight of the red launds went unto the castle and put him in the lady Lyones grace, and so she received him upon sufficient sureties, and all her hurts were well restored of all that she could complaine. And then hee departed and went unto the court of king Arthur, and there openly the red knight of the red launds put him in the mercy of sir Launcelot and sir Gawaine, and ther he told openly how he was overcome, and by whom, and also hee told of all the battailes, from the beginning to the ending. " Jesus, mercie," said king Arthur and sir Gawaine, " we marvaile much of what blood he is come, for he is a full noble knight." " Have ye no marvaile," said

[1] *Borowes.*—Pledges; sureties.

sir Launcelot, "for ye shall right well wit that hee is come of a full noble blood, and, as for his might and hardinesse, there bee but few now living that is so mightie as hee is, and so noble of prowesse." "It seemeth by you," said king Arthur, "that ye know his name, and from whence he is come, and of what blood he is." "I suppose I doe so," said sir Launcelot, "or else I would not have given him the order of knighthood; but hee gave mee at that time such charge that I should never discover him untill hee required mee, or else it be knowen openly by some other."

CHAP. CXXXVI.—How sir Beaumains came to the lady, and when he came unto the castle the gates were closed against him, and of the words that the lady said unto him.

NOW returne we unto sir Beaumains, which desired of the damosell Linet that hee might see her sister his lady. "Sir," said shee, "I would faine yee saw her." Then sir Beaumains armed him at all points, and tooke his horse and his speare, and rode straight to the castle. And when hee came to the gate, hee found there many men armed, that pulled up the drawbridge and drew the port close. Then marvailed hee why they would not suffer him to enter in. And then he looked up to the window, and there he saw the faire lady dame Liones, that said on high: "Goe thy way, sir Beaumains, for as yet thou shalt not wholly have my love, untill the time thou bee called one of the number of the worthy knights; and therefore goe and labour in armes worshipfully these twelve-moneths, and then ye shall heare new tidings." "Alas, faire lady," said sir Beaumains, "I have not deserved this, that ye should shew to mee this strangenesse; I had wend that I should have right good cheere with you, and to my power I have deserved thankes and kindnesse, and well I am sure that I have bought your love with part of the best blood within my body. "Faire knight," said dame Liones, "bee not displeased, nor over hastie, for wit

ye wel that your great travaile nor good love shall not be
lost, for I consider your great travaile and labour, your
bountie and your goodnesse, as I ought to doe; and therefore goe on your way, and looke that ye be ever of good
comfort, for all shall bee for your worship and honour, and
also for the best; and perdó[1] a twelve-moneth will be soone
gone, and trust you me, faire knight, I shall be true unto
you, and shall never betray you, but unto my death I shall
love you and none other." And therewithall shee turned
her from the window. And sir Beaumains rode away from
the castle in making great moane and sorrow; and so he
rode heere and there, and wist not whether he rode, till it
was darke night; and then it happened him to come to a
poore mans house, and there hee was harboured all that
night. But sir Beaumains could have no rest, but wallowed
and writhed for the love of the lady of the castle. And so
on the morrow hee tooke his horse and his armour, and rode
till it was noone; and then hee came unto a broad water,
and thereby was a great lodge, and there hee alighted to
sleepe, and laid his head upon his shield, and betooke his
horse to the dwarfe, and commanded him to watch all night.
Now turne we to the lady of the castle, that thought much
upon sir Beaumains; and then she called unto her sir Gringamor her brother, and prayed him in all manner, as he
loved her heartily, that hee would ride after sir Beaumains,
" and ever have him in a waite[2] till that ye may finde him
sleeping, for I am sure in his heavinesse he will alight downe
in some place and lye downe to sleep, and therefore have
your watch upon him, and, in the priviest wise that yee can,
take his dwarfe from him, and goe your way with him as
fast as ever ye may or sir Beaumains awake; for my sister
Linet hath shewed me that the dwarfe can tell of what kin-

---

[1] *Perdé.*—Literally, by God, for God's sake. A common Anglo-
Norman exclamation.

[2] *In a waite.*—Caxton has, *ever have ye wayte upon hym.* Either
reading means, keep ever watch upon him.

dred hee is come, and what his right name is; and in the meane while I and my sister will ride to your castle to awaite when yee shall bring with you this dwarfe, and then when yee have brought him to your castle, I will have him in examination my selfe, unto the time I know what his right name is, and of what kindred he is come, or else I shal never be merry at my heart." "Sister," said sir Gringamor, "all this shall be done as yee have desired." And so he departed, and rod both day and night till that hee had found sir Beaumains lying sleeping by a water side, and had laid his head upon his shield. And then when hee saw that sir Beaumains was fast on sleepe, hee came stilly stalking behind the dwarfe, and tooke him fast under his arme, and so rode away with him as fast as ever hee might unto his castle. And this sir Gringamors armour, and all that to him belonged, was all blacke. But as hee rode with the dwarfe toward his castle, he cried unto his lord and prayed him of helpe. And therwithal sir Beaumains awoke, and up hee lept lightly, and saw where sir Gringamor rode his way with the dwarfe, and so sir Gringamor rode out of his sight.

CHAP. CXXXVII.—How sir Beaumains rode after for to rescew his dwarfe, and came into the castle where he was.

THEN sir Beaumains put on his helme anon, and buckled his shield, and tooke his horse and rode after him all that ever hee might ride, through maries[1] and fields and great dales, that many times his horse and he plunged over the head in deepe mires, for hee knew not the way, but hee tooke the next[2] way in that woodnesse,[3] that many times hee was like to perish. And at the last it hapned him to come to a faire greene

[1] *Maries.*—Marshes.
[2] *Next.*—Nighest. Caxton reads *gaynest*, i. e. readiest.
[3] *Woodnesse.*—Madness; fury.

way, and there he met with a poore man of the countrie, whom hee saluted, and asked him whether hee met not with a knight upon a blacke horse and blacke harneis, and a little dwarfe sitting behind him with heavie cheere. "Sir," said the poore man, "heere passed by mee a knight that is called sir Gringamor, with such a dwarfe mourning as yee say, but I counsell you that ye follow him not, for he is one of the perilous knights of the world, and his castle is heere nigh hand within these two miles, and therefore I advise you that ye ride not after him, but if ye owe to him good will."

Leave wee now to speake of Beaumains, riding toward the castle, and speake we of sir Gringamor and of the dwarfe. Anon as the dwarfe was come to the castle, then dame Liones and dame Linet her sister asked the dwarfe where his master was borne, and of what linage that he was come, "and but thou tell me the truth," said dame Liones, "thou shalt never escape this castle, but for ever here to bee prisoner." "As for that," said the dwarfe, "I feare not greatly to tell his name, and of what kinne that he is come. Wit yee well that hee is a kings sonne, and his mother is sister unto king Arthur, and hee is brother unto the good knight sir Gawaine, and his name is sir Gareth of Orkeney. Now have I told you his right name, now I pray you, faire lady, let mee goe againe unto my lord, for he will never out of this countrey till he have me againe; and if he be angry he wil doe much harme or he stint, and worke you much wrack[1] in this countrey." "As for that threatning," said sir Gringamor, "be it as it may, we will goe to our dinner." And so they washed, and went to meat, and made them merry, and were well at ease, and, because the lady dame Liones of the castle was there, they made great joy.

"Truely, madame," said Linet unto her sister, "well may

[1] *Wrack.—Worke you wracke*, Caxton. *Wrake* is an old word signifying destruction or ruin.

he be a kings sonne, for he hath many good tatches[1] in him,
for he is a courteous and a mild man, the most suffering
man that ever I met withall; for I dare well say there was
never gentlewoman that reviled man in so foule a manner
as I have reviled him, and at all times he gave me goodly
and meeke answers againe." And as they sat thus talking,
there came sir Beaumains at the gate with an angry countenance, and his sword drawn in his hand, and cried aloud
that all the castle might heare it, saying: " Thou traitour,
sir Gringamor, deliver mee my dwarfe againe, or by the
faith that I owe to the order of knighthood, I shall doe
thee all the harme that I can." Then sir Gringamor
looked out at a window, and said: " Sir Gareth of Orkney,
leave thy boasting words, for thou getest not thy dwarfe
again." " Thou coward knight," said sir Gareth, "bring
him with thee, and come and doe battaile with me, and
winne him, and take him." " So will I doe," said sir
Gringamor, " and me list, but for all thy great words thou
gettest him not." " Ah, faire brother," said dame Liones,
" I would hee had his dwarfe againe, for I would not hee
were wroth, for now hee hath told mee all my desire I will
no longer keepe the dwarfe. And also, brother, hee hath
done much for mee, and delivered me from the red knight
of the red launds, and therefore, brother, I owe him my
service afore all knights living; and wit ye well I love him
above all other knights, and full faine would I speake with
him, but in no wise I would hee wist what I were, but that
I were another strange lady." " Well," said sir Gringamor,
"sith that I know your will, I will now obey unto him."
And therewithall hee went downe unto sir Gareth, and
said : " Sir, I cry you mercy, and all that I have misdone
against your person I will amend it at your owne wil, and
therefore I pray you that you will alight, and take such
cheere as I can make you here in this castle." " Shall I
then have my dwarfe againe?" said sir Gareth. " Yea,

[1] *Tatches.*— Qualities.

sir, and all the pleasure that I can make you, for as soone as your dwarfe told me what yee were and of what blood that yee are come, and what noble deeds ye have done in these marches, then I repented me of my deeds." And then sir Gareth alighted downe from his horse, and therewith came his dwarfe and tooke his horse. "O my fellow," said sir Gareth, "I have had many evill adventures for thy sake." And so sir Gringamor tooke him by the hand, and led him into the hall, and there was sir Gringamors wife.

CHAP. CXXXVIII.—How sir Gareth, otherwise called sir Beaumains, came unto the presence of his lady, and how they tooke acquaintance, and of their love.

AND then there came forth into the hall dame Lyones arayed like a princesse, and there shee made him passing good cheere, and hee her againe. And they had goodly language and lovely countenance[1] together. And sir Gareth many times thought in himselfe, "Jesu! would to God that the lady of the castle perillous were so faire as shee is." There were all manner of games and playes, both of dauncing and leaping; and ever the more sir Gareth beheld the lady, the more hee loved her, and so he brenned in love that he was past himselfe in his understanding. And forth toward night they went to supper, and sir Gareth might not eate, for his love was so hot that hee wist not where hee was. All these lookes sir Gringamor espied, and after supper hee called his sister dame Lyones unto a chamber, and said: "Faire sister, I have well espied your countenance betweene you and this knight, and I will, sister, that yee wit that hee is a full noble knight, and if yee can make him to abide here, I will doe to him all the pleasure that I can, for and yee were better than yee be, yee were well bestowed upon him." "Faire brother," said dame Lyones, "I understand well that the

[1] *Countenance.*—i. e. behaviour.

VOL. I.   T

knight is good, and come hee is of a noble house ; notwithstanding I will assay him better, how bee it I am most beholding to him of any earthly man, for hee hath had great labour for my love, and hath passed many a dangerous passage." Right so sir Gringamor went unto sir Gareth, and said: "Sir, make ye good cheere, for yee shall have none other cause, for this lady my sister is yours at all times, her worship saved. For wit yee well that shee loveth you as well as yee doe her, and better, if better may bee." "And I wist that," said sir Gareth, " there should not live a gladder man then I would bee." " Upon my worship," said sir Gringamor, " trust to my promise, and as long as it liketh you yee shall sojourne with mee, and this lady shall be with us daily and nightly to make you all the cheere that shee can." " I will well," said sir Gareth, " for I have promised to bee nigh this countrey these twelve-moneths; and well I am sure that my lord king Arthur and many other noble knights will find mee where that I am within these twelve moneths, for I shall bee greatly sought and found, if that I bee on live." And then the noble knight sir Gareth went to the dame Lyones, which hee then much loved, and kissed her many times, and either made great joy of other. And there shee promised him her love, faithfully to love him, and never none other, all the dayes of her life.

And then the lady dame Lyones, by the assent of her brother, told sir Gareth all the truth what shee was, and how she was the same lady that he did battaile for, and how that shee was lady of the castle perilous; and there shee told him how shee caused her brother to take away his dwarfe.

CHAP. CXXXIX.—How in the night came in an armed knight and fought with sir Gareth, and hurt him sore in the thigh, and how sir Gareth smote off the knights head.

FOR this cause, to know the certaintie what was your name, and of what kinne yee were come." And then shee let fetch before him the damosell Lynet, which had ridden with him many wilsome[1] wayes. Then was sir Gareth more gladder then he was before. And then they plight their troth unto each other to love, and never to faile whiles their lives lasted. And so they burnt both in love that they were accorded to abate their lusts secretly, and there dame Lyones counsailed sir Gareth to sleepe in none other place but in the hall, and there shee promised him to come to his bed a little afore midnight. This counsell was not so privily kept but it was knowne, for they were but young both and tender of age, and had not used no such crafts before, wherefore the damosell Lynet was a little displeased, and thought her sister dame Lyones was a little over hasty in that thing, as that shee might not abide the time of her marriage; and for saving of their worship shee thought to abate their hot lusts; and so shee let ordaine by her subtile crafts that they had not their entent the one with the other, as in their delights, till they were married. And so it past on, and after supper was made cleane avoydance that every lord and lady should goe to his rest. But sir Gareth said plainly that he would goe no further than the hall, for such places, said hee, was convenient for an arraunt knight to take his rest in. And so there were ordeined great couches, and thereon feather beds, and there he laid him downe to sleepe. And within a while came dame Lyones wrapped in a mantle that was furred with armines,[2] and laid her downe beside sir Gareth. And anon hee beganne to kisse her, and then he looked afore

---

[1] *Wilsome.*—For *wildsome*; dreary.   [2] *Armines.*—Ermine.

him and perceived and saw comming toward him an armed knight, with a great light about him; and this knight had a long gisarme[1] in his hand, and made a grim countenance to smite him. When sir Gareth saw him come in that wise, he leapt out of his bed, and gat his sword in his hand, and went straight toward the knight. And when the knight saw sir Gareth come so fiercely upon him, he smote him with a foyne through the thicke of the thigh, that the same wound was a shaftmon[2] broad, and had cut atwo many veines and sinewes. And therewith sir Gareth smote him upon the helme such a buffet that he fell groveling to the earth, and then sir Gareth lept over him and unlaced his helme, and quickly smote off his head. And then he bled so fast that hee might not stand upon his feete, but laid him down upon his bed, and there he swoned, and lay as hee had beene dead. And then dame Lyones cryed aloude, that her brother sir Gringamor heard her. Then came hee downe, and when he saw that sir Gareth was so shamefully wounded, he was sore displeased, and said, " I am ashamed that this noble knight is thus dishonoured." Then said sir Gringamor unto his sister dame Lyones, " How may this bee that yee bee here, and this noble knight so sore wounded ?" " Brother," said dame Lyones, " I cannot tell you, for it was not done by mee, nor by mine assent, for he is my lord, and I his, and hee must be my husband; therefore, brother, I will that yee wit I am not ashamed to bee with him, nor to doe him all the pleasure that I can." " Sister," said sir Gringamor, " and I will well that yee wit, and sir Gareth also, that it was never done by me nor by mine assent that this unhappy deede is done." And then anone they stanched the bleeding as well as they might. And great sorrow made sir Gringamor and dame Lyones. And

---

[1] *Gisarme.*—See before, p. 162.
[2] *Shaftmon.*—An old term for a measure, equal to the distance from the extremity of the thumb to that of the palm in the extended hand—reckoned at about half a foot.

forthwith came dame Linet, and tooke up the head of the dead knight in the sight of them all, and anointed it with an oyntment there as it was smitten off, and in the same wise shee did to that other part there as the head stood, and then shee set it together, and it was as fast as ever it was afore; and the same knight arose lightly, and the damosell Lynet led him into her chamber with her. All this saw sir Gringamor and dame Lyones, and so did sir Gareth, and well hee espied that it was the damosell Lynet which rode with him through the perillous passages. "Ah, well, damosell," said sir Gareth, " I wend yee would not have done as ye have done." " My lord Gareth," said the damosell Lynet, "all that I have done I will avow, and all that I have done shall bee for your honour and worship, and also to us all." And so within a while sir Gareth was nigh whole, and waxed light and jocund, and sang, daunced, and gamed; and he and dame Lyones were so hot in burning love that they made their covenant that at the tenth night after she should come to his bed. And because he was wounded afore, he laid his armour and his sword nigh his bed side.

CHAP. CXL.—How the same knight came againe the next night, and was beheaded againe. And how at the feast of Pentecost all the knights that sir Gareth had overcome came and yeelded them unto king Arthur.

RIGHT as shee had promised shee came, and shee was not so soone in his bed but shee espied an armed knight comming toward the bed, and therewith shee warned sir Gareth, and lightly through the good helpe of dame Lyones he was armed anon; and then they hurled together with great ire and malice all about the hall, and there was great light, as it had beene to the number of twentie torches both before and behind, so that sir Gareth strained so himselfe, that his old wounds brast out againe in bleeding, but hee was hot and couragious and tooke no care, but with his great force he strukc downe that knight, and voyded his helme, and strake off his head. Then he hewed the head in an hundred peeces, and when he had done so, hee tooke up all those peeces, and threw them out at a window into the diches of the castle; and when hee had thus done, hee was so faint that he could not stand for bleeding.

And when hee was almost unarmed, hee fell in a deadly sound [1] in the floore. And then dame Lyones cryed so loud that sir Gringamor heard her, and when hce came and found sir Gareth in that plite he made great sorrow, and there he awaked sir Gareth, and gave him a drinke that releeved him wondrously well, but the great sorrow that dame Lyones made no tongue may tell, for shee so fared with her selfe, as though shee should have died. Right so came the damosell Lynet before them all, and shee had fetched all the little gobbets [2] of the head that sir Gareth had thrown out at the window, and there shee anointed them as shee had done before, and set them together againe. "Well, damosell Lynet," said sir Gareth, "I have not deserved all this despite which yee doe to mee." "Sir knight," said the damosell Lynet, "I have nothing done but I will avow it, and all that I have done shall bee for your worship and for us all." And then was sir Gareth stanched of his bleeding. But the leeches [3] said that there was no man on live that should heale him throughout of his wound, but if they healed him that caused that strooke by enchauntment.

Now leave we off sir Gareth ther with sir Gringamor and his sisters, and returne wee unto king Arthur, that at the next feast of Pentecost held his feast, and there came the greene knight with fiftie knights, and they all yeelded them unto king Arthur. And after there came the red knight his brother, and yeelded him to king Arthur and threescore knights with him. Also there came the blew knight, that

---

[1] *Sound.*—i. e. swoon.   [2] *Gobbets.* – Pieces.
[3] *Leeches.*—Physicians.

was brother unto the other two, with an hundred knights, and they all yeelded them unto king Arthur. The greene knights name was sir Pertolope, and the red knights name was sir Perimones, and the blew knights name was sir Persaunt of Inde. These three brethren told king Arthur how they were overcome by a knight that a damosell had with her, and called him sir Beaumains. "O Jesu!" said the king, "I marvaile what knight he is, and of what linage he is come; he was with mee a twelve-moneth, and poorely and shamefully hee was fostred, and sir Kay in scorne named him Beaumains."

Right as king Arthur stood so talking with these three brethren, there came sir Launcelot du Lake, and told the king that there was come a goodly lord with five hundred knights. Then the king went out of Carlion, for there was the feast, and there came to him this lord, which saluted the king in a good manner. "What is your will?" said king Arthur; "and what is your errand?" "Sir," said hee, "I am called the red knight of the red launds, but my name is sir Ironside; and, sir, yee shall wit that heere I am sent to you of a knight which is called sir Beaumains, for he wanne mee in plaine battaile, hand for hand, and so did never no knight but he this thirtie winters, and hee charged and commanded me to yeeld mee unto your grace and will." "Yee are welcome," said the king, "for yee have beene long a great foe to mee and to my court, and now I trust to God I shall so entreat you that yee shall bee my friend." "Sir, both I and these five hundred knights shall alway bee at your command, to doe you service as much as lyeth in our power." "Jesu, mercy!" said king Arthur, "I am much beholding unto that knight, that hath so put his body in devoure[1] to worship mee and my court. Ironside, that art called the red knight of the red launds, thou art called a precious[2] knight, if thou wilt hold of me I shall worship thee and make thee knight of the round table, but then thou

---

[1] *Devoure.*—Duty.   [2] *Precious.—Peryllous*, Caxton.

maiest bee no more a murtherer." "Sir, as to that I have
promised unto sir Beaumains never to use such a custome;
for all the shamefull customes that I have used, I did it at
the request of a lady that I loved, and therefore I must goe
unto sir Launcelot and unto sir Gawaine, and aske them
forgivenesse of the evill will that I had unto them, for all
them that I put to death was onely for sir Lancelots and
sir Gawaines sakes." "They be heere now afore thee,"
said the king, "ye may say unto them what yee will."
And then hee kneeled downe to sir Lancelot and to sir
Gawaine, and prayed them of forgivenesse of the evill will
and enmitie that he had committed against them both.

CHAP. CXLI.—How sir Launcelot and sir Gawaine pardoned him,
and demaunded him where sir Gareth was.

THEN goodly they said all at once, "God forgive you and wee doe, and pray you that yee will tell us where wee may finde sir Beaumains." "Faire lord," said sir Ironside, "I can not tell you, for it is full hard to finde him, for all such young knights as hee is, when they bee in their adventures, bee never abiding in one place." But to say the worship that the red knight of the red launds and sir Persaunt and his brother said of sir Beaumains, it was marvaile to heare. "Well, my faire lords," said king Arthur, "wit you well I shall doe you honour for the love of sir Beaumains, and as soone as ever I meete with him I shall make you all upon one day knights of the table round. And as to thee, sir Persaunt of Inde, thou hast ever beene called a full noble knight, and so have ever beene thy three brethren called. But I marvaile," said king Arthur, "that I heare not of the blacke knight your brother, hee was a full noble knight."
"Sir," said Pertolope the greene knight, "sir Beaumains slew him in an encounter with his speare, his name is sir Percard." "That was great pittie," said king Arthur,

and so said many knights moe. For these foure brethren were full well knowen for noble knights in king Arthurs court, for long time they had holden warre against the knights of the table round. Then said sir Pertolope the greene knight unto the king, "At a passage of the water of Mortaise, there encountred sir Beaumains with two brethren, that ever for the most part kept that passage, and they were two manly knights, and there hee slew the eldest brother in the water, and smote him upon the head such a buffet that he fell downe in the water and there hee was drowned, and his name was sir Gerarde le Brewse. And anon after hee slew the other brother upon the land, and his name was sir Arnold le Brewse."

CHAP. CXLII.—How the queene of Orkeney came to this feast of Pentecost, and how sir Gawaine and his brethren came to aske her blessing.

SO then the king and they went to their meate, and were served in the best manner. And as they sat at their meate, there came in the queene of Orkeney, with a great number of ladies and knights. And then sir Gawaine and sir Agravaine and sir Gaheris arose and went to her, and saluted her upon their knees, and asked her blessing, for in the space of fifteene yeares they had not seene her. Then shee spake on high to her brother king Arthur, "Where have yee done my young son sir Gareth? hee was heere among you a twelve-moneth, and yee made a kitchin knave of him, which is a great shame to you all. Alas! where have yee done my deere sonne which was my joy and blisse?"

"Oh, deare mother," said sir Gawaine, "I knew him not." "Nor I," said the king, "which me now sore repenteth, but God be thanked he is proved a worshipful knight as any is now living of his yeares, and I shall never bee glad till I may find him." "Ah, brother," said the queene of Orkeney to king Arthur, and to sir Gawaine, and to her other two sonnes, " yee did your selfe a great shame when ye among you kept my sonne Gareth in the kitchin and fed him like a poore hogge." " Faire sister," said king Arthur, " yee shall right well wit that I knew him not, no more did sir Gawaine nor his brethren. But sith it is so," said the king, " that he is thus gone from us all, wee must seeke a remedy to find him. Also, sister, mee seemeth yee might have done mee to wit of his comming, and then if I had not done well to him, yee might have blamed mee. For when he came to this court, hee came leaning upon two mens shoulders, as though he might not have gone; and then he asked mee three gifts, and one hee asked that same day, that was, that I would give him meate enough for twelve moneths.

"And the other two gifts hee asked that same day twelve-moneths after, and that was that he might have the adventure of the damosell Linet; and the third was, that sir Launcelot should make him knight when he desired him; and so I graunted him all his desire. And many in this court marvailed that he desired his sustenance for twelve moneths, and therefore we deemed many of us that he was not come of a noble house."

"Sir," said the queene of Orkeney to her brother king Arthur, " wit you well that I sent him unto you right well armed and horsed, and worshipfully well beseene of his body, and gold and silver great plentie for to spend." " It may well bee," said the king, " but thereof saw we none, save that same day that hee departed from us, knights told mee that there came a dwarfe hither sodainely and brought him armour and a good courser full well and richly beseene, and thereat we had all great marvaile from whence that riches came, and then we all deemed that hee was come of great men of worship." " Brother," said the queene, "all that ye say I beleeve, for ever sithence that hee was growen he was marvelously witted; and ever he was faithfull and true of his promise. But I marvaile," said she, "that sir Kay did mock and scorne him, and gave him that name Beaumains; yet sir Kay," said the queene, "named him more righteously than hee wend, for I dare well say, and hee be on live, hee is a faire handed man, and well disposed as any is living." Then said king Arthur, "Let this language bee still, and by the grace of God hee shall be found and he be within this seaven realmes, and let al this passe and be merry, for he is proved a man of worship, and that is to me great joy."

CHAP. CXLIII.—How king Arthur sent for the lady Liones, and how shee let crie a turnement at the castle, where as came many good knights.

THEN said sir Gawaine and his brethren unto king Arthur: "Sir, and yee will give us leave, wee will goe seeke our brother." "Nay," said sir Launcelot, "that shall not neede," and so said sir Bawdewaine of Brittaine, "for as by our advise the king shall send unto dame Liones a messenger, and pray her that she wil com to the kings court in al the hast that she may, and I doubt not but that shee will come, and then she may give you the best counsaile where as yee shall find him." "This is wel said of you," quoth king Arthur. So then goodly letters were made, and in all haste a messenger was sent forth, that rode both night and day till he came to the castle perilous. And then the lady dame Liones was sent for there as shee was with sir Gringamor her brother and sir Gareth. And when she understood this message, shee bad the messenger to ride on his way unto king Arthur, and she would come after in al the haste possible. Then when shee came to sir Gringamor and sir Gareth, she told them all how king Arthur had sent for her. "That is because of me," said sir Gareth. "Now advise me," said dame Liones, "what shall I say, and in what manner shall

I rule my selfe?" "My lady and my love," said sir Gareth, "I pray you in no manner of wise be yee knowen where I am, but well I wot my mother is there and all my brethren, and they will take upon them to seeke me, as I wot well they doe. But this, madame, I would ye said and advise my lord the king, when hee questioneth with you of me, then may yee say this is your advise: that and it like his good grace ye will make a crie against the feast of the Assumption of our Lady, that what knight there proveth him best, hee shall weld you and all your lands. And if it so bee that hee be a wedded man, that his wife shall have the degree and a coronall of gold, beset with stones of vertue to the value of a thousand pound, and a white jarfawcon."[1] Then dame Liones departed and came unto king Arthur, where she was nobly received, and there she was sore questioned of king Arthur and of the queen of Orkeney; and she answered, wheresoever sir Gareth was, she could not tell. But thus much shee said to king Arthur: "Sir, I will let crie a turnement, that shal be done before my castle at the Assumption of our Lady, and the crie shall be thus, that you, my lord Arthur, shall bee there and your knights, an I will purvey that my knights shall bee against yours, and then I am sure yee shall heare of sir Gareth." "This is well advised," said king Arthur. And so shee departed from thence. And then the king and shee made great provision for the tournement. When dame Liones was come to the ile of Avilion,[2] which was the same ile where as her brother sir Gringamor dwelled, and then shee told him all how she had done, and what promise shee had made to king Arthur. "Alas!" said sir Gareth, "I have beene so sore wounded with unhappinesse sithen I came into this castle, that I shall not bee able to doe at that turnament like as a knight should doe, for I was never well whole since I was hurt." "Bee yee of good cheare," said the

---

[1] *Jarfawcon.*—See before, p. 163.
[2] *Avilion.*—Avallon, or Glastonbury.

damosell Lynet, " for I undertake within these fifteene dayes for to make you as whole and as lusty as ever yee were." And then she laid an oyntment and a salve to him as it pleased her, that he was never so fresh nor so lusty. Then said the damosell Lynet, " Send you unto sir Persaunt of Inde, and command him and his knights to be heere with you as they have promised. Also, that yee send unto sir Ironside, that is the red knight of the red launds, and charge him that he bee ready with you with all his company of knights, and then shall yee be able to match with king Arthur and his knights." So this was done, and all the knights were sent for unto the castle perillous. And the red knight then answered and said unto dame Lyones and to sir Gareth : " Madame and my lord sir Gareth, yee shall understand that I have beene at king Arthurs court with sir Persaunt of Inde, and his brethren, and there we have done our homage as yee commanded us." Also sir Ironside said, " I have taken upon mee with sir Persaunt of Inde, and his brethren, to hold partie against my lord sir Launcelot and the knights of that court. And this have I done for the love of my lady dame Lyones, and you, my lord sir Gareth." " Yee have well done," said sir Gareth, " but wit ye well yee shall be full sore matched with the most noble knights of the world, therefore wee must purvey us of good knights whereas wee may get them." " That is well said," quoth sir Persaunt, " and worshipfully." And so the cry was made in all England, Wales, and Scotland, Ireland, and Cornewaile, and in all the out yles, and in Brittaine, and in many other countries, that at the feast of the Assumption of our Lady next comming, men should come to the castle perillous, beside the ile of Avilion, and there all the knights that came should have the choyse whether them list to be on the one part with the knights of the castle, or on the other part with king Arthur. And two moneths was to the day that the turnament should bee. And so there came many good knights that were at large, and held them

286   *THE HISTORIE OF*

for the most part against king Arthur and his knights of the round table, and came on the side of them of the castle. For sir Epinogris was the first, and he was the kings son of Northumberland, and sir Palamides the Sarasin was another, and sir Safere his brother, and sir Sagwarides his brother, but they were christened, and sir Malagrine another, and sir Brian de les Iles, a noble knight, and sir Grummore Grummorsum, a good knight of Scotland, and sir Carados of the dolorous tower, a noble knight, and sir Turquine his brother, and sir Arnold and sir Gauter two brethren, good knights of Cornewaile; there came sir Tristram de Liones, and with him sir Dinadan, the seneshall, and sir Sadoke, but sir Tristram at that time was not knight of the round table, but he was one of the best knights of the world. And so all these noble knights accompanied them, with the lady of the castle, and with the red knight of the red launds; but as for sir Gareth he would take upon him no more but as other meane knights did.

CHAP. CXLIV.—How king Arthur went to the turnement with his knights, and how the lady dame Liones received him worshipfully, and how the knights encountred together.

AND then there came with king Arthur sir Gawaine and his two brethren sir Agravaine and sir Gaheris; and then his nephewes sir Ewaine le Blaunche-Mains, and sir Aglovale, sir Tor, sir Percivale de Galis, and sir Lamorake de Galis. Then came sir Launcelot du Lake with his brethren, nephewes, and cosins, as sir Lionell, sir Ector de Maris, and sir Bors de Ganis, and sir Galihodin, sir Galihud, and many moe of sir Launcelots blood, and sir Dinadam, sir La-cote-maletaile his brother, a noble knight, and also sir Sagramore, a good knight, and the most part of the round table.

Also there came with king Arthur these knights, the king of Ireland king Aguisaunce, and the king of Scotland king Carados, and king Urience of the land of Gore, and king Bagdemagus and his son sir Meliganus, and sir Galahault the noble prince. Al these kings, princes, earles, and barons, and many other noble knights, as sir Brandiles, and sir Ewaine les Avoutres, and sir Kay, sir Bedivere, sir Melion de Logres, sir Petipace of Winchelsee, and sir Godelake; and all these came with the noble prince king Arthur, and many moe, which were too long to rehearse. Now leave wee to speake of these kings and knights, and let us speake of the great array that was made within the castle and about the castle for both parties. The lady dame Liones ordained great array on her part for her noble knights, for all manner of lodging and vittaile that came by land and by water, that there lack nothing for her part nor yet for the other, but there was plentie to bee had for gold and silver for king Arthur and his knights. And then there came the herbegeours[1] from king Arthur, for to harborow him and his knights, his dukes, his earles, his barons, and all his knights. And then sir Gareth praied his lady dame Liones, and sir Ironside, the red knight of the red launds, and sir Persaunt of Inde, and his brother, and sir Gringamor, that in no manner of wise there should none of them tell his name, and make no more of him then of the least knight that there was; for hee said, "I will not be knowen neither of more nor lesse, neither at the beginning nor at the ending." Then dame Liones said unto sir Gareth, "Sir, I will leave[2] you a ring, but I would pray you as yee love mee heartily let mee have it againe when the turnement is done. For that ring encreaseth my beautie much more then it is of it selfe. And this is the vertue of my ring, that is greene it will turne it unto red, and that is red it will turne into likenesse of greene, and that is blew it will turne to likenesse of white, and that is white it will turne to likenesse of blew,

---

[1] *Herbegeours.*—Harbingers; officers sent before the court to prepare lodgings.

[2] *Leave.*—Caxton has more correctly *lene*, i. e. lend.

and so it wil doe of all manner of colours. Also who that beareth my ring shall leese no blood, and for great love I will give you this ring." "Gramercy," said sir Gareth, "mine owne lady, for this ring is passing meete for me, for it will turne all maner of likenesse that I am in, and that shal cause me that I shal not be knowen." Then sir Gringamor gave sir Gareth a baye courser that was a passing good horse; also he gave him a passing good armour and a sure, and a noble sword that somtime sir Gringamors father wan upon an heathen tyrant. And so thus every knight made him ready unto that turnement. And king Arthur was come two dayes before the Assumption of our Lady. And there was all manner of royaltie, and of all manner of minstrels that might be found. Also there came queene Guenever, and the queene of Orkeney, sir Garethes mother. And on the day of the Assumption, when masse and mattins was done, there were heraulds with trumpets commanded to blow unto the field. And so anon there came out sir Epinogris, the kings sonne of Northumberland, from the castle, and there encountred with him sir Sagramore le Desirous, and either of them brake their speares to their hands. And then came in sir Palomides out of the castle, and there encountred with him sir Gawaine, and either of them smot other so hard that both the good knights and their horses fell to the earth. And then the knights of either part rescewed their knights.

And then came in sir Safere and sir Segwardes, brethren unto sir Palomides, and there encountred sir Agravaine with sir Safere, and sir Gaheris encountred with sir Segwarides. So sir Safere smote downe sir Agravaine, sir Gawaines brother, and sir Segwarides, sir Saferes brother, smote downe sir Gaheris,[1] and sir Malgrine, a knight of the castle, encountred with sir Ewaine le Blaunch-Mains, and there Ewaine gave sir Malgrine a great fall, that he had almost broken his necke.

[1] *Smote downe sir Gaheris.*—These words are not in Caxton.

CHAP. CXLV.—How the knights bare them in the battaile.

THEN sir Brian de les Iles and sir Grummore Grummorsum, knights of the castle, encountred with sir Aglovale and sir Tor, and sir Aglovale and sir Tor smote downe sir Brian and sir Grummore Grummorsum to the earth. Then came in sir Carados of the dolorous tower and sir Turquine, knightes of the castle, and there encountred with them sir Percivale de Galis and sir Lamorake de Galis, which were two brethren, and there encountred sir Percivale with sir Carados, and either of them brake their speares unto their hands; and then sir Turquine and sir Lamorake, and either of them smote downe others horses to the earth; and either parties rescewed other and horsed them againe. And sir Arnold and sir Gauter, knights of the castle, encountred with sir Brandiles and sir Kay, and these foure knights encountred mightily, and brake their speares unto their hands.

Then came sir Tristram and sir Sadoke and sir Dinas, knights of the castle, and there encountred sir Tristram with sir Bedivere, and sir Bedivere was smitten to the earth both horse and man; and sir Sadoke encountred with sir Petipace, and there sir Sadoke was overthrowen. And there sir Ewaine les Avoutres smote downe sir Dinas the seneschall. Then came in sir Persaunt of Inde, a knight of the castle, and there encountred with him sir Launcelot du Lake, and there he smote both sir Persaunt and his horse to the earth. Then came in sir Pertolope out of the castle, and there encountred with him sir Lionell; and there sir Pertolope the greene knight smote downe sir Lionell, brother to sir Launcelot. All this was marked of noble heraulds, who bare them best, and their names. And then came into the field sir Perimones the red knight, sir Persaunts brother, which was a knight of the castle, and he encountred with sir Ector de Mares, and either smote other so hard that both their horses and they fell to the earth. And then came in the red knight of the red launds and sir Gareth from the castle, and there encountred with them two sir Bors de Ganis and sir Bleoberis, and there the red knight and sir Bors smote each other so hard that their speares burst and their horses fell groveling to the earth. Then sir Bleoberis[1] brake his speare upon sir Gareth, but of that great strooke sir Bleoberis fell to the ground. When sir Galihodin saw that, hee bad sir Gareth keepe him, and sir Gareth smote him to the earth. Then sir Galihud gat a speare to avenge his brother, and in the same wise sir Gareth served him. And sir Dinadan and his brother La-cote-male-taile, and sir Sagramore le Desirous, and Dodinas le Savage, al these he bare downe with one speare. When king Augwisaunce of Ireland saw sir Gareth fare so, hee marvailed what he might bee, that one time seemed greene, and another time at his againe-comming hee seemed blew; and thus at every course that hee rode too and fro, hee changed his colour, so that there might neither king nor knight have cognisance nor knowledge of him. Then king Augwisance of Ireland encountred with sir Gareth, and there sir Gareth smote him from his horse, saddle and all. And then came king Carados of Scotland, and sir Gareth smote him downe horse and man. And in the same wise he served king Urience of the land of Gore. And then there came in king Bagdemagus, and sir Gareth smote him downe horse and man to the ground. And king Bagdemagus sonne Meliaganus brake a speare upon sir Gareth mightily and knightly. And then sir Galahaut, the noble prince, cryed on high: "Knight with the many colours, wel hast thou justed, now make thee ready that I may just with thee." When sir Gareth heard that, he gate him a great speare, and so they encountred together, and there the prince brake his speare, but sir Gareth smote him on the left side on the helme that he reeled

---

[1] *Sir Bleoberis.—Syr Blamor*, Caxton.

here and there, and he had fallen downe had not his men recovered him. " So God mee helpe," said king Arthur, " that knight with the many colours is a good knight;" wherefore the king called unto him sir Lancelot du Lake, and prayed him to encounter with that knight. " Sir," said sir Launcelot, " I may well finde in heart to forbeare him as at this time, for he hath had travaile inough this day; and when a good knight doth so well some day, it is no good knights part to let him of his worship, and namely when hee seemeth a knight that had done so great labour; for peradventure," said sir Launcelot, "his quarrell is here this day, and peradventure hee is best beloved with this lady of all that be here, for I see well hee paineth himselfe, and enforceth him to doe great deeds, and therefore," said sir Lancelot, " as for me, this day he shall have the honour; though it lay in my power to put him from it, yet would I not doe it."

Then when this was done, there was drawing of swords, and there began a great turnament; and there did sir Lancelot mervailous deeds of armes. And betweene sir Lamoracke and sir Ironside, that was the red knight of the red launds, there was a strong battaile; and betweene sir Palomides and sir Bleoberis was a strong battaile; and sir Gawaine and sir Tristram met togither, and there sir Gawaine had the worst, for he pulled sir Gawaine from his horse, and there he was long on foote and defouled. Then came sir Lancelot, and hee smote sir Turquine, and hee him againe, and then there came sir Carados his brother, and both at once they assailed him; and hee as the most noblest knight of the world right worshipfully fought with them both, that all men wondred of the noblenesse of sir Lancelot du Lake that fought with those two perilous knights. [And then came in sir Gareth, and knewe that it was sir Lancelot that fought with the two perillous knights],[1] and then sir Gareth came with his good horse, and put them

[1] The passage within brackets is supplied from Caxton's text.

asunder, and no stroke would hee smite to sir Lancelot du Lake. That espied sir Lancelot, which deemed it should bee the good knight sir Gareth, and then sir Gareth rode here and there and smote on the right hand and on the left hand, that all the folke might well espie where he rode; and by fortune he met with his brother sir Gawaine, and there he put sir Gawaine to the worst, for hee put out his helme, and so hee served five or sixe knights of the round table, that all men said he put him in the most paine, and best he did his devoure.[1] For when sir Tristram beheld him how he first justed and after fought so well with a sword, then he rode unto sir Ironside and unto sir Persaunt of Inde, and asked them by their faith, "What maner of knight is yonder knight which seemeth in so many divers colours? Truely me seemeth," said sir Tristram, "that hee putteth himselfe in great paine, for hee never ceaseth." "Know ye not what he is?" said sir Ironside. "No," said sir Tristram. "Then shall yee know that this is he that loveth the lady of the castle, and shee loveth him againe right heartily, and this is he that wanne me when I had besieged the lady of this castle, and this is hee that wanne sir Persaunt of Inde and his three bretheren." "What is his name?" said sir Tristram; "and of what blood is he come?" "Hee was called in king Arthurs court 'Beaumains,' but his name is sir Gareth of Orkeney, brother unto sir Gawaine." "By my head," said sir Tristram, "hee is a good knight and a big man of armes, and if he bee young he shall prove a full noble knight." "Hee is but a child," said they all; "and of sir Lancelot hee was made knight." "Therefore hee is much the better," said sir Tristram. And then sir Tristram, sir Ironside, sir Persaunt, and his brother rode together for to helpe sir Gareth, and then there were given many strong strookes. And then sir Gareth rode out on the one side to amend

---

[1] *Devoure.*—Duty.

his helme, and then said his dwarfe, "Take me your ring that yee lose it not while ye drinke." And so when hee had drunke, he put out his helme againe, and egerly tooke his horse and rode into the field, and left his ring with his dwarfe, and the dwarfe was glad that the ring was from him, for then hee wist well hee should be knowne. And then when sir Gareth was in the field, all the people saw him well and plainly that he was in yellow colours, and there he rashed off helmes and pulled downe knights, that king Arthur had mervaile what knight hee was, for the king saw by his haire that it was the same knight.

CHAP. CXLVI.—How sir Gareth was espied by the heraulds, and how he escaped out of the field.

BUT before hee was in so many colours, and now hee is but in one colour, that is yellow. "Now goe," said king Arthur unto divers heraulds, "and ride about him and espie what maner of knight he is, for I have asked of many knights this day that bee of the partie, and all say they know him not." And so an herauld rod as nigh sir Gareth as he could, and there hee saw written about the helme in gold, 'This is sir Gareth of Orkeney.' Then the herauld cryed as he were wood, and many heraulds with him, "This is sir Gareth of Orkeny in the yelow armes;" whereby all kings and knights of king Arthurs part belaid him and waited for him, and then they pressed[1] all to behold him, and ever the heraulds cryed, "This is sir Gareth of Orkeney, king Lots son." And when sir Gareth espied that hee was discovered, then hee began to double his strooks, and smote downe sir Sagramor and his brother sir Gawaine. "Oh, brother," said sir Gawaine, "I wend yee would not have striken mee." And when sir

---

[1] *Pressed.*—The edition of 1634 has *proceede*, but the correct reading is here restored from Caxton's edition.

Gareth heard him say so, hee threw here and there, and with paine hee gat out of the presse, and then he met with his dwarfe. "Oh, boy," said sir Gareth, "thou hast beguiled mee fouly this day that thou kept my ring; give it mee anon againe that I may hide my body withall." And so hee tooke it him, and then they all wist not where he was become, and sir Gawaine had espied where sir Gareth rode, and then hee rode after with all his might. Then espied sir Gareth, and rod lightly into the forrest, that sir Gawaine wist not where hee was become. And when sir Gareth wist that sir Gawaine his brother was past, he asked the dwarfe of his best counsell. "Sir," said the dwarfe, "me seemeth it were best now that yee are escaped from spying, that yee send my lady dame Lyones her ring." "That is well advised," said sir Gareth; "now have it here, and beare it to her, and say that I commend mee unto her good grace, and tell her I will come when I may, and that I pray her to be true and faithfull to me as I will bee unto her." "Sir," said the dwarfe, "it shall bee done as yee have commanded." And so hee rode his way, and did his errand unto the lady. Then shee said, "Where is my lord sir Gareth?" "Madame," said the dwarfe, "hee bad mee say that hee would not be long from you." And so lightly the dwarfe came againe unto sir Gareth, that would faine have had a lodging, for hee had neede to rest him. And then fell there a thunder and raine as heaven and earth should have gone together, and sir Gareth was not a little weary, for of all that day hee had but little rest, as well his horse as himselfe. Sir Gareth rode so long in that forrest till night came, and ever it lightned and thundred that wonder it was to see. At the last by fortune hee came to a castle, and there he heard the waites[1] on the wals.

[1] *Waites.*—Watchmen.

CHAP. CXLVII.—How sir Gareth came unto a castle, where he was well lodged, and how he justed with a knight, and how he slew him.

THEN sir Gareth rode straight unto the barbican of the castle, and prayed the porter faire for to let him into the castle. The porter answered him ungodly againe, and said: "Thou gettest no lodging here." "Faire sir," said hee, "say not so, for I am a knight of king Arthurs, and I pray the lord or the lady of this castle to give me harbour for Arthurs love." Then the porter went unto the duchesse, and told her how there was a knight of king Arthurs that would have harbour. "Let him in," said the duchesse, "for I will see that knight, and for king Arthurs sake he shall not be harbourlesse. And then the duchesse went up unto a towre over the gate with great torch light. When sir Gareth saw the torch light, hee cryed all on high, "Whether thou be lord or lady, gyant or champion, I take no force, so that I may have harbore for this night, and if it be so that I must needs fight, spare me not to morow when I have rested mee, for both I and my horse are weary. "Sir knight," said the duchesse, "thou speakest mightily and boldly, but wit thou well that the lord of this castle loveth not king Arthur nor none of his court, for my lord hath ever beene against him, and therefore thou were better not to come within this castle, for if thou come in this night, thou must come in under this manner and forme that wheresoever thou meete my lord, by streete or by way, thou must yeeld thee unto him as prisoner." "Madame," said sir Gareth, "what is your lord, and what is his name?" "Sir, my lords name is duke de la Rowse." "Well, madam," said sir Gareth, "I shall promise you that in what place I meete your lord, I shall yeeld me unto his good grace, so that I may know he will doe me no harme, and if I may understand that he will, then will I release my selfe and I can with my speare and with my sword." "Yee say right well," said the duchesse; and then shee let the drawbridge downe. And so he rode into the hall, and there he alighted, and his horse was led into a stable, and in the hall hee unarmed him, and said: "Madame, I will not out of thy hall this night, and when it is daylight, let see who will have adoe with mee, he shall finde mee lightly ready." Then was he set to his supper, and had many good dishes. Then sir Gareth list well to eate, and knightly he eate his meate and egerly; there was many a faire lady by him, and some of them said they saw never a goodlier man nor so well of eating. Then they made him passing good cheere all. And shortly when that he had supped, his bed was made there, so he rested him all night. And on the morrow he heard masse, and brake his fast, and tooke his leave of the duchesse and of them all, and thanked her goodly of her lodging and of her good cheere. And then shee asked him his name. "Madame," said hee. "truely my name is sir Gareth of Orkeney, and some men call me Beaumains." Then knew she well it was the same knight that fought for dame Lyones. And then sir Gareth departed, and rode up unto a mountaine, and there met him a knight, his name was sir Bendelaine, and hee said to sir Gareth: "Thou shalt not passe this way, for either thou shalt just with me, or be my prisoner." "Then will I just with thee," said sir Gareth. And so they let their horses runne, and there sir Gareth smote him throughout the body, and then sir Bendelaine rode forth unto his castle there beside, and there dyed. So sir Gareth would faine have rested him, and he came riding unto sir Bendelaines castle, and then his knights and his servants espied that it was hee that had slaine their lord; then they armed twentie good men, and came out and assailed sir Gareth, and he had no speare but onely his sword, and put his shield afore him, and there they all brake their speares upon him, and they assailed him passing sore; but ever sir Gareth defended him like a noble knight.

CHAP. CXLVIII.—How sir Gareth fought with a knight that held within his castle thirtie ladies, and how he slew him.

SO when they saw that they might not overcome him, they rode from him, and tooke their counsell to slay his horse, and so they came upon sir Gareth, and with speares they slew his horse, and then they assailed him full hard; but when hee was on foote there was none that hee caught but hee gave him such a buffet that he never recovered after. So he slew them one and one till they were but foure, and then they fled; and sir Gareth tooke a good horse which was one of theirs, and rod his way. Then hee rode a great pace till that he came to a castle, and there he heard much mourning of ladies and gentlewomen, so there came by him a page. "What noyse is this," said sir Gareth, "that I heare within this castle?" "Sir knight," said the page, "here be within this castle thirtie ladyes, and all they bee widowes, for here is a knight that waiteth daily upon this castle, and his name is the browne knight without pittie, and he is the perilloust knight that now liveth; and therefore, sir," said the page, "I bid you flee." "Nay," said sir Gareth, "I will not flee, how! well thou be afeard of him?" And then the page saw where as the browne knight came. "Loe," said the page, "yonder is he comming." "Let me deale with him," said sir Gareth. And when either of other had a sight, they let their horses runne, and the browne knight brake his speare, and sir Gareth smote him throughout the body, that he overthrew him to the ground starke dead. So sir Gareth rode into the castle, and prayed the ladies that he might rest him there. "Alas," said the ladies, "yee may not be lodged here." "Make him good cheere," said the page, "for this knight hath slaine your enemy." Then they all made him good cheere as lay in their power. But wit ye well they made him good cheare, for they might none otherwise doe, for they were all but poore gentlewomen.

And so on the morrow hee went to masse, and there he saw the thirtie ladies kneele and lay groveling upon divers tombes making great moue and sorrow. Then sir Gareth wist well that in the tombes lay their lords. Then said sir Gareth: "Faire ladies, yee must at the next feast of Pentecost be at the court of king Arthur, and say that I, sir Gareth, sent you unto him." "Wee shall doe your command," said the ladies. So he departed; and by fortune he came to a mountaine, and there he found a goodly knight which said: "Abide, sir knight, and just with me." "What be yee?" said sir Gareth. "My name is," said he, "the duke de la Rowse." "Ah, sir, yee are the same knight that I lodged once in your castle, and there I made promise unto your lady that I should yeeld me unto you." "Ah," said the duke, "art thou the same proud knight that proffered to fight with my knights? therefore make thee ready, for I will have adoe with thee." So they let their horses run, and there sir Gareth smote the duke downe from his horse; but the duke lightly avoided his horse, and set his shield afore him, and drew his sword, and bad sir Gareth alight and fight with him. So he alighted, and did together a great battaile that lasted more then an houre, and either hurt other full sore. At the last sir Gareth gate the duke to the earth, and would have slaine him, and then he yeelded him to him. "Then must ye goe," said sir Gareth, "unto my lord king Arthur at the next feast of Pentecost, and say that I, sir Gareth of Orkency, sent you unto him." "It shall be done," said the duke, "and I shall doe to you homage and fealtie with an hundred knights with mee, and all the daies of my life to doe you service where ye will command me."

CHAP. CXLIX.—How sir Gawaine and sir Gareth fought each against other, and how they knew each other by the damosell Linet.

SO the duke departed, and sir Gareth stood there alone, and there he saw an armed knight comming toward him. Then sir Gareth tooke the dukes shield, and mounted on horseback, and so without biding they ran together as it had been thunder, and there that knight hurt sir Gareth under the side with his speare. And then they alighted, and drew their swords, and gave each other great strookes, that the blood trailed to the ground on every side, and so they fought two houres. At the last there came the damosell Linet, that some men call the damosell savage,[1] and shee came riding upon an ambling mule, and there shee cried all on high, " Sir Gawaine, sir Gawaine, leave thy fighting with thy brother sir Gareth." And when he heard her say so, he threw away his shield and his sword, and ran to sir Gareth and tooke him in his armes, and after kneeled downe and asked him mercie. " What are yee," said sir Gareth, " that right now were so strong and so mighty, and now so suddenly yeeld you unto me ?" " Oh, sir Gareth, I am your brother sir Gawaine, that for your sake have had great sorrow and labour." Then sir Gareth unlaced his helme, and kneeled downe to him, and asked him mercy. Then they arose both and embraced each other in their armes, and wept a great while or they might speak, and either of them gave other the prise of the battaile. And there was many a kind word betweene them both. " Alas ! my faire brother," said sir Gawaine, " perde, I ought of right to worship you and yee were not my brother, for ye have worshiped king Arthur and al his court, for ye have sent him more worshipfull knights these twelve-moneths then six of the best of the round table have done, except sir Launcelot." Then came

---

[1] *The damosell savage.*—i. e. the wild damsel.

the damosell savage, that was the lady Linet, that rode long time with sir Gareth, and there shee stenched sir Gareths wounds and sir Gawaine. "Now what will ye doe?" said the damosell savage, "me seemeth it were wel done that king Arthur had knowledge of you both, for your horses are so bruised that they may not bear you." "Now, faire damosel," said sir Gawaine, "I pray you to ride unto my lord mine uncle king Arthur, and tell him what adventure is befallen to mee heere, and I suppose he will not tarry long." Then she tooke her mule, and lightly came unto king Arthur, that was but two mile thence; and when shee had told him the tidings, the king bad to get him a palfrey, and when he was upon his backe, hee bad the lords and ladies come after who that would. Then there was sadling and bridling of queenes horses and princes horses, and well was him that soonest might be ready. So when the king came there as they were, he saw sir Gawaine and sir Gareth sit upon a little hills side, and then the king avoided his horse. And when he came nigh sir Gareth, hee would have spoken but might not, and therewith hee sunke downe in a sound for gladnesse. And so they start unto their uncle, requiring him of his good grace to be of good comfort. Wit ye wel the king made great joy, and many a pittious complaint he made unto sir Gareth, and ever he wept as he had beene a child. With that came his mother the queene of Orkeney, dame Morgawse, and as she saw her sonne sir Gareth readily in the visage, shee might not weepe, but suddenly fel down in a sound and lay there a great while, like as shee had beene dead. And than sir Gareth recomforted his mother in such a wise that shee recovered, and made good cheere. Then the king commanded that all manner of knights that were under his obeysance should make their lodging there for the love of his nephews; and so was it done, and all manner of purveiance purvaied, that there lacked nothing that might bee gotten of tame ne wild for gold or for silver. And then by the meanes of the damosell savage, sir Gawaine and sir Gareth were healed of their wounds, and there they sojourned eight dayes. Then said king Arthur unto the damosell savage: " I marvaile that your sister dame Liones commeth not heere to me, and in especiall that she commeth not to visit her knight my nephew sir Gareth, that hath had so much travaile for her love." " My lord," said the damosel Linet, " ye must of your good grace hold her excused, for shee knoweth not that my lord sir Gareth is heere." " Then goe for her," said king Arthur, " that we may bee appointed what is best to be done, according unto the pleasure of my nephew sir Gareth." " Sir," said the damosell Linet, " that shall be done;" and so she rode unto her sister. And as lightly as shee might make her ready shee did, and came on the morrow with her brother sir Gringamor, and with her fortie knights. And when she was come, shee had all the cheere that might be done, both of king Arthur and of many other kings and queenes.

CHAP. CL.—How sir Gareth acknowledged that they loved each other to king Arthur, and of the day of their wedding.

AMONG all these ladies was shee named the fairest and peerlesse. Then when sir Gareth saw her, there was many goodly lookes and goodly words, that all men of worship had joy to behold them. Then came king Arthur and many other kings, and queene Guenever and the queene of Orkeney; and there the king asked his nephew sir Gareth whether hee would have the lady to his paramour, or to have her to his wife. " My lord, wit you well that I love her above all ladies living." " Now faire lady," said king Arthur unto her, " what say yee?" " Most noble king," said dame Lyones, " wit you well that my lord sir Gareth is to mee more lever to have and weld[1] as my husband, then any king

[1] *Weld.*—Possess.

or prince christened, and if I may not have him, I promise you I will never have none. For, my lord king Arthur," said dame Lyones, "wit yee well he is my first love, and he shall be the last, and if yee will suffer him to have his will and free choyse, I dare say he will have mee." "That is truth," said sir Gareth, "and I have not you and weld you as my wife, there shall never lady nor gentlewoman rejoyce mee." "What, nephew," said the king, "is the wind in that doore? for wit yee well I would not for the stint of my crowne to be causer to withdraw your hearts, and I wit yee well yee can not love so well but I shall rather increase it then distresse. Also yee shall have my love and my lordship in the uttermost wise that may lye in my power." And the same wise said sir Gareths mother. Then was there made a provision for the day of marriage, and by the kings advise it was provided that it should be at Michaelmasse next following at Kinkenadon by the seaside, for there is a plentifull countrey. And so it was cryed in all places through the realme. And then sir Gareth sent his messengers unto all those knights and ladies that he had wone in battaile before, that they should be at the day of his marriage at Kinkenadon by the sands. And then dame Lyones and the damosell Lynet, with sir Gringamor, rode to their castle, and a goodly and a rich ring she gave to sir Gareth, and he gave her an other. And king Arthur gave her a rich patre of beads of gold,[1] and so shee departed, and king Arthur and his fellowship rode toward Kinkenadon; and sir Gareth brought his lady in the way, and so came to the king againe, and rode with him. The great cheere that sir Launcelot du Lake made for sir Gareth of Orkeney it was mervaile to see, and he of him againe, for there was never no knight that sir Gareth loved so well as he did sir Lancelot du Lake, and ever for the most part would be in

---

[1] *Patre of beads of gold.*—*A ryche bee of gold*, Caxton. A *pater* of beads was a set of beads, to count the paternosters by. *Bee* is perhaps for *beigh*, a bracelet.

KING ARTHUR. 303

sir Lancelots company ; for after sir Gareth had espied sir Gawains conditions, he withdrew himselfe from his brother sir Gawains fellowship, for he was vengeable and unmercifull, and whereas he hated he would be avenged with murther and treason, and that hated sir Gareth.

CHAP. CLI.—Of the great royaltie and what officers were made at the feast of sir Gareth and dame Liones wedding, and of the great justing at the same feast and wedding.

SO it drew fast to Mighelmasse, and thither came dame Liones and her sister dame Linet, with sir Gringamor their brother with them, for he had the guiding of those ladies. And there they were lodged at the devise of king Arthur. And on Mighelmasse day the archbishop of Canterbury made the wedding betweene sir Gareth and the lady Liones with great solemnitie. And king Arthur made sir Gaheris to wed the damosell savage that was dame Linet. And king Arthur made sir Agravaine to wed dame Liones neece, a faire lady, her name was dame Laurell. And so when this solemnisation was done, then there came in the greene knight that hight sir Pertolope, with thirtie knights, and there he did homage and fealtie unto sir Gareth, and these knights to hold of him for evermore. Also sir Pertolope said, " I pray you that at this feast I may be your chamberlaine." " With a good will," said sir Gareth, " sith it liketh you to take so simple an office." Then came in the red knight, with threescore knights with him, and did to sir Gareth homage and fealtie, and all those knights to hold of him for evermore, and then sir Perimones prayed sir Gareth to graunt him for to be his chiefe butler at that high feast. " I will well," said sir Gareth, " that ye have this office and it were better." Then came in sir Persaunt of Inde, with an hundred knights with him, and there he did homage and fealtie unto sir Gareth, and all his knights should doe him service and hold their lands of him for evermore, and then hee prayed sir Gareth to make him the chiefe sewer[1] at the feast. "I will well," said sir Gareth, "that yee have it and it were better." Then came in the duke de la Rowse, with an hundred knights with him, and there he did homage and fealtie unto sir Gareth, and so to hold their lands of him for ever, and he required sir Gareth that he might serve him of the wine that day at the feast. "I will well," said sir Gareth, "and it were much better." Then came in the red knight of the red launds, that was sir Ironside, and he brought with him three hundred knights, and there he did homage and feaultie to sir Gareth, and all these knights to hold their lands of him for ever, and then he asked sir Gareth to be his karver. "I will well," said sir Gareth, "and it please you." Then came into the court thirtie ladies, and all they seemed widdowes, and those thirtie ladies brought with them many faire gentlewomen, and they all kneeled downe at once unto king Arthur and unto sir Gareth, and there all those ladies told the king how sir Gareth had delivered them from the dolorous towre, and slew the browne knight without pitie, " and therefore wee and our heires for evermore will doe homage unto sir Gareth of Orkeney." So then the kings and queens, princes, earles, and barons, and many bold knights, went unto meate, and well ye may wit that there was all manner of meate plenteously, and all manner revelles and games, with all manner of musicke that was used in those dayes. Also there was great justing three dayes. But the king would not suffer sir Gareth to just because of his new bride. For the French booke saith that dame Lyones desired the king that none of them that were wedded should just at that feast. So the first day there justed sir Lamoracke de Galis, and he overthrew thirtie knights, and did passing mervailous deeds of armes. And then king Arthur made sir Persaunt of Inde and his two bretheren knights of the round table

[1] *Sewer.*—The officer who placed the dishes on the table.

unto their lives end, and gave them great lands. Also the second day there justed sir Tristram best, and he overthrew fortie knights, and he did there mervailous deeds of armes. And there king Arthur made sir Ironside, that was the red knight of the red launds, a knight of the round table unto his lives end, and gave him great lands. The third day there justed sir Launcelot du Lake, and he overthrew fiftie knights and did many mervailous deeds of armes, that all men had great wonder of his noble deeds. And there king Arthur made the duke de la Rowse a knight of the round table to his lives end, and gave him great lands to spend. But when these justs were done, sir Lamorake and sir Tristram departed sudainely, and would not be known, for the which king Arthur and all his court were sore displeased. And so they held the feast fortie dayes with great solemnity. And this sir Gareth was a full noble knight, and a well ruled, and faire languaged.

Thus endeth the history of sir Gareth of Orkency, that wedded dame Lyones of the castle perillous. And also sir Gaheris wedded her sister dame Lynet, that was called the damosell savage. And sir Agravaine wedded dame Laurell, a faire lady. And great and mightie lands with great riches gave with them the noble king Arthur, that royally they might live unto their lives end.

END OF VOL. I.

www.ingramcontent.com/pod-product-compliance
Lightning Source LLC
Chambersburg PA
CBHW030319240426
43673CB00040B/1211